# WISDOM OF
# THE HEART

# WISDOM OF THE HEART

Working With Women's Dreams

Karen A. Signell, Ph.D.

FOREWORD BY *Riane Eisler*

**RIDER**

LONDON · SYDNEY · AUCKLAND · JOHANNESBURG

Copyright © Karen Signell 1990

This edition published in 1991 by Rider
An imprint of Random Century Group Ltd
20 Vauxhall Bridge Road, London SW1V 2SA

Random Century Group Australia (Pty) Ltd
20 Alfred Street, Milsons Point,
Sydney, NSW 2061, Australia

Random Century New Zealand Ltd
18 Poland Road, Glenfield,
Auckland 10, New Zealand

Random Century Group South Africa (Pty) Ltd
PO Box 337, Bergvlei 2012, South Africa

Printed and bound by
The Guernsey Press Co. Ltd, Guernsey, Channel Islands.

A catalogue record for this book is available
from the British Library.

ISBN 0–7126–4748–1

This book is printed on recycled paper.

Dedicated in loving memory to my mother and father

Ottlie Burdick Signell
1905–1987

Lloyd George Signell
1901–1979

# Table of Contents

# Foreword

We all have dreams, and when we wake up we wonder what they mean. The ancients, we are told, thought that dreams were portents of the future, laden with messages from goddesses and gods. At the other extreme is the view of some modern biologists who see dreams as mere neurological static, devoid of any real meaning. Most of us are somewhere in between; we believe that dreams are often messages from our unconscious minds, but we usually do not know what to make of them.

Dr. Karen Signell has spent much of her professional life listening to dreams, using her training as a Jungian psychologist to help her patients use their dreams for healing. In *Wisdom of the Heart*, she tells of these dreams and of the women who dreamed them. But what makes her approach, and this book, different—and what attracted my attention—is that it is designed to empower women: to help us use our dreams to find our own sources of inner wisdom and strength.

Trusting our own inner wisdom is not easy for us, particularly if we are women. How can we look to ourselves for guidance in a society where, by and large, women's ways of knowing are still viewed with suspicion, if not disdain; where—ironically, since in both Hebrew and Greek "wisdom" is a feminine word—it is wise men, not wise women, who dispense knowledge and wisdom in both religion and science?

Karen Signell suggests that an important source of guidance

can be found in our dreams: that as society changes, so also do our inner images, and that many of women's dreams today reflect our search for our own internal truths rather than the externally imposed "truths" of male "authorities."

To me, one of the most exciting aspects of *Wisdom of the Heart* is its link to my own work. As those readers acquainted with my book *The Chalice and the Blade* know, I have over the last decades tried to reconstruct from the evidence of archaeology, mythology, religion and art history, and other disciplines an earlier age when women were not subordinate to men; a more peaceful and harmonious time before war and the war of the sexes, a time when both women and men worshipped the powers that give and nurture life in the form of a Great Goddess. During that same time, as I was putting together the findings of what the British archaeologist James Mellaart calls a "veritable revolution in archaeology" to document the possibility of a better future with roots going back to our prehistoric past, Karen Signell was also gathering information about our lost heritage, but in a very different form. For her interest was in what Jungians call archetypes, powerful images and stories they believe derive from our "collective unconscious" and are shaped by not only our personal but our cultural history. And time and time again, in the dreams of women today, there were images that Dr. Signell saw as the reemergence of very ancient archetypes of feminine power, often images of the Great Goddess herself.

*Wisdom of the Heart* is thus in many ways a reflection of women's contemporary search for self: of our search for our own inner integrity and wisdom, as we, and society, try to move toward a way of living, working, and loving that honors each one of our unique potentials.

As Signell writes, many of our culture's myths "disappoint women searching for their own feminine nature, since the myths usually feature male protagonists preoccupied with war, rationality, power over death, and the subordination of the feminine and women." These myths both reflect and reinforce what I have called a dominator rather than a partnership society, for they idealize, and thus help to maintain, the suppression not only of women but also of the qualities stereotypically viewed as "soft" or "feminine"—such as caring, nonviolence, empathy, and intuition.

I say stereotypically, because my research has led me to the conclusion that at this point in our history—after approximately five thousand years of dominator myths and realities—it is almost impossible to talk of "feminine" and "masculine" in other than stereotypical terms. Certainly in the traditional Jungian scheme, the archetypes of the "anima" or "feminine" in men and the "animus" or "masculine" in women have been embedded in these stereotypes, largely shaped by notions that view wisdom as masculine, as in the association of the animus with thinking or reason. As Demaris Wehr writes in *Jung & Feminism: Liberating Archetypes,* through archetypes that define their thinking side as masculine, women are left in "a deficit position with regard to natural female authority, logic, and rationality"—they arc effectively distanced from their thinking side, just as men are distanced from their more feeling and vulnerable side by personifying it as "feminine." And yet, unlike Freudian and other psychoanalytic approaches, Jung's work with archetypes and dreams did allow women and men to claim these qualities via their "feminine" or "masculine" side—an important first step toward a more integrated psyche for both sexes.

In Karen Signell's book we find Jungian dream analysis taken one step further. By focusing on the dreams of women in the process of personal empowerment and healing, *Wisdom of the Heart* helps us look at our own dreams for clues not only to who we are and were, but who we can become.

*Wisdom of the Heart* is not a how-to book in the conventional sense, yet it is a practical book for women seeking support in a time of rapidly changing personal and social realities. It deals with many of the internal obstacles we face in our personal and spiritual development: our fear of aggression (others' and our own), our difficulty in claiming (much less proclaiming) our positive qualities and achievements, and our impossible expectations of ourselves and our mothers (and at the same time, our lack of a mother deity, and the immense importance of the contemporary reclamation of the Great Goddess for both women and men).

It is a book about mermaids and oceans, princesses and

dragons, young maidens and old crones, as these appeared to real women who told the stories of their dreams to Dr. Signell in the course of their therapies. In that sense, it is a book about personal healing, and how we can connect with our unconscious needs and aspirations through our dreams. But most important, it is a book by a woman who really cares—about her patients, her readers, and the kind of world we can create for ourselves and our children if women, and men, are guided more by our "feminine" wisdom: the wisdom of the heart.

—Riane Eisler

# Acknowledgments

First I wish to thank the many women who have so generously shared their dreams. They are the explorers whose dauntless spirit and imagination have provided insights and inspiration for this book.

Four people in particular have unstintingly helped me throughout this undertaking: Ann MacLeod with her tactful questions, constructive advice, and generous assistance; Leslie Meredith with her thoughtfulness, diplomatic suggestions, perceptive editing, and strong support of the book; Frances Tobriner with her finely-tuned clarity about the feminine; and Judy Askew with her careful editing and discerning way with words. They have been a stalwart team at my side, giving me a sense of fellow-feeling and support through all my labors, and their work has made this a better book. They deserve acknowledgment and my wholehearted gratitude.

Substantial contributions have been made by others with their insightful editorial suggestions. Leslie Sidle gave generously of her time and thought and was a constant source of encouragement. Lynda Schmidt consulted on several chapters and enriched the book with her perceptive observations and archetypal understanding of dreams. Barbara Dean edited an early version of initial chapters and provided encouragement at a time when it was needed and also valuable perspectives on shaping the book. I am grateful for this help.

I want to express my appreciation to those who read one or more chapters and generously gave me their suggestions: Sandra Dixon, Maria Miller, Maria Nieri, Mary Ann Mattoon, Florence Grossenbacher, Madeleine Marcus, Katherine Bradway, Lila Kramer, Shirley MacIntosh, Arthur Colman, Keith Chapman, Millie Fortier, Rosemary Warden, and Jamie Brodie.

Others helped in discussions of certain dreams or portions of the text and in various ways: Geraldine Spare, Florence Irvine, Betty Meador, Jane Wheelwright, Richard Schoenbrun, Sandra Lewis, Janet Tatum, Joanne Nordlie, and Lani Kask.

I owe a special debt to my friends and colleagues Linda Leonard, Patricia Bixby, and Anne-Marie Bloch for their warm-hearted support, creative insights, and advice.

I would like to thank Gina Velasquez, Katinka Matson and John Brockman, Kay and John Scheuer, Jean Bolen, Lore Zeller, and Sandy Boucher for offering me timely and crucial support in the publication process.

Special appreciation goes to the C. G. Jung Institute of San Francisco for its scholarship grants which lightened the burden of clerical expenses in the early years of the book.

Last, but not least, I wish to acknowledge the rich legacy from my Jungian mentors and personal analysts who have handed down to me their "wisdom of the heart": Joseph Wheelwright, Katherine Bradway, Elizabeth Osterman, and Joseph Henderson.

# List of Dreams

## Early Glimpses of the Self

## Dealing with Aggression

## Sex

## The Wise Heart

The heart has its reasons which reason cannot know.
—Pascal, *Pensées IV*

                    I am not one
Who must have everything: yet I must have
My dreams if I must live, for they are mine.
Wisdom is not one word and then another.
Till words are like dry leaves under a tree;
Wisdom is like a dawn that comes up slowly
                    Out of an unknown ocean.
—Edwin Arlington Robinson, *Tristram*

            Thinking globally, acting locally.
—Hazel Henderson, *The Politics of the Solar Age*

# A Personal Preface

I still remember that moment in 1972 during the interview for admission to the local Jung Institute when the interviewer, a male analyst, said to me quite candidly, "You don't look like one of us," and I felt the sharp truth of his comment. I *was* a woman—and you could count on both hands the number of women analysts in the Institute—and I was a clinical psychologist, not an M.D. psychiatrist. Moreover, I didn't have the faraway look of a natural dreamer. I had my feet firmly planted on the ground.

I also hadn't been sitting in the traditional, well-furnished private office seeing clients for years, for I had come of age professionally in the 1960s, the time of exuberant flower children and expansive outreach to the grassroots community. In the ferment of the times, we believed in "saving the world" through self-help groups and education for the public—giving away our knowledge—in addition to helping people in therapy. I had gone out into the community, consulting at Headstart preschools and teaching housewives how to give parent-child communication courses to other parents. I knew, even then, that if I became an analyst I wanted to write a book to reach the many people who didn't have access to analysis.

"You don't look like one of us." This was also true in that I didn't come from the same background as the generation of analysts ahead of me who were brought up in family cultures of scholarship and reflection that allowed them—the pioneers—to turn to their inner lives and study for years with Carl Jung in Switzerland. My father, the son of Swedish immigrants, and my mother, the daughter of midwestern German and Scotch-Irish immigrants, had started as young factory workers, although they both managed to spring themselves from their 1920s factories and put themselves through college. Their early experiences led them to believe in progress and dedicate their lives to working on poverty and other kinds of social reform. My mother never forgot how her hands had been cut handling tin cans on the assembly line and they both remembered how frightened they had been in the Great Depression. My brothers and I were told about these things—many times—to impress upon us that since we had our education on a silver platter we must "do something useful."

My family was close to the earth. As a soil conservationist, my father loved the earth. How often he would scoop soil into his palm and say, "Fine loam!" or he would point out a gash of erosion on a hillside and flinch at the wasteful destruction of good farmland which he knew how to preserve as a soil conservationist. My mother came from farming people. She showed us how to raise vegetables and take care of our animals. We lived in a modern log house we had all built from the trees—I stripped the bark off the logs—in our woods in Maryland. Thus, from an early age I knew the hope and promise of those who cherish and plant and nurture the earth with their own hands and I saw the responsiveness, the fruitfulness, of the earth in return. In this I was fortunate.

"Did you have a fantasy life as a child?" the Jung Institute interviewer asked me. No, the possibility of having fantasies had never occurred to me. If I had been caught sitting a moment my mother would say, "What're you doing—daydreaming? There's work to be done!" This was the reality of everyday life in my childhood.

Yet I loved those stolen moments in nature—the stream, the woods, the wild animals—and I still remember certain times: holding a chicken as my mother sewed up a neck wound, helping my father be midwife to a goat as he pulled out the newborn kid's legs, holding a duck to be killed, catching a poisonous snake near my duck pond. All these—the light and dark of life—brought me close to the rhythms and truths of nature and my own inner nature—the reality of nature, not as one would wish it, but as it is.

In my thirties I discovered another frontier of nature—the inner world, the stream of the unconscious that runs underneath our known world, the world of dreams. This inner world echoed the familiar world of nature I knew, with its burst of seed, spurts of growth, and bearing of fruit, then its dying, lying fallow and waiting, and then its spontaneous growth again.

Yet I was too much of a realist in the outer world to be a "natural" like some people in the innermost world of mysteries, symbols, and spontaneous psychological growth. I had to learn this second language, become a craftswoman in a foreign land.

What the analyst said at the end of the interview gave me hope at that time. Seeing that I wasn't the kind of person to whom the inner life originally came with ease he said, "Well, when your kind *does* have dreams, they can be vivid and real." And as I became more deeply attuned to my dreams, what he'd said proved to be true for me.

I hope it can be true, too, for you readers who are natural dreamers and those who can learn the craft. And for those of you who have your feet on the ground—and those who have a faraway look in your eyes—may this book help you find the vividness of your dreams and learn how to use them in reality.

# Introduction:
## Dreams as a Source of Feminine Knowledge

## *A Search for the Feminine*

Ten years ago I set out to write a book on the feminine in women because I believed our wisdom comes not only in the traditional patriarchal way—with words, objectivity, control, and conscious knowledge—but in a much more subtle way. I believed, and still do, that women's basic source of knowledge comes from our inner feelings and images; and that our basic self-confidence comes not from another's authority and theories, but from our personal experiences in the world—what we know up close, what we know in our hearts. I'm convinced that these personal resources can guide us to remain true to our deepest selves and eventually find the strength together as women to counter world violence in all its pervasive manifestations from the molestation of a child to nuclear warfare. I believe that especially in these troubled times our life-sustaining perspectives are necessary to enhance the quality and assure the continuance of life on earth.

In writing this book I hesitated to define "the feminine" myself because, even though I'm a woman, I'm just one woman, and I've been steeped in patriarchal theories as a clinical psychologist and Jungian analyst. I decided to let women speak for themselves through the purest source I knew, their dreams. What wisdom could we glean together as we journeyed along the shore and into the ocean of the unconscious? What could we find out about our feminine natures, and what meaning could this have for our everyday lives?

For ten years I gathered dreams—not dreams as examples to illustrate theories, but dreams that seemed to speak about basic feminine nature. I wrote down dreams as women told them to me and as we discovered together what the dreams meant. I chose dreams that helped women understand their own feminine nature, dreams that might also offer insights for other women.

Four hundred dreams (two percent of those I'd heard) "caught my eye" because they had a telling image, had a valuable message for women generally, or were relatively easy to comprehend. One requirement I made was that the dream actually had been meaningful to the dreamer and useful in her life. Of the four hundred dreams, about one fourth are contained in this book. Without a preconceived idea of what would happen, I sorted dreams into stacks of similar topics, and half of these became chapters for this book.

I didn't notice many dreams about women in the roles of wife and mother, even from women who *are* wives and mothers. The explanation may lie in the fact that dreams compensate for what is overemphasized in our daily lives, so that women tend to dream about what is important to them as individuals and what was important in their own childhood. In the selection of content, I tended to choose dreams about a woman's relation with her mother more than her relation with her father[1] because I have noticed that the feminine is known more in continuity— being similar to another person, than in contrast—being different from another.

To concentrate on the feminine, I passed over most dreams about the masculine in women, the "animus." While inner male figures are often invaluable guides for women,[2] recently, it seems to me, our inner masculine side has been overemphasized; much has been written about it; and it has been viewed with so much cultural bias that it has become difficult to write about without becoming mired in stereotypes. For instance, when a woman's thoughts have been expressed with emotional intensity, often her thoughts have been dismissed as the product of her unconscious "negative animus" (stereotyped as the opinionated, power-driven, and strident side of a woman) rather than seen as an assertion of her own legitimate thoughts and feelings. Therefore, women themselves must begin to define their own masculine side in all its constructive and destructive forms as it appears in their lives and in their dreams. We need to know more about both the masculine and the feminine in ourselves. However, as an analyst, I am always drawn to notice the small voice that isn't being heard enough. In women today, that small voice is often the feminine voice.

Although I was trained in proper scientific research, I decided to use dreams and related anecdotal material collected mostly from women I happened to know. I then added whatever comments seemed relevant: explanations, general observations from experience, and personal opinions. This was not just a practical decision—to use information easily at hand—but, it seemed to me, an appropriate one. For we are in the early stages of exploring women's inner psychology: First, we must gather many examples of women's raw experience, analyze case studies in depth, make general observations from these, and finally build new theories based on women's own experience. Thus, I tried not to draw general conclusions about the feminine or define it in this book, but let the dreams tell us about what processes, attitudes, and values comprise the feminine, so that the reader can make her own intuitive assessments.

I might mention that all the "stories" contained in this book are real stories from actual women told here by the kind permission of the dreamers. Dreams are presented in the dreamers' own words[3] with only minor editing for purposes of clarity or confidentiality. Any identifying material about the women or their circumstances has been omitted or changed to protect their identities, and any names used in the text are fictitious ones.

Most dreams came from my own clients, and some came from other sources such as colleagues and friends in therapy. Most women were in analysis for their personal growth, some for healing old wounds. A particular life crisis, such as divorce or physical illness—and resulting depression, anxiety, or anger—often precipitated their seeking help. While their dreams may show a cross section of many women's problems today, these women are certainly not a representative sample of the population: They are mostly women who could afford weekly analysis.

However, they have come from a variety of life situations. They range in ages from their twenties through their seventies; they are single, married, and divorced; heterosexual, bisexual, and lesbian. Most, but not all, are educated and professional, but they come from a range of family backgrounds in terms of economic conditions, culture, religious upbringing, and emotional climate at home. Some had never worked with dreams before; some had worked on their own dreams since childhood.

I wrote this book mainly for women who don't have the opportunity or inclination to have therapy or analysis, but want to tap their own inner resources. The book is for those who want to know more about their feminine nature, and those in search of personal fulfillment and spiritual growth in their lives. It also may be of interest to men who want to understand women better as well as to understand the feminine in themselves. Other people may also be interested: therapists and clients who want to deepen their understanding of women's inner lives; teachers and students of psychology and women's studies; feminists; poets and artists; social service workers; professionals and academicians in literature, the arts, religious studies, and spiritual counseling.

## How to Read This Book

In writing this book, I did not follow the tradition of a logical progression of abstract theory, well-refined concepts, and a few illustrations. Instead, I took a voyage of discovery, starting with many specific dreams that sparked my interest, to see what might be of general interest; that is, I took the inductive route. Therefore, you, too, can meander through this book, following your interests and gradually building up your knowledge over the course of the whole book.

After the first chapter, "Understanding Dreams," which gives you some background for working with your own dreams and for understanding the language of the unconscious, all the rest of the chapters use women's dreams as a point of departure. I followed my inclination about the order of those chapters, and found that, unconsciously, I had more or less followed the path women often take in analysis. First, a woman finds a guide, someone she trusts or her own inner guide, the Self. So the beginning chapter on dreams is about finding "Early Glimpses of the Self" and the hope that comes from that commitment. I felt compelled to write the following chapter on "Dealing with Aggression." Whether in the form of threats or constraints imposed on women, the subject of how to deal with others' aggression often comes up early in analysis because we must usually handle fear and oppression before we're free to assert who we really are. This brings us to the subject of the next chapter, "The Shadow," which deals with parts of ourselves we haven't recognized, the negative qualities that have been attributed to us and that we sometimes unconsciously accept, as well as the positive qualities—the positive shadow—we can dare to claim as our own strength and potential.

The middle section of the book concentrates on intimacy, a major topic in analysis. "Relationship" is a long chapter representing the many dreams of women about the people around them. It shows how important relationships are in our lives, and the hard work that is required for fulfillment. The exploration of intimate relationships is continued in the following chapter, "Sex." Some dreams recall childhood and young adulthood when family or cultural attitudes restricted autonomy and sexuality, but most deal with such current issues in adult life as women trying to integrate sexuality and spirituality, and trying to reclaim their bodies as their own, not as objects for others.

The last section consists of a long chapter called "The Wise Heart," which shows the culmination of the gradual development of inner harmony and wisdom of the heart. In this chapter you will find dreams where a wise old woman in some form appears to inform a woman about the nature of the universe. You will also find that as women mature and listen to the inner voice, their dreams reflect more mature manifestations of that center, the Self: a symbol such as a circle of great beauty—perhaps a rose window—or the transcendent experience of grace in a dream.

I wrote this book expecting that you may want to follow the progression of the chapters, but it is written so that each chapter and dream can stand alone. Thus, if you prefer, you can follow your inclinations in learning to work with the unconscious. Because the unconscious wanders, so can you! For example, if you scan the List of Dreams at the beginning of the book and an image catches your eye, that may be the place for you to start, for your unconscious is "alive" to that image. Let yourself enter the experience with the dreamer of what the dream meant to her, and hear what resonates within you. Imagine, if it were your own dream, what it would mean to you, what would it say about your life? For, if you wish, you can treat any dream as your own, since dreams draw upon layers of the unconscious and human experience common to us all. The ability to analyze dreams is not acquired in a systematic way. It is helpful to pause now and then to hear the sounds coming from the depths and discover what meanings reverberate within you.

I've used few psychological terms and little jargon; what terms I have used are explained in the first chapter or in context. Major themes which recur from chapter to chapter and dream to dream are cross-referenced in the text. Prominent symbols are listed in the overall Index of subject matter at the back of the book. If you wish to explore Jungian psychology further, you will find an annotated listing of Resources at the end of the book: sources of information about books, journals, and local workshops.

Many books present general insights neatly packaged with everyday examples. This book isn't like that. You can't just take it like a box of cornflakes off the shelf for immediate use. You need to ponder and absorb unconscious material by following a spiral path, first wondering, glimpsing, knowing more, then wondering anew, until the unknown gradually becomes more familiar, more accessible. It is never really known, however. You probably can't read this book at the usual pace and with the focused attention with which you usually read and learn new ideas

This book does not provide a clear highway, deep into the jungle of the unconscious, direct to where the gold lies. Your conscious mind can't be in control, can't be in charge, or goal-oriented. You won't have your usual rewards and sense of accomplishment on this journey. The following chapters won't give you obvious signs along the road telling you where you are or how far you've come, for this is an inward, very personal journey. While the conscious mind likes to count things—three aspects of a symbol, four elements in a dream, ten steps to knowledge—and the Western mind likes definition and boundaries, in this jungle everything interweaves by nature. Any one dream spreads in many directions, and any dream can follow another. For instance, you won't find sex all in one chapter; it may occur naturally in a dream in the last chapter on the Wise Woman. Try to give up consciously driving for a while, and let your dancing girl, your inner wanderer, who enjoys being curious and surprised, lead the way for you. Follow the other women down the footpaths, wander in the dense undergrowth, find your way along the streams. You may find the greater waters and the deeper currents in your life.

Learning interpretation techniques is not the key to understanding dreams. You gain a general sense of how to approach dreams by experiencing many dreams, by learning how to cultivate your imagination and gaining confidence in your own intuition. This book shows you the *process* of understanding dreams in an intuitive way, using the dreamer's—and your own—imagination and experience as the main resources. This is the way a person learns in Jungian analysis and, generally, in life. This is "the way of the small": You accumulate knowledge bit by bit not through reading about concepts, not through intellectual understanding, but through many small personal examples, each one keeping intact the feeling tone and the truth of the individual case and its particular context. By listening to how each woman understands her dream, step by step throughout the book, you can gradually absorb how to do it yourself.

This book, by necessity, is limited in scope and makes no attempt to give a comprehensive exposition of symbols, not even of the ones that appear here. Symbols have personal meanings which you must discover yourself. We don't know yet the general meanings that various symbols have for women. Knowledge accumulated in symbolic literature during the last few thousand years often reflects the meanings that symbols have had in men's psyches. These traditional meanings sometimes don't fit women, especially our feminine side, which is the focus of this book. We are just beginning to explore what certain symbols mean to women, so reading this book is embarking on a pioneering voyage of discovery!

What can you do if you want to investigate further any interesting images you find in the book or in your own dreams? Even though your intuition is still your best resource, you may find it helpful to supplement your own work with at least one symbol dictionary to provoke further thought. Therefore, I've suggested some reference books you might find useful under Recommended Books at the back. If you want more generalizations about patterns in dreams and more specific techniques for analyzing dreams, you can also find there Jungian books on dreamwork and books containing very readable descriptions of Jungian psychology. I've also listed books on the feminine.

Since I concentrate on analyzing dreams in this book, you may wonder if the analytic process consists only of dreamwork. In actuality, the dreamwork took place within the context of a therapeutic relationship and the exploration of each woman's early history as well as of her family, work, and social relationships. Thus there was always the background of a dreamer's life for understanding what a dream meant, and an atmosphere of openness and empathy within the safe container of analysis. When reading this book, you might try to re-create a similar setting for yourself: a quiet place, a leisurely pace, a spirit of receptivity that sets free your imagination.

As you begin the next chapters, remember that the dreams do not yield their secrets readily. Dreams say things we don't already know. That's the main reason why they're worthwhile: They complement what we already know consciously and lead us to new, deeper knowledge. We enter an unexplored wilderness where there are no clear guideposts. Only the dreamer can be the final arbiter on what a dream means to her, although I've tried to clear a path through the thicket so you can discern some general patterns from each dream. Looking at a dream is like looking at a poem, a treasured picture, an impressionist or surrealist painting. You have to look at it in your own way, let it move you, see what it stirs up in you. I found that, when I worked with these dreams, the more times I looked at them, came back to them, the more I could see.

I invite you to read the dreams in this book with easy eyes that wander and rest upon images that interest you, to see how they make you respond, what they mean to you, and what commentary happens to resonate with your experience. Remember that even one image can evoke many different images, feelings, ideas, and memories—including contradictory ones—and dreams can have many meanings, only some of which have been touched upon in the text.

## Some Moving Dreams

As a preview to the many dreams you will find in this book, I conclude this introduction with some examples of dreams informing life. First, an example of letting dreams affect your everyday life, for it is more often in small ways that we find our way and progress than in the rare illumination. I went to a remote island to write this introduction. Overviews require great effort for me, and weeks went by. Then I dreamed one morning:

> **I was keeping a group of women waiting, with men nearby to join them.**

I knew what it meant: I must write the introduction to my book. Yet, I quailed before the effort and sat down to edit my chapter on sex, something much easier to do. But the ethical imperative—to listen to the dream—made me waver a moment, and that moment somehow tipped the balance and I found myself writing the first sentence. In the night the tide had turned, and the energy was, indeed, moving in this direction. My unconscious itself, during the night, had somehow prepared me; I was ready, for the energy came.

A dream was crucial to a remarkable woman in recent world history, Cory Aquino. When the Filipino people began to turn against Ferdinand Marcos, she was asked to accept the nomination for the presidency. While she was trying to reach a decision, she had a recurrent dream that she was

> **going to a church and seeing a casket that she expected to contain Ninoy's [her assassinated husband's] body. But the coffin was empty: Ninoy, she felt, had been reborn in her.**

She remembered what he had said before his fatal return to the Philippines: that he'd never forgive himself if he didn't do all he could for his people. She said, "I feel I owe the country something." She felt unprepared for the presidency and wanted to return to her private life, but after receiving a petition signed by 1.2 million people and going on a retreat, she made her decision.[4]

A dream can warn us about something we have overlooked. For example, I recently took a refresher course in underwater diving. Twenty years earlier when I had been diving, I had prided myself on being the last one to run out of air underwater, so in the refresher course I took a smaller tank of air than the others. During a dive one day I thought that I noticed leaking air, but I dismissed the worry as my unfamiliarity with modern equipment. Down deep, at mid-dive, to my astonishment my tank was almost empty. Eyes wide with alarm, I found the diving instructor, who shared her air for our return. When my equipment was examined, it passed inspection for my future use, so I passed off the incident as puzzling, and continued with my old confidence as an experienced diver. One night I had a corrective dream with the following image:

> **A mother donkey is lying beside the road, sides heaving, eyes glazed in helplessness. She's old and has given up. I look at her and think, "That's the reality of life." Beside her is a young donkey with its legs cut off at the ankles as a lesson for others. I feel great compassion for the young donkey and outrage that its**

**legs have been so ruthlessly cut off and its life cut short.**

This dream woke me up at night, and also woke me up to my overconfidence and lack of vigilance. The dream grossly exaggerated, as dreams often do, and upset me enough to make its point. My old mother donkey, my own maternal side that should take care of me and my body, was indeed twenty years older and was not very alert. The "reality of life" was that I might have to admit some infirmities of aging and perhaps give up diving. The younger donkey referred to the youthfulness I still have, and the ruthless fact that if I have too much youthful daring (act like a young donkey, act like an ass) and lose contact with hard realities (legs not connected to the ground), the terrible truth (lesson) is that my life could indeed be cut short.

What effect did the dream have on my life? It led me to have a physical checkup and to be far more cautious when diving: to check my air gauge, to stay close to my underwater buddy, and to double-check my equipment. This extra carefulness actually resulted in the discovery of a subtle air leak in my diving gear.

It is an exception rather than a rule to be guided by the unconscious in modern Western society, yet there have been societies throughout humanity's 4,000 years of recorded history (and undoubtedly in over 30,000 years of unrecorded history before that) in which people have relied on dreams. In ancient times, people were more in touch with the unconscious and could dip into that reservoir of knowing. The major religions of the world relied on dreams and visions for revelation. People looked to dreams and ritual for knowledge and healing. On the coast of Turkey near a temple dedicated to the early Greek goddess Demeter, a version of the Great Mother, you can still stand today in a long, arched passageway of stone, a "dream tunnel," where people once stayed to dream and be healed.

In more recent centuries, leaders, composers, artists, and scientists have found insight and inspiration from dreams and images. Today—especially outside the influence of modern Western civilization—there are people who still rely on dreams for warning and guidance. Some years ago, Peace Corps volunteers working among mountain people in the Andes were captured by guerillas and held a short time until they escaped. Afterward, a mountain woman asked one of the women volunteers, "But didn't you know that would happen? Weren't you listening to your dreams?" I am grateful to that mountain woman from the high Andes for her faith that we can find our lost heritage. We *can* be in touch with nature and its wisdom, and we, too, can look to our dreams and know again.

# 1

# Understanding Dreams

## Working with Your Own Dreams

Since you may be interested in working with your own dreams—
tapping your own personal natural resource—I will mention here
some things I've found useful.

### Catching Your Dreams

Research shows that everyone dreams every night, so the
first problem if you are unable to remember them is to "catch
your dreams." Some people wake up during the phase of sleep
when dreams are more easily recalled. It takes some effort and
discipline but I've found it worthwhile, sometimes, to catch
dreams during the night, so I have a flashlight, dream notebook,
and pen at bedside. Some people find it easier to keep a notebook
in the bathroom.

Morning is a good time to remember dreams. I find that if
I keep my eyes closed when I awaken and don't move my body,
I'm more likely to stay in a semiconscious state where I can recall
at least one image. It's like catching a mouse by the tip of the
tail as it slips around the corner. If you can grab the tip, you can
pull the whole dream back, bit by bit. Then I let my thoughts and
feelings gently settle. Sometimes in this state an idea comes to me
about what the dream means. Sometimes, in fact, an idea comes
without my remembering the dream at all. I linger awhile around
any vague sensations that I notice in my body and see if any

feelings or memories emerge. As long as I keep my eyes closed, or stay in that dawn state, I stay in touch with the inner world. Perhaps that is the meaning of the image in folklore that, as soon as the cock crows, all the ghosts disappear. Then I open my eyes to more concentrated thought and write down the dream, amplify the images, and let the dream speak to me.

## Amplification

In analyzing dreams, most people are more familiar with the Freudian method of "free association" than the Jungian method of "amplification" of dream images. In free association, you take the original dream image and see what association—second image or thought—freely appears from your unconscious. Then you look at the second association and see what third image or word it evokes, until you have a string of associations usually going back to a childhood origin. A typical Freudian sequence would be a chain of associations: church steeple–big penis– father's penis–specific childhood memories or fantasies of father's penis–conflicts about sex or aggression.

In the Jungian method of dream analysis, the "amplification" of dream images is similar to free association in that we let various associations appear freely without censoring them or the mean- ings they contain, and they sometimes go back to problems in childhood. The process is different, however, since we stay with the original image because we believe it contains a great richness of meaning within itself and has a lot to tell us directly from another world—our own personal inner world and the universal realm of symbols and myths that we share from the cultural heritage of humankind. We amplify the original image by seeing what second image appears, then back to the original image until a third image appears, then back to the original one, and so forth. A typical Jungian sequence then would be associations radiating from a central image: church steeple–big penis–church steeple– pointing to heaven–church steeple–my big hopes–church steeple–spiritual yearnings–church steeple–gleaming and sharp, etc. It is similar to the Eastern meditation technique "The Thousand-Petal Lotus," where one central symbol can lead out in many directions in an expanding circle to a multiplicity of other images.

To amplify an intriguing dream image of your own, you can concentrate lightly on it and see what other image floats up from your unconscious. Then return to the original image and see what image, thought, feeling, or memory appears next, and keep returning this way for a while to explore what the original image might mean to you. Then, if you're especially fascinated by the image, you may want to sketch or paint it, or look it up in a symbol dictionary.

Because dreams come from the unconscious, they share the same language of symbolism as art, myths, folklore, and religious ritual, which all spring from the imagination. Some of these symbols speak to us across cultures and across time. Therefore, another form of amplification typical of Jungian dream analysis is finding universal themes in myths and folklore that are parallel to images found in dreams. It is challenging, especially for women, to find truly universal meanings in the myths we grew up with, since they often offer insights about the human condition which have been shaped to fit certain cultural and religious biases. Western culture has relied heavily on Greek myths, and since we live in a patriarchal culture, those myths do indeed represent our general heritage and world situation. However, they often disappoint women searching for their own feminine nature, since the myths usually feature male protagonists preoccupied with war, rationality, power over death, and the subordination of the feminine and women. In general, myths sound distant and abstract to us, and often reflect the psychology and the politics of those in power.

In contrast, fairy tales, folk stories, ballads, and ritual often come from ordinary people—including women—trying to fathom the nature of everyday life, love, and the unknown. Early versions of stories must be ferreted out, because when the stories were finally written down, they were often altered by individual authors to reinforce cultural norms. For example, Wilhelm Grimm edited his collection of fairy tales to promote the moral teachings of his society: that girls and women should be passive and conforming, and old women should be silent. Jungians[1] and other scholars[2] have been searching for the feminine in early myths of Greek goddesses and in other literature—sometimes back to prepatriarchal times—to unearth symbols that sprang from women's own nature and still speak to us today. We, too, can look at myths, fairy tales, poetry, art, and stories to find again our feminine knowledge of how nature changes and regain our awe of life with all its hardship, passion, and mystery. We are finding echoes of these early motifs in women's dreams today.

Sometimes in this book I amplify a dream by telling about parallel stories from folklore: a fairy tale such as "Cinderella," a children's story such as "The Ugly Duckling," or an image such as the Mermaid. The earliest origins of such stories, or a feminist interpretation, can shed light on the essence of the feminine in a dream and underscore its special meanings for us today. You might notice whether your own dreams ever remind you of a myth, a fairy tale, or a story from childhood. You might discover the myths or universal themes that are also prominent in your life.

The shift from the oral to the written tradition centuries ago has skewed the general process of interpreting stories so that we focus on their images, which can be described in words (as in the text of this book, too). We neglect the other half of any symbol or story: the feelings. Similarly, people usually concentrate on the *images* in dreams and pursue them for meaning, but it is also important—if not more important—to be aware of the *feelings* elicited by dreams. Sometimes the feelings are dramatically obvious: You wake up frightened with a pounding heart or holding your breath in anticipation. But often feelings are more subtle.

How do you know what your feelings are? Since your body registers the slightest nuances of unconscious feelings, listen closely for a while to any tensions or other vague feelings you may notice in your body. If you use this "body sense" you can become attuned to your feelings and they will become more and more clear to you. You may discover early memories, even preverbal ones that have been held back in your "body memory." For example, a tight feeling in your throat and a constriction in your upper chest might seem like a suppressed cry and call forth a vague memory of whimpering alone in a dark room as a child.

Getting in touch with a feeling can start a spontaneous process of amplification. Sometimes a feeling releases a burst of other feelings or fresh images that interplay with the original feeling, which tells you more about it. For example, if you awaken with a knot in your stomach and concentrate on that feeling you may suddenly remember how scared you were in your dream giving a speech, and the knot shifts and loosens enough to release flashes of other images and fears about earlier performances. Another example is a dream that leaves a residue of tension in your elbow. If you exaggerate that muscle tension, you might discover yourself raising your arm in anger, and realize how angry you were at a particular character in your dream or at a particular person in real life. For an image and a feeling are two sides of the same coin. It's good to know both, if you can, because each completes the other half. Finding the feeling that goes with an image (or the image that goes with a feeling) adds depth and reality to the experience of your dream.

Your body sense can also tell you which images and meanings are truly important to you out of your myriad associations. You know you're on the track of something when you feel mounting curiosity and excitement. Then, you know you've finally touched what's important when you think, "Aha!" or you feel some shift in mood. That's the moment when unconscious thoughts, feelings, or meanings have finally broken through into consciousness. Then you may suddenly feel a change in your body: a release of tension, surprise, amusement, laughter, or crying. To find out something you didn't know before, even if it's negative, usually brings a flow of life and energy.

## Further Steps in Analyzing Dreams

If you have a "big dream," one that tells a story and seems especially vivid, you may want to analyze it thoroughly. After noticing and perhaps writing down images and feelings, you can also look at the general structure and movement of the story for clues to meaning. Sometimes a dream is like a stage play, with a setting, a cast of characters, a conflict or problem, a decisive moment or dramatic action, and some kind of resolution or ending. The setting is often a clue about when and where an issue first occurred, such as the family dinner table in your childhood home, a dating scene from high school, the first time away from home, the birth of your first baby, a distressing job interview, the first year of retirement.

The unconscious is also uncanny in choosing characters to represent parts of yourself. A rule of thumb is that if a character is someone you know well, the dream is pointing out some quality you haven't noticed enough about the real person, such as recent sadness you've overlooked in your best friend. However, if a character is someone remote in your history or someone you don't know, then the person probably represents a more remote aspect of yourself that you haven't acknowledged enough, such as your own sadness. In either case, ultimately, your own dreams are talking about you. They're bringing to your attention certain qualities you don't know consciously about yourself and consequently can't perceive clearly in others.

A dream can be understood in two ways: what it says about your outer life, and what it says about your inner life. In analyzing dreams for this book, usually I first present the implications of dreams for everyday life and emphasize that aspect, since it is more easily understood in our extraverted culture. Then I present what dreams mean about what's happening within the dreamer's own psyche because dreams are also talking about the dreamer and her inner life, trying to convey some truth about her.

Don't be discouraged in this undertaking of analyzing your own dreams. It is a difficult process whether you are a beginner or a seasoned analyst. It's like trying to decipher hieroglyphics for which the codebook has been lost. Even if a dream seems to be about someone else, it is ultimately telling us something we don't know about ourselves, our own lives, or about life in general. Our conscious mind, arrogant and used to being in charge, often hears only what it wants to hear or hears only that which confirms what it already knows.

Although it does take some effort to do dreamwork, you go further with an attitude of ease rather than one of grim determination. There are periods when it is easier to recall dreams, such as vacation time. You don't always have to labor at it. You don't have to look for a dream every night nor wrest the meaning out of every dream. Dreams do their job; the little elves do their work at night whether you acknowledge them or not, though it's nice to have the shoes they make—the practical results of dreamwork for your life.

Just taking a few moments to think about a dream gives energy to your inner life and allows additional meaning to filter through to the conscious mind. Writing down or tape-recording a dream helps, too, as does working with images and analyzing them. Dreams are often weeks, months, or years ahead of your conscious understanding, so if you review your dreams now and then, you can sometimes perceive sequences and themes. It's surprising how an early dream suddenly can become more understandable. No matter how experienced you are in working with dreams, however, another person can be helpful. Just telling the dream to a friend, counselor, therapist, or analyst can clarify it for you even if the other person does not comment. It impresses the dream upon your psyche, and the dream comes alive.

Therapy, counseling, or analysis is not available nor the choice for many people. I have had many years of very helpful analysis, but I can also attest to the great value of working in a small dream group with friends. I think a leaderless dream group with a total of three people meeting for an hour and a half each week to discuss dreams can work quite well for some people. One possible format for a meeting is for each person to tell a dream; then, in turn, the other two group members comment on the dream—and this is important—as if it were their own, telling what it means to each of them. Since dreams often contain universal elements, others may find meanings and perspectives the dreamer has overlooked. Also, in this way, others are not telling you what your dream means; they are not imposing interpretations on you, so you are free to listen and absorb from others what rings true. This is a gentle way to work with dreams, similar to the women's tradition that has arisen from consciousness-raising groups.

## Temenos: Creating a Safe Setting

From earliest times people have demarcated a magic circle as a protected space within which sacred ritual could take place; they have set aside a taboo area or sacred ground to honor a deity placed in the center, or have enclosed a special area for prayer or contemplation. Jung found echoes of these protected spaces in people's dreams about special inner containers: a circle of protection, a mandala, a garden with a fountain in the center with healing waters from below. Jung used the Greek word *temenos* (tem'-e-nos)—the precincts of a sacred temple—to indicate the kind of safe, protected container required for the deep inner work of unconscious development, and Jungians today regard analysis as a special container, a "temenos."

How can you create such a setting for yourself to do inner work, such as dream amplification? If it's possible, you might try to find a time and place protected from intrusion from the outside, such as morning time in bed. You also need a safe atmosphere. Some people must keep still and be alone. Some people prefer to be in motion surrounded by familiar sounds: at home doing chores with others quietly nearby, gardening, or taking a walk. Sometimes, if you're in a setting with a hum of familiar distractions, you can enter a state of diffuse awareness so that your mind can wander or even reach deep contemplative levels. Other people find that the safest atmosphere for confronting dreams and the unconscious is being in the comforting presence of a trusted confidante. When another person listens with empathy and respects the importance of dreams, sometimes you can then experience the vividness, the reality, of your own dreams and feel inspired to explore them further than you could by yourself. The idea of the temenos applies to when you confide your dreams to a friend or mate. Just as analysts keep careful confidentiality to guard a person's own inner process from outside disturbance, likewise it is good to ask your listener to preserve your unconscious material within the circle that you form together.

If you can't find a situation that feels safe to you and you're too afraid of being overwhelmed by the unconscious, it's important to wait until you do feel safe and have access to someone who knows the unconscious. It is wise to know your limitations and follow your inner sense of timing that cautions you. There are times in life you should hesitate at the water's edge until you feel ready to go more deeply into your unconscious, especially if you might stir up very troubled waters. For example, you should take warning, stop dreamwork for a while, or seek help, if you dream of blithely going down a stairwell and opening up the door to floodwaters, wildfire, quicksand, or sinister monsters that over-power you with no escape possible; if you find yourself waking up from nightmares preoccupied with overwhelming fear, fore-boding, rage, or sadness; or if you see that the more you work on your dreams, the more confused or disoriented you get.

Notice when a particular image or emotion seems "too hot" to work on. Honor your reluctance to tell anyone about it until you know deep inside that you're ready to face it yourself and that you have found someone trustworthy enough. You may want to make a note of a dream, but put it "on a back shelf" to incubate, perhaps for as long as a decade or more. If there's something you must know for your current development, probably the uncon-scious will repeat it, in dream after dream, until you hear the message and deal with it in your life.

## Active Imagination

In the course of working on dreams, a person may occasion-ally use a variation of amplification called "active imagination," a direct encounter with the unconscious while awake. Through this kind of fantasy work you can augment your dream images and integrate them into consciousness. You will find that a few times in this book a dreamer uses active imagination. Since it is an advanced method and I can't describe it fully enough here for your own use, I refer you to a book by a Jungian author, Robert Johnson,[3] for your further exploration. However, since you might be interested in using some form of it, I will describe briefly the different kinds of active imagination. Active imagina-tion reveals a special attitude toward the unconscious, which shows the essence of Jungian work.

The most common kind of active imagination is mental imagery work. When you consciously let yourself enter an inner landscape, you might encounter an inner figure—have a dialogue with the Trickster, the wily side of yourself. You might give a physical form to an inner emotion—ponder your grief until it appears as a wounded bird that must be cared for in some way. Or you might decide what you should do with an important symbolic object, such as a golden egg, perhaps guard it properly. Other kinds of active imagination are painting, sculpture, movement, automatic writing, poetry, music, and sandplay—where you place objects in a box of sand. Unlike the process of art, where skill and products are important concerns, here you are working with your unconscious in an imaginative way only for yourself.

Active imagination is not like conscious problem-solving, where your conscious mind—what you think of as "I," the ego— is pursuing a goal with its knowledge, focused attention, stream of conscious thought, words, and insights. In active imagination, the conscious mind collaborates with the unconscious to work through deeper issues necessary for your own development.

I can best convey the attitude behind active imagination by explaining what might happen if you were to experience it. Imagine entering this kind of storyland and see what you're likely to encounter. Like a brave traveler to a foreign land, your conscious mind—the ego—gets ready and knocks on the door of the unconscious to see who its inhabitants are and what's happening there. This requires some daring, but also some humility. The real key to entering this realm of intuition, though, is your playful spirit that opens the flow of inner spontaneity and creativity. Once inside this inner realm, you—the main actor in this drama—will encounter something, perhaps a winged dragon, but you don't have to handle it alone. You can ask for help from the sovereign of that land, the Greater Self—and see what images or intuitions come forth. The ego, ruler of the conscious world, and the Self, ruler of the unconscious,[4] each with its own autonomy and its own weight, must work together since each has knowledge in its own realm. That is, your ego knows about the realities of the outer world, and you use your common sense to sift through solutions, ask for more help when needed, and, like a heroic figure from fairy tales, concentrate and persist until a resolution is found. The special guide, the Self, the center of transcendent power, offers wisdom and healing from the inner world.

A person's active imagination may sound like an authentic fairy tale, because it comes from the same place where fairy tales and dreams originate, and gives rise to similar resolutions that ring true emotionally. To continue this story, if you ask for help from the Self, a magical bird, a messenger from your deepest intuition, might appear, and perhaps you decide to follow its advice—to make an alliance with the winged dragon. When deep symbolic work on an inner problem like this has taken place, you may then feel truly "moved" emotionally, as if relieved of an inner burden. Something would be settled inside, and although you might feel tired from the work, you'd probably feel a sense of renewed energy for your everyday life.

Active imagination is soul-work. The crux of the Jungian attitude is to respect the unconscious and the guidance of one's center—the source of one's deepest intuition, feelings, and values. Active imagination therefore differs from most visualization work. In the latter, the ego is more of a conquering hero seeking to use the unconscious material for its own goals, but not being truly affected by the unconscious. Jungian work requires faith in the unconscious, but not to the extent that the ego relinquishes its sense of purpose and sustained effort, for then you would experience only passive fantasy—where unconscious images pass by as if in a movie—or, like the fairy-tale hero who can't keep awake, you risk being overcome by the unconscious.

## The Language of the Unconscious

### Dream Images as Metaphors

While dreams often reassure us and resolve problems, they also sometimes frighten and wake us up. Typical dream images of anxiety are natural phenomena—floods, tidal waves, earthquakes—or the sensations of falling or crashing. These images inform us that we are troubled underneath. Often this is helpful. The dreams are trying to resolve problems we have been reluctant to admit or bring to our conscious attention so that we can actively handle them. But dreamwork is not helpful when it opens us up to such strong emotions that they intrude on daytime life. Then, it is better to wait a while on the good firm land of consciousness and everyday life.

A dream may frighten a person unnecessarily when the conscious mind doesn't understand its language. The language of the unconscious is alarmist! It exaggerates to make itself heard, like a child who has to scream to get attention. For example, killing someone in a dream is usually translated as being angry with someone or wanting to get rid of some part of yourself.

Dreams usually express things in images, but these should be understood *metaphorically*, not concretely. A burglar breaking into your house or a stranger chasing you may mean that some new element in your psyche is trying to break into consciousness, trying to reach you and be acknowledged. While a dream about intercourse may indicate that you actually desire to be with someone sexually, it often is metaphoric, meaning that you are coming close to, coming together with, embracing or receiving a special quality within yourself that the person in the dream represents. A dream of giving birth may express a wish to have an actual baby, but it often can be metaphoric, meaning a new development in your own psyche. Being naked in front of someone in a dream probably doesn't mean you're secretly exhibitionistic or seductive; rather it could mean that you're being open and vulnerable, being yourself without pretense, protection, or cultural accoutrements.

Dreams about death can be frightening and misunderstood. If you dream someone dies, it usually refers to metaphoric death, such as a loss or something missing in your relationship. But, since dreams almost always refer to yourself, it also may mean you have lost or miss the quality in yourself that the person represents. Thus a dream where you mourn the death of an exuberant, artistic childhood friend (when you are actually work-weary) is pointing out to you the loss of your own exuberant and artistic spirit. On the other hand, if you dream of your own physical death, it is undoubtedly symbolic, referring to a transformation, a great change taking place in your life. Analysts have generally found that dreams are unreliable about foretelling actual death. In fact, physical death in a dream is usually metaphoric and prepares a person for some great change in life, such as leaving behind one stage in life for another; whereas symbolic or ceremonial death—passage to another world in a dream— prepares a person actually facing death, such as someone terminally ill, to understand and inwardly accept physical death.

Analyzing dreams in a spirit of play will help you, especially when you are just starting to notice them. Dreams can be very difficult to understand at first. The dream voice, when you begin to hear it, seems like a bumptious teenager who only says, "I don't know" or mumbles obscure expressions to frustrate and puzzle you. However, as with a new teenage friend, if you don't rush in to tell the dream what it means, but listen patiently, the inner dream voice will emerge more eloquently and feelingly, not necessarily telling you what you'd expect to hear, but the truth of what it knows. If you befriend the unconscious, it becomes your ally.

You will find that dreams truly inform you in little ways, and sometimes they gradually lead you to follow the deeper currents of your life. This happens when certain dreams grip your attention. You no longer just look at them with detachment as if they were interesting movies, but you are moved by them. To be in tune with the deeper layers of your psyche, your own arrogant ego, the conscious mind, starts to take into account this new, informative inner companion commenting on life. Similarly, if you truly befriend a teenager, you can hardly remain unmoved by his or her strong wishes and fresh insights. As your inner voice develops and speaks with maturity and wisdom, you may begin to feel the ethical imperative to let it affect your life. Thus, the conscious mind yields to wisdom from the deep, while yet retaining its captaincy in translating what the unconscious says into what makes sense in the outer world of practical realities and ethics.

## History of the Archetypal Unconscious

Most dreams, and many of the dreams in this book, come from the more accessible layer of the unconscious, the "personal unconscious," which consists of experiences from childhood and current everyday life. Since Freud concentrated on the personal unconscious, and his view is the most familiar to people, I'll describe it briefly here as a point of departure. Freud considered the personal unconscious the entire extent of the unconscious. It was the repository of "preconscious" thoughts and memories that were close to awareness or forgotten, and also more repressed instincts and conflicts, which had never reached conscious awareness. The repressed material could try to find expression in "wish-fulfillment" fantasies and dreams. However, the main function of dreams, he thought, was to disguise this repressed material and keep it from conscious awareness. In fact, an expert was required to understand the hidden meanings of images.

Jung, who originally collaborated with Freud, came to believe that the function of dreams was not to obscure but to bring unconscious contents to awareness, a view that now generally prevails. In Jung's view, images and symbols appear in dreams because they're the natural language of the unconscious, and he saw that they could be understood through translating the dream language. Moreover, he observed that the unconscious is more than a repository of unacceptable material. It contains content that compensates for whatever one-sidedness the conscious mind happens to have. In fact, the unconscious seems to select what messages a person *needs* to hear.

Jung's major departure from Freud was his discovery of contents in the psyche beyond the personal unconscious—the archetypes. In fact, differences over this issue precipitated the break between these two early collaborators in the study of the unconscious. In 1909 when they were both lecturing in the United States, Freud and Jung had been analyzing each other's dreams. On the return voyage, Jung had a dream about a "house" which revealed to him that beneath the personal unconscious were deeper layers of the unconscious. To summarize the dream and his interpretation from his memoirs: The top floor of the house, which was inhabited, represented his conscious mind. In the dream he descended the stairs to an uninhabited ground floor with medieval furnishings and a brick floor; he explored every room. This floor stood for the first level of the unconscious. The deeper he went, the darker and more alien the scene became. He found a heavy door which led down to a cellar from Roman times. His interest grew intense as he looked at the stone slabs on the floor, and discovered a ring in one. He pulled it, and descended stone steps into the depths of a cave cut into the rock. Thick dust lay on the floor, and in the dust were scattered bones, broken pottery, and two skulls that were very old.

Freud concentrated on the skulls and saw them as death wishes Jung had toward people in his personal life, but Jung saw a deeper meaning. He wrote later that the dream "constituted a kind of structural diagram of the human psyche; it postulated something of an altogether *impersonal* nature underlying that psyche . . . and the dream became for me a guiding image which in the days to come was to be corroborated to an extent I could not at first suspect. It was my first inkling of a collective a priori beneath the personal psyche. This I first took to be the traces of earlier modes of functioning. Later, with increasing experience and on the basis of more reliable knowledge, I recognized them as . . . archetypes."[5] Jung called this deeper layer "the collective unconscious"[6] to show its universality and distinguish it from the personal unconscious. He launched his fifty-year study of philosophy, archaeology, mythology, art, religion, and alchemy; through this study he discovered universal patterns and themes fundamental to the psyche, so that he could understand the meanings of archetypal symbols that he found in dreams. In addition, as a conscientious researcher, Jung analyzed 67,000 dreams before he attempted to theorize about them for his series of books.

## What Are Archetypes and Where Do They Originate?

Occasionally in this book and in your dreams you will encounter archetypes (ark'-e-types)—symbols that are fascinating, mysterious, and usually charged with intense energy. These are the unconscious images and feelings that are the basis for our most meaningful and moving experiences in life. It is important to recognize archetypes whenever you can so that you can find their deeper meanings—meanings that are common to various cultures and peoples—and distinguish them from personal symbols, which pertain more to your everyday life. Traditionally, the names of archetypes have been capitalized (e.g., the Grim Reaper) because they represent fundamental truths about the human condition, or they've been given Latin or Greek names (e.g., the *puer aeternus*, the eternal boy; the *anima*, the feminine side of a man; *Aphrodite*, the goddess of love), which show their mythic origins and universality.

You may be familiar already with certain *traditional* archetypes found in dreams, myths, and art, which often take the form of special figures in dreams: the Great Mother, the Devouring Mother, the Witch, the Divine Child, the Great Father, the Hero, the Wise Old Man, the Trickster, the Clown. Archetypal images can also be plants and animals of symbolic importance (a tree, a flower, a swan, a spider); natural forms in the universe (the sun, the moon, the earth, fire, water); meaningful objects (a hidden treasure, a pearl); and geometric patterns (a pyramid, the spiral). Some archetypes represent important inner processes: meaningful developmental transitions (an initiation or marriage ceremony); intense emotional experiences (awe, anguish, merriment, harmony); parts of the psyche that participate in inner change (the shadow, the Self, the animus—a woman's inner masculine figure); and processes of transformation themselves (growth, decay, alchemical distillation, death and rebirth).

Don't worry if you don't know what archetypes are, or what the different names mean. This knowledge comes only gradually, through experience, and is always limited because archetypes can never be logically or rigorously described or actually seen. You can only glimpse their images in dreams or active imagination, or feel the force of their energy. You can't define them any more than you can define the wind, but you can see their effect. Since archetypes are so important, however, I'll further describe different views of them, which will highlight their various aspects. From these working definitions, then, you can build up a general picture of the many forms archetypes can take.

One view is that archetypes are psychological counterparts of biological instincts. Just as instincts are universal, underlying patterns of complex behavioral potentials existing in the body from the beginning of life, so, too, archetypes are underlying patterns in the psyche from the beginning of life. Like instinctive behavior in animals (imprinting, migration, nest-building) which unfolds in time and is triggered by certain stimuli in the environment, archetypes are evoked by major transitions, universal human experiences, or "archetypal events" in life. I think the parallel between archetype and instinct is especially obvious in those psychological events that are also physical transitions, such as puberty, marriage, giving birth, nurturing a child, aging, and dying. These events provide opportunities for psychological and spiritual growth, and can be profoundly emotional and deeply meaningful experiences.

Sometimes Jungians seem to imply that archetypes are inherited ideas or symbols in the collective unconscious of humankind, since certain myths and motifs appeared universally across various cultures and throughout history. In my own clinical experience, I have been shaken to see the spontaneous appearance in modern people's dreams of ancient archetypal symbols with which they were not familiar, which surprised the dreamers and were strangely apt: an elaborate sun wheel, a golden light of healing, the Third Eye of transcendence, the vulture of death and completion picking the bones clean, a labyrinthian journey of initiation, a cleansing ritual of purification, the imperious Snake Goddess on her throne. I doubt that these complex symbols were transmitted genetically, but they may be the products of the creative functioning of the archetypal unconscious, which begins with elemental patterns and combines them throughout life into more complex forms. Evidently we begin with some innate images and patterns (the newborn baby's response to simple pictures of a human face, the inborn capacity to develop words and language), but these are elementary patterns and must be elaborated by outer experience and inner creative processes.

Of course, we come into a world that already has a rich cultural heritage of art, traditions, and stories containing complex archetypal symbols and themes which have been preserved, elaborated, and shaped by many psyches through the ages. Some of these archetypal symbols still speak to us in our time because they strike an inner chord as they did when they originally appeared to someone—in a dream, a fantasy, or in the course of artistic creativity. However, many symbols of the past 5,000 years—the patriarchal era—no longer move us, especially as women; consequently, we are turning to subjective experience to find those universals of human life that have been neglected and that form the archetypes that are "alive" to us today.

As I listen closely to women's personal impressions of their childhood experiences, I wonder at times whether many archetypes might actually be vague memories of early childhood. After all, preverbal experiences can only be registered in images and emotion, the same language as the unconscious uses. Perhaps all parents seem to be "giants" and "gods" to children. Could this account for the universality of many archetypes, their power and emotion? I don't think, however, that archetypes can be reduced to being merely names for these early experiences. I think that we perceive our earliest intimate relations through a filter of innate patterns and emotions. The kinds of real-life experiences we have, in turn, affect how archetypes evolve; experience and archetypes shape each other throughout life.

## Archetypes in Women's Dreams

Jungian tradition has emphasized the primacy of *images* in the manifestation of archetypes, and has only briefly acknowledged that intense emotions often accompany them. The main function of the archetype has been seen by many Jungian analysts as one of combining and integrating seemingly paradoxical thoughts or ideas, transcending opposites such as light and dark, negative and positive (the Tao is one example), masculine and feminine (male/female union; androgynous gods), life and death (a cross). Archetypes seem distant or cool since they loom large to us and make us feel small. They feel "numinous" with awesome mystery and authority because they represent important principles in life, truths about the unknown, spiritual essence, and knowledge, such as the Self, the Buddha, or the Great Father. Often such archetypal images bring shifts in thinking about the nature of the universe or a perspective on life and death.

Just as the emotional side of human life has been denigrated by authority figures who overvalue rationalism, the emotional component of archetypes has also been undervalued. Perhaps one reason the emotional side of archetypes is often ignored is that emotions are hard to put into words. I've been impressed with the intense charge of many archetypes and the great energy they bring people. I believe that archetypes originate in our innate, primary *emotions* such as contentment, sadness, fear, anger, and feelings of rejection—emotions which are found universally in children and adults across all cultures.[7] I can often identify archetypes in women's dreams by the freshness of the moment and the feeling tone of the dreamer. I picture an archetypal ocean of primal emotions—turbulent waters, tidal currents, and still waters. Under this ocean is the changing topography of the ocean floor with its flat plains, deep trenches, mountains, and great continental shelves. In life, we mainly see what is on land, in consciousness. But the drama of outer life is always being registered in the unconscious—in the shifting currents, movements of great fishes, and ever-changing ocean floor. However, this picture is just part of a larger image of the archetypal world—the entire earth with its core of molten energy and its place in the universe. This molten core is *psychic energy*, a general energy for Eros, to love and be related, and Logos, to explore and to know.

So, by and large, you will have to be alert to the feeling side of any archetypal image which is alive to you and let it speak directly to you. On the other hand, some archetypes have such strong and clear emotional force that we can name them by it, such as Great Despair, Great Indifference, Great Neglect, or Grace which you will find in dreams or discussions in this book.

Other dreams actually feature the feeling side of archetypes, but you have to decipher the code. The clues lie in certain imagery that symbolizes feeling. Since feelings are formless, they're often expressed by images of texture, colors, fluidity, and, in rare instances, sound. Textures express very intimate (or distant) feelings, such as the soft fur of a rabbit, the rough bark of a tree, or cold, hard metal. Colors are the main medium for expressing feeling in images, from the intense primary colors to the subtlest variations. Archetypal colors range from red blood to the highly differentiated rainbow, an array of color formed of misty air. In fact, the rainbow was the archetypal symbol of the ancient goddess Iris (the predecessor of Hermes/Mercury), who was the messenger from the unconscious and bringer of creativity.[8] Water is an age-old archetypal symbol of the life-giving forces and the flow of feeling in general, and it figures often in women's dreams: the ocean, the river, the rain, the deep well, the waterfall.

I have been impressed, also, with archetypal symbols of energy breaking out in women's dreams. You can sense primary energy expressed in archetypes of fire, wind, storms, and boiling water. Energy is expressed in more complex motifs of freedom and movement: the *puella aeterna* (the eternal girl, she who dances forever in our psyches), the Big Cat who pounces, and movement that transcends the ordinary—flying through the air, skiing, and swimming.

I was intrigued by the combination of freedom, movement, and color in an image—mermaids in many subtle colors—in a woman's dream that appears in the "Relationship" chapter. This was not the usual mermaid seen through men's eyes, but an archetypal Mermaid, which has fresh meaning for a woman today about her own sensuality and her own flexible body at home in the waters of the unconscious, that is, the fluidity of her own feelings. When feeling and energy become more differentiated and integrated, they bring us archetypal symbols of value, meaning, healing, and transcendent spirituality. These can be intricate combinations of colors, or special ones such as golden or white light.

In our feelings lies our humanity—or inhumanity—and I'm especially interested in the complex emotions that have positive energy to sustain and heal us as well as unite us with others. For instance, trust and daring, which originate in our earliest shared moments of looking, touching, and laughing, become Love and Playfulness—sources of energy for us throughout life. The archetypes of the Self and the puella aeterna have their roots deep in these emotions. Although such archetypal images often appear more prominent in dreams than do feelings, the feelings are always moving beneath the images. Thus, whenever possible, it is important to be open to the emotional side of archetypes, since the main function of archetypes is to handle emotions, to express the richness of emotional experience, and to integrate emotion and image. This is what I discovered in the women's dreams in this book, and this is the theme behind the title "Wisdom of the Heart."

## Traditional and New Archetypal Figures

In dreams, the most familiar archetypes are personifications of human potential in the form of gods or goddesses, kings or queens, heroes or heroines, wonderful or terrible figures whom we may recognize from myth, folklore, art, and religion. You can tell that figures are archetypal because they feel larger-than-life and wield special power, wisdom, or authority beyond the ordinary. In fact, the figures do have qualities beyond us, deep in our unconscious, which we feel compelled to learn about, and they also have energy we can draw upon.

Some traditional Greek gods and goddesses are still "alive" to women today, such as the three early goddesses who were complete in themselves: Artemis (Diana), goddess of the moon, the wilderness, and all creatures, who demonstrates freedom, adventure, and our own untamed nature; Hestia, goddess of the hearth and inner wisdom, guardian of continuity in the home and family, and keeper of the sacred fire at the center; and Athena, goddess of wisdom, who embodies our natural right to strength and authority in the world. Sometimes figures in our dreams look like the familiar Greek statues, but usually they take less obvious shapes. In dreams, Artemis can be a young Native American woman, a woman naturalist, veterinarian, or zookeeper, a Girl Scout leader, or a Crone roaming the forest; or she might be an independent woman, a feminist, Wonder Woman, a mother bear, or a deer. Hestia might be a woman at the fireplace or the stove, a priestess lighting a candle, or fire itself. Athena might appear in a dream as a confident, active woman, or an owl. Alive to women today are other goddesses neglected through time and now returning in dreams: Demeter, the Earth Mother, sorrowing for her daughter's return and the renewal of the earth; Inanna, powerful and sensuous Sumerian queen, going to the depths of the Underworld; Quan Yin, the lively and playful Far Eastern goddess of compassion, who protects the family and its children, and listens to the cries of the world.

Sometimes women's dreams show the hero who meets a challenge and does the task, the Knight in Shining Armor or other traditional male archetypes, or the traditional female figures of Mary and Joan of Arc, or prominent historical figures— Cleopatra, Madame Curie, and Mother Teresa. But more often our dreams today feature the Imprisoned Woman Within, or the Wounded Girl Within—the Missing Child, the Neglected Girl, or the Victim.

I've been struck by how many women's psyches and dreams are dominated by the archetypes of the Abused and the Abuser. The archetypal forms that the victims of physical and sexual abuse take in dreams attest to the devastating effects of assault and secrecy: mutilated and slashed bodies, a blinded baby, a locked room, or a dark, evil place. The depiction of the Abuser as monstrous and sinister, masked or faceless, or as a group of tormenting, mocking, scornful devils underscores the victim's experience of dread, inhuman cover-up, and helplessness. Sometimes a complex image of the Abuser shows the many contradictory emotions of a victim's unconscious experience, such as the dream figure of the Abuser who's impeccably well dressed, seems warm and kindly, but also strangely detached and sinister. Women's dreams sometimes have figures of a helpless bystander or paralyzed onlooker who, in later dreams, becomes the one who knows, the Witness.

Women who are victims of certain kinds of emotional neglect by their mothers can have dreams dominated by other kinds of sinister figures: a woman with glazed eyes in a trance, a flamboyant witch, a woman with cobwebby hands, or ghostly figures. These express a daughter's archetypal reaction to the mother who was "not there" for her emotionally because the mother was heavily medicated, addicted, or severely depressed. These strange figures poetically highlight what's so devastating for the daughter—the mother's dissociation from genuine feeling-relatedness.

Various figures of the wounded or imprisoned side of women call forth from within us other archetypal figures to help: the Rescuer who helps and protects, the Woman of Compassion, and the Liberator who's free and sets us free. Our personal experience and our cultural heritage haven't yielded many heroines acceptable to women now, so they're usually represented in dreams by special women we have known, such as a kind-hearted neighbor who loomed large as a vital presence in childhood. Sometimes new archetypal figures of mythic proportions emerge in a dream: a huge old Black Goddess, solid and warm, with strong and callused hands, wielding an axe as a sign of power, with the armor of rage and laughter to survive herself and also be a champion for the dreamer. Contemporary dreams also reveal other new forms of archetypal feminine strength: an archetypal sisterly companion (the helper from the unconscious); a special group of older women; and a community of women, often in a circle, sometimes dancing. You can name archetypes like these when you find them. Let's call these last three the Sister, the Crones, and the Circle of Women.

Women are showing new and different figures in their dreams. There are those who depart from the norms and don't mind if they affront society: the rebellious teenager, the punk girl, the fiercely independent Bag Lady (who can also be a skeletal figure of homelessness, starvation, and harsh realities). Many of women's archetypes are life-affirming, such as the baby— harbinger of fresh life in us. Often women express archetypal qualities not by human figures but by objects or settings: the kitchen—center of nurturing; the toilet—the place for leftover feelings; the bowl, clay pot, cave, or womb—the container of creativity; the river—the course of life.

Although this book concentrates on female images, I might mention some archetypal male figures prominent in women's dreams today: the boyish puer, the careful Saturn, the powerful but philandering Zeus, the Good Father, the Wise Man, the harsh Authority, the Man Carrying the Light, the Earthy Man, the Lover, the Man of Heart, the Brother, or the Companion. Some of these dream figures have fresh and complex combinations of qualities: Jacques Cousteau, a warm-hearted Hell's Angel, a big Polynesian man.

## Animal Archetypes

Animals are prominent in women's dreams because they are models of natural potentials within ourselves and our original wholeness. Historically we have been told so often what we should be that by now we hardly know how we feel and who we truly are. In contrast, animals can be who they are and we respect and enjoy them for their genuineness. Because they're so free and close to their own instinctive knowledge, animals often represent the wisdom we've lost in becoming too conscious. So they are important messengers in our dreams from the unconscious. They show us wisdom that arises from our own natural instincts, the intuitions of our body, our spontaneous feelings and energy. Because animal dreams are so significant, you will find in this book many dream images of animals which have personal and sometimes archetypal meaning.

How can you tell if an animal in your dreams is archetypal? An animal carries special energy and meaning when it seems beyond the ordinary—exciting, intriguing, awesome, unforgettable. For instance, when you dream about a cat you know well, it probably signifies a particular quality of that cat, which may be of symbolic importance, and even have archetypal implications. But I've no doubt that it's an archetypal image when a dream is about a larger-than-life cat with wondrous eyes or an owl in the middle of a circle of women! Then you may find it worthwhile to ponder what the animal means and perhaps look it up in a symbol book to see what it has meant to humankind through the ages.

You always have to see what feelings and meanings a particular animal archetype stirs in you, but there are some general meanings animals have acquired through the ages which still ring true. Certain animals convey archetypal spiritual power because of their special qualities. They have been worshipped themselves or have been the companions of goddesses, linking us—through nature—to our spirituality. For example, animals who have the uncanny power to see in the dark, such as the cat and the owl, often symbolize to us wisdom of the mysteries and the afterlife. Familiar or domestic animals have acquired many meanings through the ages. The cat has represented contemplative wisdom, the good mother who nurtures her young, playfulness, cruelty, and, above all, the independent feminine spirit. Among its many meanings the dog, who guards the door of the house with its alert senses and protectiveness, still represents today—as it did in Egyptian times—our loyal companion who guards the threshold to death and helps us across. Since Paleolithic times the horse has been admired for its great vitality, and in women's dreams today it usually symbolizes energy and sexuality that's free and natural—like the wild horse—or useful and constructive—like the domestic horse. The horse can appear in its negative aspect as the mythic Centaur (half man/half horse), which represents the destructiveness of primitive drives that aren't yet integrated, or it can appear as the White Horse or White Mare, which is associated with the spirit and the source of creativity.

Animals often carry paradoxical meanings, since all parts of nature and all archetypes have positive and negative sides. Usually, the more remote the animal in the phylogenetic scale of development in the animal kingdom—such as the slug or the shark—the more primitive, fundamental, or undifferentiated the feelings and instincts it represents: for example, inertia, disgust, raw sexuality, or aggression. But also the more different the animal is from us, the more distant spiritual meaning it can bring to us. For example, the snake, with its body close to the earth, its eyes always open, and its venom, is the embodiment of basic earthiness and our fears about unknown powers, as well as an ancient symbol of physical and spiritual healing.

The most highly evolved animals next to humans, the other primates, are especially important in dreams. A group of monkeys may symbolize freedom from civilization and represent the impulsive, mischievous, playful, or free spirit, whereas an individual monkey may carry deeper archetypal meaning. It reminds us of our commonality with the animal kingdom and, at the same time, what makes us distinctly human. A monkey is often a good omen. It symbolizes the very beginning of a person's deep inner instinctual and spiritual evolution that eventually will be integrated into real life. Similarly, if a woman dreams of a frog or a butterfly, archetypal animals that change their forms in life and thus are heralds of transformation, she is undergoing a great developmental transition in life. Other animals that are almost always archetypal are any winged creatures—the bird, the winged dragon, the winged horse. If you are open to them, they may bring you hope and inspiration.

## The Self

The most important, fundamental, and central archetype is the Self. Jungians usually reserve the word "Self" for this Greater Self and capitalize it to distinguish this archetypal Self from the "self" of other psychological theories. In those theories, self generally refers to a person's conscious identity, the sense of who I am, the "I" who thinks and acts, the continuous stream of thoughts, one's self-worth. Jungians designate the term "ego" for that kind of focus of personal awareness. You might picture the ego as the "eye of the day," the center of consciousness, and the Self as the "eye of the night," or the "all-seeing eye," the center of the unconscious and the whole personality.

The Self has many aspects. Jungians have traditionally emphasized *pattern*, and the origin of pattern, as the most basic and yet unknowable aspect of the Self. It is the archetype of all the archetypes, the blueprint of the blueprints, the mosaic behind all patterns. You could think of it as the cell, or the DNA, which contains the pattern of all other cells. Jung called the Self "the God within us." You can imagine the Self as the unknowable essence that lies behind the crystal-forming process. It is the source of the progression of our deepest development: all the patterns that unfold from the center. Archetypal images representing this aspect are those of divine essence, form, pattern, and order: the One, the pneuma or spirit, the seed, a pyramid, the plan of a city, the mandala—a squared circle. Closely akin to this aspect of order, form, and pattern is the traditional Jungian emphasis on the Self as a *transcendence of archetypal opposites*: the Sky Father and the Earth Mother of creation, the Tao of light and dark or yin and yang, and the royal marriage of King and Queen.

Parallel to this traditional emphasis, but perhaps more common in women's dreams, are archetypal images of *wholeness*: a circle, a circle with a dot in the center, a sphere, the earth, an integrated array of colors (a rainbow or rose window), and the dreamer's own house, mansion, or castle. These reflect the all-encompassing nature of the Self and the integrating force of the archetype—your original wholeness and the wholeness of all you can be—not the usual ego-ideal of the kind of person you wish you were. Nor does wholeness imply perfection, which would exclude parts of yourself. To be whole is to know and integrate all of yourself, your faults as well as your highest potentials. The more you know each piece-of-the-pie of who you truly are, the more centered you feel. Then your well-being, your actions, your decisions come from your wholeness and your center.

This brings us to the most familiar form of the Self, the *inner guide*, an inner voice of authority, often one of transcendent compassion, pictured as a Bountiful Woman, Mother Nature, Great Grandmother, a Wise Woman. Related to this are two other forms: *union*—the capacity to know wholeness with another person and to know the essential unity of all things; and *love*—personal and transcendent.

How can you experience the Self? You know you are in its presence when you feel tremendous energy and emotion, for the Self has *numinosity*, an aura of wonder and mystery. It is the source of the life-force, creativity, love, and healing. You can experience this special energy as the buoyancy of the playful spirit, a feeling of certainty in yourself, the excitement of creativity, the warmth, tenderness, and passion of love, the feelings of grace and harmony that can come from the transcendent power of healing. The pure energy-force of the Self, and the primal feelings that flow from it, are sometimes too powerful to encounter as forces and too fluid to comprehend; they often take form as images, which we can understand and handle more easily.

Our early experiences mold our primary emotions so that they evolve into more differentiated feelings and acquire images to represent them. The unfolding of the Self is the essence of psychological development. That is why this book begins and ends with chapters on the Self: its early forms in the first chapter and later, more mature forms in the final chapter on "The Wise Heart." Early Self images in dreams suggest that the earliest experiences of wholeness are in the sound and rhythm of your body, your and your mother's heartbeat, and suggest that throughout life you can have access to the fundamental energy to be yourself and be with another by being centered in your body, following your natural bodily rhythm and pace. Correspondingly, in your psyche you can listen to your own inner drummer and move at your own pace, gain confidence in yourself, and sometimes find transcendent energy. Other early manifestations of the Self are images and feelings of remaining close to the personal mother and the Great Mother, while also separating, such as a dream image of a young Nature Woman emerging from a madonna-and-child figure. The archetypal treasure of the Self is symbolized in women's dreams as gold retrieved from the earth or pearls from the sea. Another dream image is the Unicorn, archetypal figure of the early feminine Self, free and solitary, yet also highly vulnerable. You can sense the Self now and then behind other archetypes and behind other images in your own dreams and in the dreams throughout this book, for it is the inner guide and energy, the integrating force, the director behind the stage play of all dreams.

More mature symbols of the Self show greater integration of

feeling, more developed feminine and masculine qualities, and movement toward expansiveness and a sense of union with all life—but at the same time movement toward more independence, too. In the last chapter of this book you will see symbols of passion, compassion, wisdom, detachment, and transcendence. There are grandmother figures; the bear and the cat; the Holy Spirit and other abstract images of the transpersonal dimension. There is also the symbol of a rose window, which seems to me the quintessential Self symbol for a woman: an array of beautiful, luminous colors within a circle, a symbol of wholeness coming from the differentiation and integration of myriad feelings.

## The Ego and the Self

The process of maturing is one of both strengthening the ego and aligning yourself more and more with the Self. The ego and the Self lend support to each other. Each informs the other about its world, and gives the other energy to develop further. The island chief (the conscious ego) needs to know what's rumbling deep below inside the mountain to tap its molten energy and make good use of volcanic steam. Conversely, the Self also needs the ego: When the Self receives conscious attention, the inner voice gains strength and continues to develop further.

The kind of relationship between the two is crucial. The ego must relate to the Self with deference and respect, while holding its own. If the ego becomes too entranced with the Self and the inner world, it can fall into the fiery center and get burned up, or fall off the island into an ocean of feeling or dissolve in the Greater Self. For example, you can see that the ego has lost its identity and position in reality for a person who thinks he or she is Jesus Christ, or who is fervent with idealism at the cost of personal relationships.

Also, the ego must be independent enough to identify the False Self—addictions, cravings, or inflated feelings of importance that draw you toward abusive and destructive situations. The ego must veto the False Self to see what you really want and what's good for you as a whole. The ego must also interpret the Self in terms of the ordinary ethics it knows. If the Self seems to propose that you should have an affair, take a great risk in your life, or kill someone, the ego should not take this literally, but understand its metaphorical meaning and translate it into something that makes sense in terms of ethics and real life consequences. For only in relationship can the ego and the Self complement each other, put their energy and expertise to use, and together strike the right chord. How do you do this? Listen to your dreams, listen to the small voice—carefully—but also retain confidence in your judgment of realities.

For the great decisions in life—love, work, family, and home—you need to consult both the ego and the Self. Your reasoning may lead you toward one choice, but you also need to sense what's truly important to you, consult the Self—an impulse or intuition from your deepest center so that you *know* what is the right decision. Your ego must then check your choice, verify it with common sense, and ensure that it's possible.

At a pivotal time in my life I was offered the job for which I'd been preparing ever since I was young—and I didn't automatically accept it. Something made me pause. I was puzzled that I didn't feel excited or happy deep inside. And despite a list of good reasons why I should accept it, I heeded my "gut reaction" against the job. I couldn't have explained or justified my choice to myself or anyone else, but I put my faith in the "spark of life" I felt inside me about a new field. I decided to trust—shakily so—a little voice I could barely hear that *knew*. This was a struggle between the ego—what I thought and felt I had wanted—and "the Way"—a path frightening for me to take on faith, but one that, although it required more training, held promise and turned out well in my life.

How can you tell the difference between guidance from the conscious or the unconscious? You know it's the ego operating when you have a driving kind of energy to have "your own way," whereas the Self draws you toward the Way. The ego strives for your individual identity; the Self stands for your essence, your soul. With your ego, you make decisions and work hard to establish your role and place in society; the Self shows you your mission in life and gives you the energy for it. Since most work requires the conscious discipline and effort of your ego, you feel you deserve credit for it. However, imagination, intuition, inspiration, creativity, and special energy "come" to you from the Self, so that you feel more grateful and lucky to have access to it.

We all wish to be special, but the Self knows you are special—and also ordinary—like everyone else. With our conscious mind we worry and feel insecure; the Self is our core of security within, our "safe place." We all want a sense of belonging and we fear alienation, but through the Self we can know our commonality with others and can also tolerate being different because we're being true to ourselves. We consciously seek a mate, but the unconscious knows our soul-mate; and both ego and Self are needed to choose.

With our ego we see the world through a focused lens. We see things sharply and feel confident. With the Self, we see through a wide-angle lens. Everything is more hazy and out of focus; we don't have the confidence of sharp definition but a more general confidence from seeing the whole picture. Paying attention to the Self, then, requires a more general kind of faith. We have ready access to the conscious mind because it uses words and reasons; we have to learn how to be attuned to the Self, to know what it means.

## Useful Distinctions Between the Personal and the Archetypal

Since the Great Mother is one of the most important archetypes, let's begin with the difference—and relationship—between the personal mother and the Great Mother. Out of the ocean of the unconscious comes primal Love and its loss, the Void. A baby first experiences attachment and feelings of joy gazing into the mother's (or father's) eyes, and feeling the warmth of her body. The baby is "at one" with another, before she knows she's a separate being. This is the primal experience of the Great Mother who is "always there." This inborn capacity to feel the harmony, confidence, and contentment of being in union with another later becomes the ability to have empathy with others and form deep bonds. Through her mother, then, a girl can develop the positive aspect of this archetype. However, if the mother is not positive enough, the girl feels sad and empty, and the negative side of the archetype is evoked, the Terrible Mother or the Void. In her life she will probably feel cut off from the flow of love and life-giving forces from deep within her. Then she will have to contend with her negative feelings about her own mother, and she may have to confront the Terrible Mother within. She will also try to restore love through personal experiences of trust and caring in her life. To do this she must activate love from deep within herself. The positive Earth Mother, who is always there, may come to her through her dreams or fantasy. For if she is open to the inner world, it can replenish and inspire her, rather than just deplete or threaten her. Each realm of reality helps the other: Just as personal experiences activate the Great Mother, so, too, archetypal images and feelings of love make you more receptive to personal experiences.

It can be helpful at important times in your life to distinguish whether a quality is personal or archetypal so that you don't mistake one for the other. For example, if, later in life, you lose someone you've loved, you may mistakenly think you have lost your deepest inner capacity for Love; this is not true. You can love again, for the archetypal wellspring is always there, even if you've lost contact with it for a while. Another mistake would be to attribute your own personal sadness to the state of the real world, as if it contained only the stark absence of love, the archetypal Void.

Another example is the difference between death and Death. When an acquaintance dies, you may feel loss at the absence, but when it's the first death in your life, or a parent's or spouse's death, then you may confront Death: anxiety about the great unknown. Archetypal knowledge can help you handle your feelings and thoughts about the Abyss. One archetypal symbol of Death is the Cross, which expresses the suffering in dying, the sacrifice of life, and the hope of transcendence over death. Another archetypal symbol, with origins close to nature, is the

Grim Reaper, who expresses our dread that death will cut life short; it also expresses confrontation with the hard fact, the inevitability of death, which can lead to an acceptance of nature. Those symbols can help people ponder Death and reconcile themselves to a particular death, their own death, the fact of Death.

Also, women are finding again—in their dreams and in the well-rounded and multidimensional symbols of prepatriarchal times—ancient archetypes of Life and Death that are especially helpful today. One is the Great Tree of Life, which expresses faith in nature and the continuance of the life-force after death. The Great Mother is bringer of life, protector, and destroyer. Another symbol is the ever-simmering Cauldron of Life, which expresses knowledge about the transformation and continuity of life. These images have helped people accept death through the ages. If people don't find archetypes that seem alive to them and help them with their fear of the Abyss, there is danger that they will identify with false archetypes of Death and Power, such as the Bomb, which expresses both the terror of annihilation and the power of dealing out destructiveness.

### Exercise: The Personal Mother vs. the Great Mother

You may like to try an exercise from my own training to illustrate the difference between the personal and the archetypal. Write the heading "mother" on a piece of paper, and next to it the heading, "Great Mother" (or Mother Nature, a Fairy Godmother, a Great Grandmother). Then list under each heading whatever qualities spontaneously come to mind. You're likely to find more personal and human-size traits under "mother," such as "giving," "warm," "always there," "critical," and "depleted." These come from your *conscious* experience—the cultural image of a mother, your perception of your own mother, and perhaps your own experiences of being a mother. However, under "Great Mother" you will probably find more extreme traits of great dimension or intensity, such as "all-giving," "always there," "all-embracing," "infinitely wise," "safe," "fearsome," and "devouring." These express your *unconscious* knowledge of Great Mother qualities—

the innate, powerful, essential, archetypal mothering—from which more conscious mothering springs.

Some other interesting points can be made from the similarities and distinctions you find in this exercise. Notice any close—but not identical—parallel items in the two columns. Say you are a person who described the mother as "giving" and the Great Mother as "all-giving." This shows the natural outcome of the fact that the personal reflects the archetypal in a modified way. A mother's "giving" *comes* from her deepest archetypal and instinctual source, so the power of the "all-giving" archetype is felt behind her giving, yet she mediates its power in a personal way and is capable of only limited giving. You know well, and can accept, that aspect of the archetype that is passed on to you in your personal experience. You know the archetypal, yet you wisely only expect human-size giving.

On the other hand, if you're someone who never experienced much "giving" from your mother, you may have put only rejection or criticism under the mother column, and therefore might have seen the Great Mother only in her terrible aspect. Or, perhaps, to compensate for the ordinary mothering missed in actual life, you may have great longing for the archetypal "all-giving" Great Mother. In this case, you would have elaborated on the generosity of the Great Mother and this inner image would have even greater power and force in your unconscious than if it had been mediated by the personal mother. It can be a good thing, eventually, that the unconscious always retains the archetypal quality like this, but here and now it can create problems for a woman who seeks in vain for the Great Mother in the real world, or is overwhelmed by her archetypal power within.

A second thing to do is to notice complete parallels, where you haven't distinguished the personal and the archetypal. In the above example, say the "always there" quality of the Great Mother is also attributed to the mother. This quality can never be fulfilled by a real person. A woman who tries to fulfill this expects someone to be "always there," or expects herself to be "always there" for her husband or children—an impossible task!

You might find it useful to remember this exercise when

special figures appear in your dreams or certain people loom large in your life. For example, you might explore the parallels between a figure of Pan in your dreams and an intriguing new lover, or a figure of Scrooge and a miserly, heavy-handed boss, a fairy-tale Princess and your own new feelings of success. If you can sort out the difference between the personal and archetypal, you can recognize human-size qualities within yourself and others and also respect the deeper archetypal dimensions that reverberate within yourself and between people.

# 2
# Early Glimpses of the Self: The Treasure Within

As you turn attention inward and remember your dreams, you may find early signs of the treasure deep in the recesses of your unconscious: your innermost guide, the Self. The Self holds the promise of hope and confidence that comes from your center, the Other within you. Feeling attuned to nature, having a sense of individuality and a sense of oneness with the universe—these are all experiences of the Self. Like an artesian well it flows for those who seek it, a source of energy beyond yourself.

## The Unfolding of the Self

A woman's first experience of the Self is given to her as a child by her mother, grandmother, or another nurturing person who encircles the child in loving arms and gives her feelings of trust and security. At this time early in life, the most important archetype—the Self—can be characterized as a child's inner readiness to receive the warmth and security of the mother and to experience wholeness through her. Later, as the Self unfolds, an adult woman experiences wholeness *within herself*. Just as in nature a tree thrusts roots downward, reaches branches outward, and grows toward the light to reach its fullness, so, too, a human being can draw strength from the inner regions of the Self to stretch out into the world and flourish.

If this first experience of the Self—a profound experience of security, intimacy, and love—is missed in early childhood it can still be nurtured in adulthood by a loved one, a therapist, a teacher, or a religious guide. Sometimes the Self—as a sense of your own direction and worth—must be wrested from the family. The first dreams in this chapter show how you must search for a deep sense of self-worth if your parents have made themselves the center of your life or have attributed the Self—love and specialness—only to a favored brother or sister. Sometimes the Self must be asserted against a wider culture, if it has denied your worth as a girl or placed you in the position of being a satellite to others because you are a woman. In this case, you are searching for more than the personal self—a conscious sense of identity, belonging, and self-worth in everyday terms. You are also searching for something vitally important, the greater Self—your core of well-being, integrity, authority, and personhood.

The unfolding of the Self in adulthood is a lifelong process. It can be experienced through nature—Mother Earth herself; through spiritual experiences; through the arts—poetry, painting, music, dance; or through dedication to meaningful work—caring for a family or fulfilling a mission outside the home. The Self can also be found through dreams, a rich source of unconscious archetypal images available to any woman anywhere.

## Symbols of the Self

In her dreams, a woman may first encounter early symbols of the Self as it emerges from the unconscious such as: a hidden treasure deep in the ocean, an egg, a tree, a beautiful meadow of flowers, a pregnant whale, the birth of a baby, the madonna and child, the maiden who stands alone, a house of one's own, an elf-priest. These images reflect how close the early Self is to nature and how close it remains to its origins in the Great Mother archetype that symbolizes nature in all its abundance and destructiveness, and personal mothering in its positive and negative aspects.

Later, as you will see in the last chapter, as a woman reaches the deeper resources of her unconscious, more abstract and archetypal forms of the Self may spontaneously appear: a jewel, the Capital City, a Holy Woman, a sacred heart, a circle, the Snake Goddess, a Greek cross, the Buddha, a temple, a golden glow.

Static images alone can't adequately express the Self, because they tend to imply that the Self is only a goal or end-state, whereas the Self is also the process of development itself, the "becoming." So the Self is often represented by symbols of movement: a journey, a quest for something unknown or special, the seasons of the year, the stream of life, the Way of the Tao, the spiral shape of a seashell or winding staircase.

As a woman journeys further on her path toward knowing the Greater Self, she may experience some of its healing energy percolating into her daily life. She may find within herself a feeling of things settling into place. She may feel more acceptance of her own light and dark nature and that of others. She may know transcendent feelings of oneness with others while also retaining her own autonomy. She may experience harmony and grace that somehow encompass discord and darkness. And as an older woman, she may know life and death with the unblinking eyes of the owl.

Often the energy of the Self is utilized or made known as a woman commits herself to the deeper course of her nature, as she begins to listen to her dreams, or as she begins analysis. When this happens, she may feel a gathering of her inner forces, a great quickening of energy inside herself. Something moves her, and she lets herself be moved. This also happens at moments of closeness with another person or moments of ecstasy. At other times, such as a woman's darkest times alone, the Self may seem like a light in the darkness. It is the "something" she cannot name that sustains her at times in her life when she faces the great unknowns, the threats that could uproot her—an operation, illness, death.

## The Loss of the Self and the Negative Side of the Self

You can also suddenly become aware of the Self by its apparent absence—in your wilderness of indecision before you know what must be done at times of upheaval, in the unendurable loss of the person who holds the Self for you—your mother, grandmother, child, mate, minister—until the Self comes home to you again and you recover your centeredness and buoyancy. You can feel as if you've lost the Self when you lose your homeland, lose your way of finding meaning in life, or lose your sense of belonging in the world, as if your wholeness and continuity as a person has disappeared into a "black hole" of depression and utter hopelessness.

The Self has positive and negative potentials, just as any archetypal—universal and profound—life experience does. In fact, the essence of the Self is the integration of light and dark. At times of dark transitions in life, if you can't consciously accept inner or outer realities—you're too afraid to yield yourself to the negative facts of life, the new, and the unknown—then the negative Self may pursue you. The more you brace against the negative side of the Self, the more it hounds you or even possesses you—until you face it and acknowledge it.

During times of stress or personal upheaval, symbols of the negative Self can be represented in dreams as archetypal—deep and powerful—forces contrary to wholeness within yourself, or forces of disintegration and destruction in the world: dismemberment, fragmentation, chaos, a tornado, a Nazi swastika, a whirlpool, a person burned up by the sun, the earth split open by an earthquake, a nuclear explosion.

As a person matures and develops a more conscious orientation toward the negative aspects of the Self, accepting inevitable limitations and losses in this world, then the toxic quality of negative forces can become neutralized. For example, by admitting some fear, anxiety, anger, and helplessness in life, usually you can inoculate yourself against falling into panic, terror, or vengefulness. But you can't handle the darkest aspects of life with your conscious ego alone, with its reasoning and its ideals of how things "should be." The assistance of the Self is required to integrate the negative within a larger sense of the whole—and this can be experienced as a welcome relief. How does this happen? Conscious commitment to self-exploration and the truths of the outer world are important steps. The inner symbolic process in dreams, meditation, and fantasy can also take you along the way. Pondering symbols of the Self in dreams and in the culture can also help you integrate the negative side of things and accept nature as it is. These symbols do not deny the negative but encompass it within a greater pattern of positive and negative that transcends what seem to be incompatible opposites, such as the love and hate that you can feel for the same person. One of the best representations of how embedded the negative and the positive are in each other is the circle of the Tao sign, in which a black area with a small white center intertwines with a white area with a small black center.

Some symbols of the light-and-dark side of the Self give us perspective on nature and the Great Mother archetype. These symbols—and images in our lives—unsettle and settle us; for, through them, we can perceive that we are part of greater cycles and patterns of harmony and stability and chaos and change. Some common symbols in our dreams, fantasies, and mythology are: the waxing and waning of the moon, landslides and volcanoes, the hatching of an egg, an underground stream, spring and winter, fresh-cut flowers, an ancient tree, a great-grandmother rock, a star falling to earth, a spider weaving its web, the Fates, the cauldron, the ascending or descending spiral.

We women have "blood knowledge" of Mother Nature in our premenstrual upset, flowing blood of menstruation, and upheaval of menopause. We carry mystery in the fluids of our bodies: welcoming wet vaginas, stirring of life in our bellies, breaking waters of childbirth, spurting of warm milk from our breasts. We know in our bones the reality of the symbols of the feminine mysteries, the Great Unknown: decay, devouring death, the snake goddess, a beckoning old hag, priestesses, the cat, ashes of our grandmothers, a special room in an old mansion, the wise old owl. These we know as part of the Self, the grand design.

Upon recognizing the reality of negative archetypal powers, one can be tempted to attribute great evil to the dark side of the Self. This would be a misunderstanding of the Self, as I see it, and a misuse of Jungian psychology, which should actually help one sort out individual responsibility. What, then, is evil? The problem lies in the willful ego not being in proper relationship to the negative Self. The ruthless swipe of a grizzly bear's paw is not evil, but rape is. If one must call anything "evil," one can call evil those human acts which neglect, exploit, degrade, dominate, or violate the wholeness of nature—our own human nature, other people, or our earth itself. What instinctively feels alien and evil are images of violated nature: on an individual level—child neglect, addiction, physical and sexual abuse, rape, and sadism; on a societal level—pollution, torture, rampages of war, the massacre of old women as witches, the Holocaust, Hiroshima, the spectre of nuclear annihilation, and the extinction of peoples, cultures, flora, or fauna in our Western society, in the Brazilian forests, Vietnam, or Afghanistan. These images represent not so much the dark side of the Self as the darkest side of humankind's arrogant ego.

When the ego (our conscious mind, the "I" who thinks, wills, and acts) does not honor the negative side of the Self, does not know our human nature or Mother Nature in her random, cool, impersonal aspect, the ego often unconsciously identifies with power. On a personal level, people can become all-controlling and aggressive in their relationships and work—as if human nature were controllable. On a societal level, they can unconsciously identify with the great impersonal forces of nature to produce their own imitative and inflated forms of power, such as technological weapons of destruction, as if they could control vulnerability. Then, instead of feeling awe at the power of nature, people take into their own hands weapons that are terrifying. Instead of confronting the reality of death, absorbing the Wise Old Woman's knowledge about the inevitability of death within the greater continuity of life and death, people recoil at the symbol of the harvest scythe, the Grim Reaper, and unconsciously try to avoid death, control death, conquer death. But since the power to preserve lives is limited, sometimes people bend their efforts toward the power to destroy.

We have lost what we once knew in the ancient times of the Great Goddess, when the passages into life and death were equally respected. We have also lost our own Wise Old Woman knowledge of the cycles and seasons of human life, the earth, the cosmos. Instead of being in alignment with the course of nature, we are ignorant, negligent, oppositional, and thereby endangered. So we need to know again the negative as well as the positive Self to be true stewards of our planet Earth and all its life.

The following sections describe dreams in which women found glimpses of the Self: The Early Self and the Family, The Self Passed Down from the Mother and the Great Mother, Refusing the Early Self, Acknowledging the Negative Side of the Self, and Sustaining the Feminine Self in Relationships.

## The Early Self and the Family

From the very beginning of life, how good it feels to move at our own individual pace and in accordance with the wider rhythms around us, and how alienating to our personhood to be restricted in our movement or speeded up, discordant with our surroundings. Finding our own natural rhythm is a crucial experience of the early Self: being attuned to Nature, its rhythms, and attuned to one's own inner nature. These are all early manifestations of being in accord with one's deepest center, one's environment, and even the Great Round of life and death.

This brief dream came to a fast-paced woman who was ordinarily very busy, but who had been ill with a moderate flu for many weeks. She had been sick long enough that she had become somewhat attuned to an inner quiet. Because of this, she consciously decided to take sick leave in order to allow her body complete rest, with the hope that perhaps in the process she could find some help from her own center of healing, the Self.

> *The Drummer.* I look over and see my brother Fred beating on a drum. But then I realize that it's really me. I'm the one drumming out the beat.

In real life, her brother was literally the drummer. He had played the drum in the high school band when they had been teenagers. But the dream was also figurative: Ever since she was little, her brother had set the pace, and she had tried to keep up. She hardly knew her own pace, she was so afraid of being left behind, left alone. And in the home the brother was also "the drummer." The whole family was charmed by him—his ease, his humor, his daring. It was no wonder that he became the drummer for a marching band, because in some unconscious way, the family had prepared him for that position. He seemed special; he "had it"—all signs of catching the projection of the Self from others. In contrast, the girl was not considered special in this way. She did not feel she "had it," so consequently she worked endlessly to "catch up."

Often one member of a family unconsciously becomes the carrier of the Self—the one upon whom the sun shines, a source of joy or well-being. Sometimes it is even the family's dog or cat. If this member is lost, or fails, it is as though the light has gone out of the family's life together.

This dream broke the spell for the woman. It allowed her to pause in her busy, stressful life and try to gain perspective and find her own Self, her own true pace. In the dream she became the drummer, drumming out her own beat. When she awoke the next morning, she said, "I woke up strong, as if I'd emerged reborn from weeks of hibernation."

In the following dream, another dreamer wrests her own pace and the Self and its energy away from her mother and the cultural unconscious—the culture's stereotyped image of a woman.

> *Running Ahead with Ease.* **I'm running with some women who are dressed in those jogging suits—the kind my mother tries to buy for me even though I don't like them. I say, "That's why I had a hard time getting into running, because of those clothes." Actually, I'm wearing track shorts and a tank top—the kind I really like. I'm running along, trying to keep pace with the other women. My feet feel weighted down. I'm pushing hard, and I've a feeling I can't keep it up.**
>
> **Then I become aware of a figure behind me, pacing, matching her pace to mine. At times I glimpse that it could be easy. Suddenly I thought of Tai Chi [a meditation dance] and I shot ahead. It was effortless,**

easy to run, and it felt good! I hadn't tried to pull ahead, it just happened. It was the difference between making my legs move and moving myself from the center. I'd shift back and forth so the two styles were clear to see. I didn't quite believe it—that it'd make that much difference—but it did!

This reminded her of a dream she had three years earlier:

*Side by Side.* I was racing through the forest. It was dusk. There was a driven quality to it. I couldn't look where I put my feet. I was crashing into things. Someone was running with me; she wore one of those ersatz running suits. It was scary because of the headlong rush. I couldn't see where I was going. We were side by side, keeping pace with one another, each monitored by the other.

First of all, she heartily disliked "those jogging suits" the other women were wearing in the current dream and "those ersatz running suits" in the Side by Side dream. "That's the kind of jogging outfit my mother likes," she said. "They're babyish pastel colors. My mother had one herself and it was as if she wanted me to be a twin—one reason I didn't want one! They're not even in cotton like men's—to be taken seriously like theirs—which can absorb sweat."

Clothing is often a matter of disagreement between a mother and a daughter. It can symbolize a choice between staying with the mother and the cultural unconscious or moving out into one's own separate consciousness—the freedom to have one's own body and one's own taste, the freedom to express one's own individuality in the world and, ultimately, to have one's own Self. The kind of clothing a mother prefers for her daughter reveals the image she projects onto her. In her "babyish pastel" associations to the clothes in the dream, the daughter perceived that her mother unconsciously wanted to keep her close to her as an infant, to continue to "monitor" her. In real life, she said, her mother did indeed have this attitude, which bothered her a great deal.

But the daughter "doth protest too much." The problem is not just her mother's. It is hers, too. Whenever a woman expresses great distaste or repugnance toward her mother, it is usually a sign that she is unconsciously disgusted with herself and her own clinging. This is especially true if she allows the mother to remain center stage, that is, she focuses more on what she dislikes about her mother than what she wants for herself.

As the actor in the dream, the woman could actually feel herself shifting between her mother's pace and her own. She was changing from her familiar position of being her mother's satellite to taking the lead from her own center of gravity. This dream illustrates vividly the burst of freedom and the ease, the quality of sheer energy, that come when you consciously align yourself with the Self.

Taken together, how do the dreams apply to her life? In the Side by Side dream three years earlier, she was running at a frantic, blind pace, scared and off-balance because she was caught up too much in another's pace instead of her own. The more recent dream, Running Ahead with Ease, showed her that she still gets too caught up in outer activities and meeting other people's demands, losing her sense of wholeness. She needs to move with her own spirit, at her own true pace, which happens at the end of the dream. This is the wisdom of the unconscious.

## The Self Passed Down from the Mother and the Great Mother

If you have been given enough good mothering and have had the inner experience of knowing that someone was almost always there, you probably have enough experience of the Self naturally passed down to you that you have some resilience and direction as you go out to meet life. If you have been given a great deal of mothering from someone who was always there, you may be content to stay by the hearth quite a while or you may be restless to venture forth. In any case, you have been given a profound sense of someone backing you up, and throughout life you can retain a connection to an inner island of security, the Self.

However, when archetypal events occur prematurely in life, such as a death in the family, this natural process of keeping in touch with the Self can be disrupted. The sense of Self can be lost momentarily or never regained. Or the Self can emerge—as it sometimes does in times of great need—to support you through the crisis, and thus be greatly solidified to sustain you through life. In fact, if this happens early in your life, you can seem marked with a certain intensity that comes from being strongly in touch with the Self, and can seem strong or wise beyond your years, which, in a sense, is true. However, you cannot stay in that rarified atmosphere all the time, so you also need to come down to earth from this inevitable inflation and be an ordinary human with ordinary feelings.

A woman whose mother—and father—were positive, accepting, and "always there" had her family life shattered as a teenager when her father was suddenly killed. At the time, her mother faltered, and as the eldest, she had to maintain the family. Decades later, in middle age, she dreamed about this teenage event. It showed how she had felt then, when her mother had faltered.

> *The Indian Maiden.* I'm bicycling and my mother is on the back of the bike. It's her turn to pedal and mine to ride, but she won't do it. I say, "When it's *my* turn *I* have to pedal, but how come when it's *your* turn, *I* have to pedal too?"
>
> I have to steer the bicycle through some barriers before someone closes the gates. It's tricky, but I weave in and out and finally get out. I can't stop or we'll both lose our balance!
>
> Then I'm with a teacher who gives me a delicately shaped piece of wood and tells me to make something. I carve it, and when I've finished the art object it has a madonna-and-child shape, but it's really an Indian maiden. It's light brown wood. The teacher looks at it, looks at me, and says, "I expected that from you." I say, "But it's in the wood, it's shaped that way

anyhow." I recognize, though, that someone else could have wrecked it.

This dream reminded the daughter of her father's sudden death years earlier when her mother became immobilized, and she, as the eldest child, had to make all the arrangements and keep the balance in the family. She had been too young for such responsibility and needed to do her own mourning, but her mother could not cope with the situation. At the time she mustered her inner strength and carried the Self for the whole family. In the dream—where she protests that her mother won't do her share of pedaling—she is registering how difficult it had been for her to carry all the burden at that earlier time.

An important question to ask with most dreams is, Why now? What is happening in outer life that brings up these issues in a dream? And what bearing, then, does this dream have on current life?

The woman suddenly remembered that her mother had been seriously hurt in a car accident a week before; she had not realized how much it had upset her. When a sudden event such as a serious accident or illness occurs, a person often denies its impact and relegates it to the unconscious, which is what happened here. This dream, a few days after the accident, reflects the dreamer's deep inner response to it, as well as her response to her father's death, the earlier trauma that it reactivated.

When the dreamer was asked what the dream said about the meaning of her mother's accident, she realized why she was anxious in the dream "to steer the bicycle through barriers before they close the gates." The gates were the "pearly gates," the threshold between life and death, and she was anxious about losing her last remaining parent. She said, "All my mother's relatives have died since my father died. Who's next?"

As those who have lost a parent know, it is a deeply jarring event. Whether you were especially close or you weren't, whether the death was sudden and violent or a natural passing, the earth is knocked from its axis. And the possible loss of the last parent has special archetypal meaning: You will be left to stand alone with no one between you and death. When those great changes that are part of the human condition occur, they often stir up material left over from the last time you encountered a similar event. In this case, the daughter is meeting archetypal Death, and she must lay the old event, her father's death, to rest as well as she can before proceeding to the current crisis.

Moreover, the reality she has to confront in her outer life is that she can't count on her mother "backing her up," or being there forever. The daughter is afraid of the gates (pearly gates) closing on her some day, too. As in the dream, the daughter herself must have enough momentum in her life to keep her balance, and move forward with her own life. She has to keep up momentum because life is precarious and she could fall—fall into anxiety, depression, or an accident of her own.

But she needs something more than her own efforts to retain stability. Her deepest sense of security in the world, her connection—through her mother—to the feminine Self, has been shaken and needs to be restored. In the dream, a teacher gives her material from nature—wood—from which she can find a symbol of the Self to help her. She perceives an early form of the Self in the wood—the madonna and child—and from this early sacred mother-child form she finds a more independent natural form to help her now—"the Indian maiden," the young Native American woman who stands alone in nature.

Interesting things can be learned from this dream in exploring the teacher's remark, "I expected that from you." It turns out that others' expectations can be a trap. Early in life, this woman accepted the expectation from her mother that she would carry the Self for the family. This was a trap, especially for a person as young as she was. A steady sense of your own place is needed whenever others—whether parents, teachers, coworkers, or mate—have conscious expectations or unconscious projections that you can carry the Self for them, too. In the dream, the woman retains a proper stance. She replies that "it's in the wood, it's that way anyhow." She knows that the inner strength of the Self is there in the first place, in the natural substance of the wood, and that she can only give it more form—that is, she can bring the Self to consciousness at times and acknowledge its presence, know that she can count on herself.

PERSONAL INFLATION.   In order to understand the last part of the dream—"someone else might have wrecked it," which implies a slight air of superiority over others—we must explore the general phenomenon of inflation. When the Self archetype touches your life, as when your parents see you as the Self for the whole family, you feel blessed with a special sense of wholeness, well-being, and importance that you would not otherwise have. The Self buoys you up like a magic carpet, exhilarating, inspiring, and sustaining you; and others may respond to this by viewing you as special because they glimpse the Self through you. But it is arrogant to become inflated with your importance and think that you are indeed destined for special burdens or privileges.

Some momentary inflation inevitably occurs when you encounter any archetype, especially the most powerful and all-embracing one, the Self. You feel a strong wave of expansiveness and intensity that touches your life and then recedes, leaving a residue of security from the Self to sustain you. In fact, some inflation is necessary at times to sweep you into a new vision of your potential as a person, your mission in life, your capacity to meet challenges. Inflation becomes a problem, and even a danger, only when it persists: You could become so attracted to the excitement that you remain in that state, lose your groundedness, and lose perspective on yourself as an ordinary person. You might experience this as a "buzz," a heightened sense of reality, a feeling of elevation. Then the ego has made the mistake of identifying too closely with an archetype, of not respecting it enough. You identify with the Self as if it were your whole being, as if you *are* the Self. Then you feel special compared to other people, perhaps oblivious of ordinary consideration for others and everyday realities. You should recognize inflation—and the betrayal of power—whenever you see a person in authority feeling a golden entitlement to sexual, monetary, or other privileges and therefore abusing those in his or her charge. Another example would be performers (or other artists) who can become so addicted to feelings of high intensity, creativity, and self-importance on the stage that they abuse drugs to continue the feeling of being larger-than-life off the stage.

This dream of the Indian Maiden warns her about inflation.

If the dreamer were to think that she actually possessed the Self, she could become inflated with her powers. She might think that she could accomplish great things by her conscious efforts alone. But, like any other ordinary human being, she wouldn't be able to sustain complete contact with the Self indefinitely. Eventually, then, inflation would lead to deflation, feeling depressed at the loss of the Self, and feeling diminished before impossible expectations.

In the dream, this woman—someone genuinely humble by nature—realizes that the Self is in nature, "in the wood." But she almost slips at the end of the dream in the aside that "someone else might have wrecked it" with its hint of superiority over others. The "someone else" could be an inner figure of hers, an inflated ego that could be destructive by assuming it had the Self at its beck and call. So the dream shows us that anyone can block access to the Self through inflation, deflation, carelessness, or faltering, and thereby lose the sense of the Self, even at a time like this when it is most needed.

THE HUMBLE BICYCLE: AN EARLY SELF SYMBOL. The most memorable aspect of this dream is that it reveals the bicycle as a symbol of the emerging Self in a woman's dream. If one looks closely at the image of a bicycle and its meaning in this dream, we also learn something about early forms of the Self.

A circle is the fundamental symbol of wholeness, the Self, and one with a point in the middle represents centeredness. When this becomes a rotating wheel, then there is movement and change—additional aspects of the Self. The image of a circle with a cross in it symbolized in prehistoric times the earth in movement, lunar time, and often solar time: seasonal, cyclical change and cosmic forces of renewal. Through millennia, a rotating wheel, with its moving perimeter that revolves around a still, unmoved axis, came to symbolize changing and unchanging fate as well as eternal transformation. In recent linear and rational patriarchal times, the great symbol of the wheel has come down to us as the wheel of fortune, meaning simply fate or luck. A wheel that moves forward implies outer progress, while one that moves counterclockwise—turning inward toward the unconscious, an ancient symbol of lunar goddesses and Kali meaning both dissolution and creative transformation—now implies to most Westerners only the sinister forces of destructive power, because of the Nazi use of the swastika symbol.

However, the circle and wheel symbols of our ancient forebears are still alive in the deepest recesses of our unconscious, and our dreams reveal interesting elaborations of original underlying meanings. A connection between two wheels in motion represents a profound coordination between two deep centers, as in an inner bond between parent and child or between marriage partners. This is sometimes represented in dreams today by a humble, everyday image—the bicycle!

In this dream there is an unusual variation on this image: a bicycle built for two. The wheel behind represents the mother's Self backing up the daughter's Self—an image that captures the universal situation of a mother passing on her centeredness, the Self, to a daughter. In this particular case, there was a shift to the daughter pulling the mother forward when she faltered. Then, in inner preparation for the possibility of losing her mother, she went from the symbol of the wheels to her own figure of the Self that emerged from the Madonna and child—the young Native American figure. This woman had enough sense of Self passed on to her originally by her mother, the wheel behind her, that she could shift to a natural symbol of the Self (the Indian Maiden) who could stand on her own, apart from the mother.

When a woman does not have a sense of having received the Self from her own mother because their relationship was lacking or negative, she can still find her heritage from the deep unconscious, the archetypal source itself, the first mother, Gaia, Mother Earth. After the following dream, the dreamer expressed the feeling that she had received her spiritual heritage, as if it had been passed down to her from centuries of Women.

> *Gold from the Delta.* At the place where a wide river met the ocean, I went out onto the broad spread of the delta. I waded deep into the soft, wet, alluvial plain to find something important. I reached down

**deep into the fine wet soil, layers upon layers having been spread there through the centuries. I found gold pre-Columbian figures and brought them back with me.**

As a child, the dreamer had not been given the warmth and security she needed from her own mother, nor had the feminine been valued in her family. Slowly, through years of analysis and through kinship with other women, she gained hard-won confidence in herself. Yet she still didn't have easy access to that solid sense of well-being that is the legacy of someone who had a golden childhood of being cherished. All her positive experiences of recent years finally coalesced into an inner core of self-worth through the mystery of this dream. She had to reach for the gift, the thing of lasting value in the great river of life, and hold it in her hands so that she would know it was true—that the gold was hers.

It is also significant that she didn't just pick up something she found lying on the ground. She had to reach deep into the fine rich loam, layers and layers of soil built up by the rhythms of the river, generations of women's history. She had to go back to pre-Columbian times, before the Western invasion and development of modern cities, to the time when the Indian culture prevailed in the Americas, when people were closer to the earth, the feminine. Just as some women have special jewels passed down to them from their mother or grandmother, in this dream she found her inheritance from the mothers in the pre-Columbian gold figures. Ten years afterward, "reaching into the loam for the gold figures" was still a vivid and sustaining image for her.

## Refusing the Self

The dreams described so far have shown a daughter receiving or wresting the Self from the mother, the family, or the cultural unconscious. These women were receptive to the Self. However, sometimes a woman feels in opposition to the Self. This can happen when parents and other important people in a woman's life have so failed her that she fears and distrusts all outer authority. She usually hasn't known anyone whom she respects and loves who has followed a deep inner sense of personal authority, so she feels cynical and recoils at the possible tyranny of her own inner voice. The inner voice of wisdom is perceived as only a harsh voice of judgment and coercion. A woman's conscious ego then must establish its good authority before she can distinguish positive archetypal authority. The next two dreams show such a time in a woman's life, when she refuses the offer of the Self from her unconscious because she is not yet ready. Note that the second dream occurred a month or so after the first one.

> **Tarnished Pearls.** I go to the bottom of the sea and find beautiful pearls. I bring them to the top of the water, but they're tarnished when they get to the air.

> **Chasing the Wise Old Woman.** I'm chasing the Wise Old Woman, ridiculing her, making fun of her. I feel superior to her, stronger and faster.

This young woman "had everything" but felt empty. She was very capable and doing well professionally, but year after year she couldn't pass her professional licensing examination. Dream images of her childhood home showed ice and snow and icicles, and her mother collecting things to put in boxes piled on the side of the house. These images tell us how little warmth she must have received from her mother.

She saw her mother as weak. As often happens for a child when one parent is seen as weak and the other as strong, she unconsciously sided with the strong one, her father. As he did, she denigrated dependency and emotion. When she would see tissue paper in the wastebasket in the therapy room, she would say, "Well, I can see the tearjerkers were here today." She made devaluating remarks about therapy, her therapist, and especially about feminine qualities in the therapist. But something within her had kept her coming faithfully to therapy for a year, and both she and the therapist knew she was committed to her search for the missing elements in her life.

These dreams eloquently show how the feminine and its wisdom is there for the dreamer to grasp if she would. In the first dream, she goes to the bottom of the sea, deep into the unconscious, to find pearls, archetypal symbol of the feminine Self. From earliest times, pearls—round, lustrous, natural treasures that develop in the womb of oysters—have been associated with the Great Mother as goddess of creation, sea and tides, Moon Goddess, Mari, Isis. Early Aphrodite, born of the sea, held a sacred pearl in her hand as a symbol of feminine wisdom—wisdom from nature, wisdom from the unconscious, whence the phrase "pearls of wisdom." In the dream, though, when the pearls reach the air, they are tarnished, as if by the dreamer's own conscious thoughts. Similarly, in the second dream, she chases the Wise Old Woman and feels superior to her.

Why does the dreamer consciously reject feminine wisdom? She doesn't dare to identify with the feminine for fear of falling into her mother's kind of weakness. As yet, she can't believe that her inner source of feminine strength, the Self, is indeed there to guide her in a true way. Instead, she must still prove that she is stronger than what she sees as the negative mother. In her unwitting arrogance, she believes that her ego must dominate the Self. Evidently she needs to do this for a while; she must build her own ego so that it is strong enough to receive the Self.

One does not leap, even at grand offers in life, if one has other tasks to do first. One needs to establish one's own individuality and strength. Just as in fairy tales where a heroine must sometimes journey far, perform endless tasks, and befriend the animals, that is, find her own strength and trust her own instincts again, so this dreamer must follow the natural order of things. She needs to learn to trust again. It takes a long time to melt ice, snow, and icicles, and a long time to unpack a mother's boxes.

Thus, in the process of proving herself, the dreamer loses the Self (tarnishes the pearls, banishes the Wise Old Woman), and that is just what she is doing in the outside world: She can have things, but cannot savor them, she cannot drink the full cup of life yet. But deep down in her own unconscious her Wise Old Woman is waiting and will be there when she is ready to go down the path with her.

## Acknowledging the Negative Side of the Self

The archetypal Self can be experienced as a symbol of wholeness. On rare occasions, another aspect of the Self may appear—the power and force of impersonal nature—an awesome presence to be respected but not embraced. An older woman who had suffered greatly since childhood from a painful illness met such an image in a dream during the second year of her analysis:

> *The Snake Looked at Me.* Something was calling me to the basement of the house. I went down the stairs—down and down and down. Finally I wound up in the cellar.
>
> There was a snake: a medium-sized one, raised up like a cobra. It had the ability to stand up and look at me. I looked at it and it looked at me. A real looking at each other. And I left it there.

When the dreamer awoke, she knew that she had done the right thing in the dream—to leave the snake there. She said, "It would have been foolhardy to dance with the snake or smash it." That is, she knew that she should not get entangled with such a powerful force, nor should she try to get rid of it. She had the instinctive wisdom to face it squarely, acknowledge its place, and keep it at bay.

This woman had gained wisdom through her life, and her dream tells us here something profound about ourselves and our place in nature. For many decades, through daily suffering and meeting the trauma of operation after operation, she had forged an ego strong enough to persevere and enable her to have a full life. She had also been graced with the presence of the positive aspects of the Self filling her with a buoyancy of spirit. All this had helped her know the darkness of Great Despair, and not succumb. This dream about the snake tells us that something else has also helped her in life: She has met and come to terms with another aspect of the Self—Great Indifference.

As archetypal earth animal, the most ancient symbol of earthly existence and the continuance of life, the snake here represents the cold, impersonal forces of nature. Sometimes we and our loved ones suffer meaningless pain, and certainly we will die, not because of any particular reason or evil intention within ourselves or outside ourselves, but because we are bodies on earth, we are part of the material universe and take our place in nature. Like other animals, plants, and rocks on earth, we are part of the great cycle of material transformation, as we are, too, in the even greater cycle of the universe: the origin and the infinity of the stars.

The dreamer has met and accepted this earth-bound aspect of the Self, her fate, and that is what has really sustained her in life. In the dream, she and the snake regard each other. They are not adversaries; no other action has to take place. Each is "just so"; each is a reality. The dream ego is not overwhelmed, destroyed, repulsed, or fascinated. In her life, this woman has learned not to struggle and rail against pain, disability, or fate; she has not become entangled with the snake but has learned to accept its presence. She does not play unconscious counterpart to the snake: the mouse mesmerized by the eyes of the snake, captive to an unconscious spell of feeling helpless—or grandiose—in a great victimization. Nor does she unconsciously identify with the indifference of nature, fall unconscious captive to the Wise Snake, and try to manifest its great qualities in herself as the very human qualities of passivity, indifference, or cynicism. This brush with the power of the snake is like an inoculation. She *knows* the snake, she has some of the wisdom of the snake.

Others less wise may let themselves be hypnotized by the snake, captivated by the excitement and drama of awesome archetypal power. They may lose themselves, fall in, and be drawn into a bottomless downward spiral, as one can be drawn to things dark, powerful, forbidden, or dangerous out of curiosity or the desire for a thrill. Presumptuous of one's own conscious power and personal immunity, unaware of the greater compulsions and powers that exist, one can eventually become helpless.

So there are awesome aspects of the Self that can make their appearance; like the snake they should be acknowledged but are then best left alone, if possible. Or, if you must, encounter them at your peril, as in the outer world you encounter only, if you must, the overwhelmingly destructive force of hurricanes, mass persecution, bombing raids, epidemics, cancer.

## Sustaining the Feminine Self in Relationships

This section contains four dreams by one dreamer. The first dream is about an early image of the Self—a unicorn that had such a shimmering presence that it burst through a woman's dream world right into her bedroom. She knew that it must have some important message, so she entered analysis two weeks afterward to find out what it meant.

At the time, she was in the throes of love with a man who wanted her to be emotionally committed to him, but she held back because she wanted him first to make some concrete promises about their life together. In their daily life, she was tired of always giving to him, as well as giving in to him. "It's as if he wants me to be a rag doll," she said. In anger, she had finally thrown something against the wall, and in response, he had slammed out the door and left.

Such turmoil is natural in the early years of a relationship because people often choose for a mate someone with whom they have a deep dark connection, someone who repeats the same problem they have had in early life, but who has some promise of being redeemable. That is the great hope and the anguish of being in love, and the task.

In various scenes in this first dream she works on her current problem with her boyfriend and her similar pattern of entanglement in her early family history—with the help of a Self figure, the unicorn. It is a complicated dream, but you don't need to understand all the details to gather meaning from it. The essential movement of the dream is from the "rag doll"—the antithesis of the feminine Self—to the Self rooted in feminine individuality.

*The Unicorn and the Witch.* My boyfriend is telling me that he really cares for me, and that I should live my life. There are no recriminations and he just floats off.

My mother is weeping. She doesn't know what to do. My sister has died, and she doesn't want me to go [to the funeral] in such a dramatic costume—black crepe with a splash of orange on it, and a medieval conical cap with a veil. So I slip off the orange part. She calms down. I'll put it back on later, I thought.

I go into the bedroom with my ex-husband. I'm naked, but he's in his clothes, which is just like him. We have sex and afterward he talks about the sex, "That wasn't bad, not great . . . blah, blah, blah." I thought, "How stupid!" and went to my own bedroom.

I'm naked on my bed and pull the sheet over me to go to sleep. Suddenly a hand flips up the sheet. I turn to look. A baby has been thrown into the bed. I shriek. Someone's trying to make me crazy!

Semi-awake: In fact, I'd shrieked out loud and it woke me up from the dream. I sat up in bed. In the shafts of moonlight from the window I saw a unicorn—in the middle of the room. It was as big as a horse, like a zebra in the play of light. I thought, "You're a hallucination!" I slammed my hand down on the bed and thought, "Enough symbols in one night!"

The opening scene in the dream gives the stage setting where the immediate problem lies—in the relationship with her boyfriend. In the dream, he has the capacity to care about her and let her have her own life without making her feel guilty about it. She wondered what in the world this meant, because she was in constant turmoil with him about these very issues. The dream suggests that he has this capacity, or at least she has inner permission to have these things for herself now.

The first question to ask in understanding this dream—the

question you might remember to ask when working with most dreams—is: What qualities do the various characters in the dream have in real life? The boyfriend, the mother, the sister, and the ex-husband all seemed to her to be "takers," especially her sister—"the black sheep in the family, a talented artist, but a despicable parasite." By default, then, this left to her the role of "the giver," the good one in the family who would placate those who were more assertive or aggressive. Eventually her resentment about her own forbidden self-interest would burst forth as it did the evening before the dream when she found herself throwing something against the wall.

While talking about these people in the analytic session this young woman became truly angry about things she should be angry about and cried about someone who had died and whom she needed to cry about. Remember: It is not just intellectual understanding of a dream that is important. The process of trying to understand, of brushing up against the people who are important to you and the archetypal images they stir up—this process shakes loose your feelings and releases you to a shift in feeling, a change of heart. With some dreams, you may not find so much clarity of thought as you find clarity of heart.

How does the dream show her change of heart and correct this position as "the giver"? As the "dream ego" (the active one in the dream), she takes several corrective actions. When her sister dies in the dream, she gives up her projection onto her sister of all the badness in the family and dons the black and orange Halloween garb of the witch herself. That is, she consciously owns up to her own feminine powers—angry assertion, the independence of the lone woman, her own artistic talent. Another correction in the dream is that she doesn't get entangled in the man's concerns, but goes to lie naked on her own bed, open to taking care of her own inner concerns. Since she is an introverted woman, the first shifts in character will come not from taking outer steps but will come naturally from within. Two images came to her: first, a baby, harbinger of a new development in her psyche, which then emerges as the unicorn, a symbol of the early feminine Self.

Two of the archetypal images that stand out in this long and difficult dream are the witch and the unicorn. You might think further about symbols like these on the rare occasions when they occur in dreams to see what feelings they evoke in you, and you might look up what they mean in reference books. The witch and the unicorn are nighttime, lunar images, symbolic of important qualities in women from the long-lost feminine realm of centuries ago. Dreams are often ahead of a person's conscious understanding by weeks, months, or years; and this was true for this woman as she continued in her analysis to explore dreams and experiences to bring these feminine elements—her birthright—into her life.

Her search for the meaning of the witch and the unicorn culminated a year later in three dreams that appeared to her in the same week:

> *Candles and Incense.* I'm standing on a hill in medieval times. Women are in black with a front surplice in white and a cross. There's a holy war. Barbarians with pitchforks come over the hill toward the women. The women don't have weapons in their lean-tos; instead they defend themselves with candles and incense. They are calm. I'm a disinterested observer, but oh, I can't watch!

> *The Unicorn.* The unicorn is standing there as though in a picture. The background is a rich, deep blue sapphire, lush. The unicorn turns, and I can see her from all angles, whereas a year ago she was only in profile.

> *Mother Hissing.* I'm coming to see you [the analyst] for my appointment. My mother followed me, so three of us are in the room. You [the analyst] say to me, "So you think the root of the problem is that women in your family are too submissive to men?" I say, "Yes." My mother makes a hissing sound.

Her thoughts about the unicorn were that "It can stay in the forest, no mate, no family, like eternal spring that sallies forth. It can live forever, unless it's caught." It is a young and innocent, pure feminine spirit safe and free in its unconscious forest world by virtue of its being elusive to others, but highly vulnerable if caught.

Thus, while she thinks that her boyfriend is the only one who will not commit himself, she herself is captivated by an unconscious attachment to Solitary Splendor. She feels guilty about this, does not feel entitled to her freedom. The problem is to make her own wish for freedom more conscious, so that she can carry her true feminine autonomy into her life and relationships.

The unicorn in all its beauty has come into her consciousness so that she can respect its qualities and carry them forward in her life, rather than be unconsciously captivated by the unicorn and live her life in one of the two opposites it represents: in solitude or in utter vulnerability to another, as the unicorn is to the hunter.

The problem for this woman is more complicated than what she had at first thought: the interpersonal struggle about whether she'll be a "rag doll" for a man. The problem also lies within her at a deep archetypal level. It seems to her as if the choice is between being ruled by her unicorn spirit or yielding her soul and allowing it to die. Instead, she needs to know it well. This has started to happen for her. In the latest dream she says, "The unicorn turns, and I can see her from all angles, whereas a year ago she was only in profile." She has been unconsciously ruled by the vague archetypal forces of the young maiden and the early Self in the form of the unicorn. She has been under its spell, shimmering with its power and also fascinating to men because of her elusiveness. Just as she is possessed by the unicorn, so men want to possess it in her. But they may crush her in the process, the same way a child—excited by holding life in its hand—might crush a small bird. On the interpersonal level, perhaps this was the "rag doll" that she was afraid of becoming, that she smashed against the wall so that the unicorn could emerge in her dream that night. She did indeed sense her lover's intrusiveness into her inner sanctum. So the dilemma is how to yield in life, but not submit.

For an introverted woman, the unicorn has a special fascination—solitary and free, reserved and shy, close to nature and the mysteries of the woods—because it is close to her innate nature. She needs to remain true to this deep feminine center, for when she yields to a relationship, she is especially vulnerable to the opposite, the aggressive hunter. She needs to preserve this quality of inner freedom to be "her own woman" in life. For instance, in an argument with a man, when she cannot explain how she feels with words, she may need to remain silent like a doe, safe and strong within herself.

For the more extraverted young woman, the unicorn may be hidden deep within. Ordinarily outgoing and interpersonal, she may discover the shy unicorn in herself when she meets someone she is very interested in. The shy unicorn may emerge as a woman feels sudden wariness at first glimpsing her capacity to be deeply touched by another person, her desire to yield and join another and yet retain her deepest sense of separateness, wholeness within herself, the Self. The unicorn is especially precious for her and can easily fade into the woods and be lost. This happens if she loses herself through being too responsive, through her capacity for immersion in others and their accomplishments. For instance, if she falls in love with a man and identifies with him and his accomplishments, she might suddenly be startled awake by her inner unicorn to remember her sense of Self: her own "horn," the spiral of the Self that points forward into the world, her uniqueness, her own cornucopia of creativity, her realm of relationships, her own mission in life.

In the modern age, our instinctual animal spirit, the unicorn with its quiet innocence and supernatural way in the forest, needs a complementary figure to accompany her—the witch who represents more power, independence, and crafty knowledge. When the doe emerges from the forest and hesitates to cross the freeway, she needs the witch who can foresee and plan and be bold.

What can this dreamer learn from the witch in her dreams to help her maintain her sense of herself out in the world? Instead of being too submissive and then resentful and hissing, she needs to know the archetype of the witch in its positive and negative aspects. In her dream a year earlier, The Unicorn and the Witch, she had donned her sister's black and orange medieval garb, could take it off when it became too disturbing to the mother, but could also put it on again later. That is, the dream helped her claim her own dark side more consciously instead of disparaging her sister and projecting it onto her. In the dream a year later, the women in black, the witch-priestesses, represent a more positive force of collective and independent feminine power from more powerful spiritual realms.

The image of these witch-priestesses was a corrective cultural image for her, reminding her of earlier times in history when women's powers were known and respected. Thus, in the dream, she returns to an early era to observe witch-priestesses in black and white with candles and incense strong enough to protect them against pitchforks. She observes their calm in contrast to her own fears. She's too scared to look at the outcome herself.

The dreamer—like many of us today—needs these women's power. She needs their solidarity of feminine strength to stand her ground, trust her judgment, and fiercely defend feminine separateness as part of a relationship. This ancient heritage has come forth in her psyche as a counterforce to her family culture where women were "too submissive" to men. In everyday terms, if her boyfriend lapses into wanting a "rag doll," or if he mistakes her independence as rejection or a desire to control him, then she doesn't need to catch these projections. She can see that they are actually his own desire to control or his own fears about being rejected or controlled. At the same time, she must avoid becoming inflated by the witch archetype, unconsciously identifying with her dark power, getting caught up in the potency and abuse of feminine power. She needs to beware of the witch's cackle and hissing.

A woman's task with the archetype of the feminine Self, such as the image of the unicorn or witch, is to make it more conscious: to know its presence and let it take its rightful place in human life. Then she can bring forward her birthright—her true feminine independence—into her life. She can yield to relationship and not have to protect herself with an unconscious, elusive unicorn or hissing witch, but still possess their conscious wariness and power to maintain her feminine autonomy in a relationship.

When we look through the window of our dreams, we see confirmation of our innermost strength as women: the drummer beating her own rhythm, the runner bursting forth at her own pace, the Indian maiden who is there from the beginning, the hands reaching down through the centuries of women to bring forth gold, pearls from the sea, the woman who can look at the snake, witch-priestesses with candles and incense, the unicorn of Solitary Splendor. When life brings us harsh realities and we might falter, these kinds of images sustain us; when we plumb our depths to the truth of who we are, they reveal our center; when we go forth to meet life or death, they show us the way. These images are glimpses of the early feminine Self.

# 3

# Dealing with Aggression: Vulnerability, Self-Protection, and Strength

Since women have traditionally lacked power and been objects of aggression—ranging from subtle social slights and criticism through such widespread practices as acquaintance rape, to even fatal assault—often one of the first issues for women coming to therapy is learning how to meet the reality of others' aggression for their own self-defense. This also eventually leads to their learning about their own aggression and other means of self-assertion.

"Aggression" in the broadest sense can include attacking, dominating, and intimidating others without regard for their feelings or rights, often using power, authority, and anger to get one's own way.

Women live in a world dominated by aggression. Men's instinctive assertiveness has become exaggerated by thousands of years of patriarchal culture and male prerogatives. We have been subject to the patriarchal values and ethics of achievement, competition, and individualism, and the patriarchal structures and processes of hierarchy, power, authority, struggle, and conflict. Thus an aggressive edge prevails in the way people treat each other in every facet of life: the home, the streets, school, the workplace, national politics, as well as international disputes. One consequence of this atmosphere is that many women live with the constant threat of intimidation, resulting in feelings of some degree of mistrust, fear, powerlessness, despondency, and anger. The male prerogatives in our culture have sharply limited women's opportunities to feel self-respect and pursue full lives.

Since the 1930s, Freudian analysts and some research psychologists have believed that frustration causes aggression, which can then be displaced on others. This belief has prevailed in the general culture. Certainly early frustration can make children rageful; and later frustration can make people angry so that they take out their frustration on each other, men often displacing their dissatisfactions onto women, and women displacing theirs onto other women and children. However, we are broadening our understanding of how aggression develops. How do children learn to act out their feelings of aggression against others? One way they learn is to adopt the behavior of important people and other models in their lives who are aggressive. They also act aggressively because it's rewarded; it gets them what they want. Contemporary research on men's violence toward women[1] attributes the violence to men's socialization, which leads them to believe that they have a right to control women. The tasks, then, for women are to know our own rights, find alternative models of being assertive ourselves, rather than aggressive, both in the family and in society, and, meanwhile, through collective and individual action, not let ourselves be targets.

The devastating effects of the extreme end of aggression—physical violence against women—are finally coming to public awareness. Beginning with Brownmiller's[2] documentation of the prevalence of rape, and how the fear of rape permeates women's everyday lives and limits our freedom of movement, through the present explosion of popular books on physical and sexual abuse by family members, friends, neighbors, and groups of teenagers, as well as trusted authorities—teachers, ministers, and even therapists[3]—we all are realizing what deep wounds these tragic events inflict on body and soul. Many therapy hours are devoted to trying to heal the shattered sense of Self, the loss of a safe place in the world, the confusion, the terror, the suspicion, the guilt, and the helplessness that result. In this process, dreams are sometimes helpful, since victims can go into emotional shock at the time of physical or sexual abuse, so that the incident is inaccessible to consciousness. Dreams may be the first indication of the trauma, revealing the circumstances and the blocked feelings to the dreamer. Dreams can also help a person work through the trauma, as you will see in the dream Spooks in the next chapter, "The Shadow."

Since much has already been written about such dramatic incidents of violence and recovery, this chapter will concentrate on the small, everyday instances of mistreatment that affect all women but might be otherwise overlooked. These are milder forms of psychological intimidation that exist throughout life and chip away at a woman's self-confidence and being, and whose cumulative effect can be profound. Other omnipresent facts of a woman's life at home and elsewhere are: teasing, poking, and name-calling by brothers; disparaging remarks, judging, and being overlooked by fathers and other authorities; and constant blaming and criticism by mothers who pass on their poor self-image, finding themselves and their daughters lacking, compared to cultural ideals.

In fact, we have been so shaped by the aggressive ways of our culture that we hardly know how we would handle things differently if we were to follow our own feminine nature. But we are beginning to find out. Carol Gilligan's[4] groundbreaking research on the differences between men's and women's ethical development reveals that boys develop an "ethic of rights" that values achievement and separateness, while girls develop an "ethic of caring," which values intimacy and interdependence. The ethic that would deter a man from acting against someone, then, would come from a respect for another person's rights, whereas for a woman, it would come more from a wider sense of responsibility and empathy—a desire not to hurt others in getting her own way. We see examples of this all around us, especially where women gather together.

As we women have more chances to do things our way, we are discovering new ways of working together and resolving differences. These reflect our very different values and structures: our emphasis on mutuality and harmony of feeling, egalitarianism, cooperation, inclusiveness, and our preference for informal networks of loyalty and friendship rather than formal power structures. We also find out, however, that doing things our way can lead to other kinds of problems, such as indecisiveness and unfairness.

A good source for finding our natural ways of handling things is our dreams. This chapter explores, through a small sample of dreams, what creative solutions can come from our deepest feminine nature about how to respond to aggression and how to handle our own aggression.

The first section of this chapter will address the fact that women often don't perceive or recognize men's aggression. Sometimes we pretend that it doesn't bother us. These dreams expose aggression for what it is and offer some suggestions for mobilizing our inner and outer resources to face it more effectively, to claim the right to our own authority and assertiveness, and to enlist a feminine spirit as an aid.

## Responding to Men's Aggression

### Breaking Free of Unconscious Denial

An earlier illustration of our denial of aggression appeared in the Unicorn dream at the end of the last chapter, a dream that woke a woman up to her boyfriend's oppressive expectation that she'd be a "rag doll." Further dreams led her to an assertion of her own feminine strength. This section concerns confronting aggression in our families and culture, starting with dreams where women encountered their true feelings about situations involving their brothers, a father, and other authorities. Because of these dreams, they became more aware of aggression directed toward them as well as their own habitual responses to intimidating situations. And they became more effective in dealing with external aggression and asserting themselves.

A pervasive problem for women is how to respond to the barrage of small, everyday verbal remarks that patronize, disparage, or diminish us as persons. This starts in the family, where older brothers and others consider girls easy targets of aggression and girls learn how to hide their hurt feelings.

A woman, whom I'll call Sarah, had the following dream about dealing with subtle aggression:

> *Swallowing the Needle.* **While I'm eating, I find a threaded needle in my mouth. I exaggerate the look on my face and the person across the way notices. Then I find lots of needles. I hope I haven't swallowed any!**

Sarah was completely puzzled by this dream until she remembered that the evening before the dream she'd had an insight about how much she'd been dominated by her brothers' aggressiveness while she was growing up. Then it occurred to her that the "needles" were all the needling she had gotten from her older brothers. Sarah said that she usually ignored needling, pretended it didn't hurt, and swallowed her anger until she finally overreacted.

This dream depiction of what happens to Sarah is useful. It alerts her, with an image she probably will not forget, that, full of all the hurts of the past, she will swallow more than she can manage if she is not careful, then blow up with anger. Sarah remembered that she is often criticized for "overreacting."

In most first impressions of a dream a woman discovers what she already consciously knows, to some extent, as Sarah did in this dream. Her first interpretation takes her only so far—to the problem of her own reactions. Whenever a woman uses the word "overreaction," this should alert us to the fact that she is probably accepting a cultural disparagement of emotions and repeating it as self-blame. Women often tell themselves that they should not "overreact" to needling, or at least not show it, that they should not be so sensitive, that they are *only* reacting to the accumulated feelings of the past.

However, this dream says more than that. It says that just as you need to stop when you're eating and pick out fishbones, instead of unconsciously swallowing them, you need to stop and notice needling. Often dreams compensate for personal or cultural attitudes, that is, they make up for, or counterbalance, one-sidedness in conscious thought. In this case, where the general attitude is that you should "just swallow it," the dream shows the opposite. We all need to go through this phase of being alert, extra-sensitive, or extra-feisty to counteract usual victim responses, and to begin to move away from being an object of aggression.

THE WITNESS. What other ways can we handle barbs, teasing, or belittling remarks directed toward us? The dream suggests a further position to take in dealing with aggression: the *witness* who notices what happens to us, the dream figure who observes from a distance with a more conscious, objective attitude. This inner witness can help us perceive provocations like needling as what they are—not humorous quips or harmless cultural habits, but small, sharp aggressions slipped in unnoticed. The witness can also help us change our habitual responses so that we "name it," we acknowledge aggression when it occurs. To free ourselves from being unconscious victims of aggression, we must take this crucial step—break through cultural denial and "call it." There is power in naming something, in this case, aggression—attack and domination in disregard of our feelings and rights.

We are also empowered by other witnesses' empathy. As women we gather emotional strength from talking with good friends or other witnesses who listen with kindred feeling. Those of us who have experienced the consciousness-raising groups of the 1970s, or women's groups since then, have experienced the great healing value of being among a group of women who mirror back to us the validity of our individual experiences. When others resonate with our accumulated feelings, we feel less isolated and self-blaming, and our feelings become less overwhelming and more tolerable. This affirmation also makes us expect that our feelings, our personhood, should be respected in the future, which can lead to individual or collective action.

Furthermore, since it is inevitable that victims sometimes unconsciously copy an aggressor when circumstances allow, our own inner witness can be alert to notice our own aggression—our needling others without noticing it.

BEYOND AGGRESSION. The final elusive question in this dream was: Why was the needle threaded? In answering this, Sarah learned how to go beyond aggression. Just as a sharp needle can jab, so, too, can it sew together rifts between people. The thought that came to her was that sewing is compensatory to aggression itself, an assertion of feminine values in her life against the overemphasis on the masculine ones in her family, with her brothers' preoccupation with aggression and the establishment of their positions and dominance. Her task, then, was not just to handle skirmishes in the game of aggression and dominance, but to find "her own game." Why play football all her life?

Sarah said that although she was not fond of sewing per se, it did seem to her an apt metaphor for a constructive and contemplative process of "putting things together"—repairing or creating something bit by bit at her own pace for herself or her family. The deeper message she found in the dream, then, was that if she emphasized her own feminine tasks, things of importance in her psyche, then needling and the whole game of aggression—something less relevant for her—might recede into the background.

One of the most challenging tasks for women surrounded by aggression, and haunted by aggression from the past, is to stop staring at it. As long as we allow it to occupy our minds, we are caught by it, whether we are offensive or defensive, successful or not. Instead, we should pick up the threads of our own lives, turn our attention to what we really want, find our own direction and take our first steps on the path—our own feminine path.

In this next dream, Sarah is given an ominous warning about more primitive instinctual aggression—the extraverted kind that is ruthless, and the introverted kind that stings without warning. The dream alerted Sarah to the existence of this kind of aggression so that she could learn how to protect herself and others.

*The Stingray.* I'm in a circle and a researcher hands out a word for each person to define. Mine is "vindictive."

The scene shifts. A man I know—very aggressive and outspoken—has a machine to cut a swath through the silt on the ocean floor. It makes a channel from far out in the ocean into the shore. "You can hear it operating if you listen," he says, and sure enough, I can hear it. It makes a channel, but I can see that it also kills any sea creatures, even the rare ones.

I go closer to see it. Then I operate the machine to save a small fearsome beast—a grayish stingray—and some crustaceans. I empty a box, then catch each sea animal and let it go. An animal is okay if it doesn't touch the sides of the box. They're all poisonous, but each one is special. They have a distinctive rattle sound like a rattler, and they blush into colors when they have feelings.

Sarah had just taken an oral examination for a professional promotion, for which she felt well qualified. She had been treated badly in the interview, and she had been thunderstruck at the unfavorable judgment at the end, which she later discovered to be based on prejudice against her different style and philosophy. She felt depressed, and thought about sending a strong letter of protest. The dream is trying to tell her something about her unconscious anger, her fear of her own anger—something many women have trouble dealing with—and her innocence about life she needed to become aware of.

UNCONSCIOUS DESTRUCTIVE ANGER IN RESPONSE TO AGGRESSION. Her first conclusion was that the dream was telling her that she "should not be so vindictive." The dream started out by saying that each person has a problem and hers is vindictiveness! It told her quite directly that she needed to understand that she had an automatic impulse toward revenge. The dream underscored for her something she already knew to some extent—that she held on to vengeful feelings and found it hard to let go of them, even if she wished she could forget about something that seemed unfair. She sometimes felt as if she were in the grips of some relentless drive.

The "stingray" suddenly gave her an idea about what had happened in the oral exam: She had expected to do well, but instead had found silent, unreceptive, and impersonal interviewers who stung her at the end. The grayness of the stingray expressed their apparently feelingless sting that evoked an unconscious counterpart in her—a gray, feelingless, depressive reaction with her own vindictive stingray lurking beneath. She was recognizing their unconscious rejection, and was responding with her own unconscious anger—anger turned inward as depression and anger turned outward as vindictiveness.

MORE CONSCIOUS ANGER: CUTTING A CHANNEL. Sarah realized, too, that she was not only depressed and vindictive underneath (which is like her swallowing the needle in the dream before) but also very angry. And when very angry, as she was here, she was afraid she could unleash her aggressive, machinelike side to cut a swath of blame of others for all the "poisonous" things that had been done to her all her life.

In understanding this dream, Sarah is affirming the general cultural attitude toward women and anger—that she should not be so vindictive, much less aggressive—but should instead contain her anger and poison, as in the box in the dream. But the dream says that the aggressive machine not only cuts a swath which can be destructive, but also a channel from the ocean floor of the unconscious to the shore of consciousness, something that is constructive.

We women need to know what is going on deep in the unconscious, so it does not just remain there gathering silt. And we need to clean out the sludge now and then—the cold, muddy, depressive feelings that are anger turned inward in unconscious self-blame. We can then allow the fire and energy of outspoken anger and blame to cut through the depressive storehouse of all the negative things we tend to ignore so we can see them clearly and handle them.

How do you detect your unconscious anger, especially if you're a woman like Sarah who's not aware when she's angry? When you're in a thick, heavy mood you're probably stuck in a "muddy" kind of unconscious resentment, perhaps going back to your early history. Unconscious anger takes many forms. When you suddenly feel "in a cold spell," as if you don't care what happens to you, when you avoid others, or show them only your sharp edges of "Don't bother me," you're probably feeling distant and detached as a substitute for your real feelings of anger and rejection. If critical thoughts keep repeating themselves in your mind, blaming yourself or others, if irritable remarks keep slipping out, you're using intellectual judgments that cut you off from feeling anger. Sometimes you can sense unconscious anger in your body as stifled "fight" responses: a clenched fist, a swinging foot, a tense jaw, or tight throat. Your dreams might exaggerate your anger so you can see it, by showing you primitive animals or a scene of violence. The first phase, then, is becoming aware of your anger as a reality.

The next phase may come slowly—to identify the source of your discontent and feel the actual heat of your anger, such as Sarah's protesting the unfairness of her examination. Experiencing anger like this is an important phase to redeem things from the cold, muddy realm of depression and unknowingness. When Sarah began to feel her real anger at the interviewers, it helped her emerge from the quagmire of her depression and feeling criticized. That is, she went from turning her destructiveness inward to feeling the full force of her destructiveness turned outward as vindictiveness and blame toward others.

In this extraverted phase of angry protest, you experience the potency of having your own intense feelings, and by coming up against others, you establish your own separateness and individuality. As a result, you feel your own power and feel less vulnerable to others' aggression. And, in the flood of your anger, all your dark thoughts of blaming others also burst forth, and you expose your *unconscious thinking* to the light of day. In the process, you can distinguish what blame is justified and what isn't. This confrontation with reality is a necessary step. Just as your primitive unconscious feelings become more useful as they become more conscious through inner distillation and outer expression, so do your unconscious thoughts.

EXPOSING THE INNOCENCE OF THE PUELLA. The process of examining unconscious assumptions about others can lead you to some painful confrontations with yourself as well. The awakening can be abrupt, disturbing, and humbling before it eventually becomes empowering. This is what happened to Sarah when she failed the examination. At first she felt dazed. She couldn't understand what had happened because the reality did not match her thoughts and expectations about the world. She had felt vaguely unsettled and wary during the examination, but had not expected to fail!

Whenever we're surprised like this, it means that there is something about reality we haven't known about, and this suggests the deeply unconscious innocence of the puella aeterna—the eternal girl who expects good from the universe. We each need this aspect of ourselves, which gives us buoyancy in our lives. However, if we identify too much with this archetype and put the puella in charge of our lives, we might not be wary enough and can step on a stingray, like Sarah did! She had to admit that in a puella fashion she had overlooked her differences with the interviewers in philosophy, values, and style and somehow naively expected acceptance from "the mothers and the fathers." A puella needs to learn that "there are no mothers or fathers," and that she has to become the protective adult herself.

A woman who stays identified with the puella lives under a magically protective umbrella. She has such attractive spirit that people naturally skip along with her, enjoying her feelings of well-being and harmony with others. Sooner or later, though, she will evoke the opposite—an abrupt and harsh rebuke—as a result of trying to deny reality and the true differences that exist between people, thus leaving it to others to confront her with them. Blithely unaware, she may not notice her employer's growing dissatisfaction, her best friend's exasperation, or her lover's infidelity until she's abruptly confronted with dismissal, rejection, or divorce. When she finally comes up against these realities, it seems sudden—the jolt of the surprise, the clash—an aggressive intrusion into a pleasant world.

In this case, as Sarah thought about the examination and bumped her head against the hard reality of what had actually happened, it eventually led her to see the realities of power. Judges are not necessarily fair or accepting of differences. The fact is that they can be one-sided, and, given their power, they can impose their standards on others, right or wrong.

Although Sarah considered her performance sufficient, she realized that she also needed to show them what *they* needed to see. It was, after all, their game, although she might wish—and strive—for more mutually respectful exchanges in the future. The result was that Sarah had more perspective on the letter she had fantasized about and decided not to send it, but rather to pursue other, more effective means of gaining recognition of her capabilities in the long run.

DISTINGUISHING AND PRESERVING USEFUL AGGRESSION. We are more accustomed in Western culture to extraverted ways of confronting unconscious problems than introverted ways. While the outer phase of being angry and confronting differences was useful, the dream itself showed a further alternative: an inner phase of integrating knowledge about aggression. In the dream, Sarah is concerned about the wholesale destruction of the sea creatures by the machine (the interviewers' drive as well as her relentless drive), and she consciously takes control of the machine so she can preserve these creatures of rare value. She looks closely and finds a box to contain the aggressive creatures. Then she lets them go. That is, she finds a protective box—a safe place—to bind the wounds of the past that the angry phase has uncovered so they can heal; then she can let them go.

This dream suggests that the temenos—a safe container for incubating deep unconscious material—can be helpful. Through reflection, you can distill your feelings and refine your thinking. For instance, in meeting aggression, you can call upon your inner resources to focus on circumscribed threats and re-experience anxiety in a more conscious form—in words, feelings, images, or fantasy work. In this way, the reality of threats and anxiety are acknowledged, while at the same time they don't have unlimited, overwhelming potency.

You can see this process portrayed in Sarah's dream. As she approached closely and looked, the box allowed her to see each fearsome creature more clearly as special and real. Then she noticed distinguishing qualities. Some gave warning (rattlers) and others showed different feeling-tones (colors). These alerting signals could help her discern others' aggression as well as her own.

The dream says that these creatures representing our primitive aggressive instincts are not to be destroyed; they are rare and valuable. We are so overly civilized that we need to study the natural world and its creatures to know about our own natural forms of aggression, forms we no longer see in ourselves and others, i.e., the awkward and primitive aggression of the crustaceans, the sideways irritability of the crab, the menacing claws of the lobster, the incredible adaptability of the octopus who blushes the exact color of his hiding place in order to be unnoticed.

All dreamers can learn from other living animals. We can warn people by giving our own primitive signals of aggression or recognize these signs of unconscious aggression in others: coughing—like the rattles warning of differences; a stiffening posture—like a crab rising up defensively; or the changes in feeling-tone—like an octopus changing colors, silently withdrawing into hiding or using its smokescreen. All these are instinctual "body alerts" to our own and other people's unconscious ways of protecting their vulnerability.

This dream reminds us that we must be careful. There are indeed poisonous creatures within and without. They are usually harmless unless we are very unconscious of their presence. And the harmful ones can at least be avoided, or met with our own conscious aggression and thus rendered less likely to be dangerous.

## The Lighter Spirit vs. Subtle Aggression

The next dream also involves denial of aggression—in the form of a father's dominance. Fathers usually loom large to daughters, and if their aggression is overt and severe, violence and helplessness feature prominently in their daughters' dreams, as in their lives. However, sometimes a father's dominance or aggression is more moderate, covert, and difficult to detect. It may be seen in culturally acceptable forms for a man such as heavy-handed authority, high standards, critical judgment, the withholding of affection, or being oblivious of others' existence or feelings. A daughter raised in this heavy atmosphere may become too sensitive to authority and can internalize the judgments into self-criticism, self-blame, and self-discipline. Like her father, she may eschew feelings and weakness, become overly rational and strive for feelings of success and approval, which probably never come, or if they do, aren't fulfilling enough. A woman needs her feminine core, which thrives on a more bountiful atmosphere. She needs her positive puella, who has generosity of spirit, heartfelt feeling, spontaneity, playfulness, and daring. She needs the narcissistic side of her little girl who wants to be center stage herself, and who can dance with someone or can dance alone. She also needs the stubbornness of her puella, who can be willful and resist what she doesn't really want, who is impulsive and disorderly by nature. She needs the laughter and the wildness that are parts of her nature as a woman.

This dream uncovers a family's unconscious collusion in a subtle form of aggression—in this instance, a father's imposition of high standards that serve to keep him center stage in the family. The dream depicts unconscious submission to this kind of insidious aggression, and shows how the lighter spirit can help a daughter free herself from its effects.

> **Father and the Toast.** We're at the breakfast table back home. My father pushes his toast away. My mother asks, "Anything wrong?" He responds, "Oh, no." But he doesn't touch it. My mother wonders, Why doesn't he eat his toast? She feels anxious, like a failure, like "I've done it again."
>
> I feel love for my mother as I sit there at the table. I also feel sorry for her and think my father is mean. I have an impulse to tell him off, but I go ahead and eat and just try to shut it all out. I'd like to leave.

When the dreamer first talked about the dream, it seemed as if all the characters were fixed in the roles they had to play out, and as if she, too, were stuck. She couldn't do anything but continue to sit and eat and feel bad and try to "shut it out." She described this as a sense of paralysis, a feeling as if she "just wasn't there anymore." This is a state of unconsciousness, or "dissociation" that a child may enter when she finds a situation intolerable to bear, yet physically inescapable. Often it is hard even to remember and work on what happened during those times (such as child abuse) except through dreams and fantasy work.

Within her therapy session, this woman did an "active imagination," trying out various fantasies to see what might happen if the conscious and the unconscious could work on the problem together. She closed her eyes and imagined being at the breakfast table. Then (this is the "active" part), she was invited to "ask for something to be different this time, ask for something or someone to be of help, then see what happens. Check with your deepest center to see if that's the right thing, and if it is, do it." This is a technique people occasionally use with dreams that seem unfinished, unsettled, or unresolved to them.

> *Active Imagination.* My mother has just asked, "Is something wrong with the toast? Want me to warm it up?" And my father is about to say, "No, it's all right."
>
> I ask for something to be different this time: If he says no, she's just going to drop it. If he says yes, she'll do it, she'll warm it up, but not so frantic, not pop up and let her own food get cold. It's not that important.
>
> She's out from under his judgment, and is free from her usual sense of failure—that has always kept me sympathetic with her and hating him.

When asked to check with her deepest center to see if that was the right thing to do, she said it wasn't, so she tried again and asked for help.

> I get angry. I ask my father, "Why don't you warm up your own toast?" He'd be shocked; Mom'd be surprised, hurt, and send me to my room. I can't do that. [Pause.]
>
> I'll see what else can happen. [Pause.] I notice my brother. He just sits there, as I do, but later he tells me he felt the same way I did. It makes me feel closer to him; we've been suffering the same way. And it confirms things: that my father judges, and my mother sets him up.

When she opened her eyes and thought about what had happened, she concluded that what the situation needed—in addition to the crucial confirmation by her brother—was for her mother to be less frantic to please, less anxious for a "crumb of approval," and for her father to be more open to "what is," rather than what "should be." And what she needed was to keep herself from being drawn in: to keep some distance with her new perspective, but not cancel out her feelings by dissociation. She said, "I need more 'So what!' in my character."

And the moment she said "so what," she suddenly recalled an incident one Thanksgiving Day. Her mother was carrying the turkey on the platter across the kitchen when it slipped onto the floor. "My mother placed it right back on the platter, looked up and said to me, 'What they don't know won't hurt them!' I was surprised and amused; it was so unlike her." This was her mother's imp who could say, on rare occasions, "So what!" Now this imp was out of the bottle and the daughter could have it, too.

In our culture, daughters don't often get to see their mothers' and fathers' imps, or tricksters. Instead, parents tend to exaggerate and be overly dramatic to a daughter in teaching the rules of how to be acceptable in our society ("You must never . . . !"), and girls are often overly impressionable, overly receptive to the feeling-tone, the heavy intonations. In general, parents oversimplify rules for children, and children themselves don't yet have perspective on rules.

The main parental influence, though, is not what parents say, but what they do. They are a model of how to treat others. Children believe what they see and unconsciously use their parents as models; they react in ways similar to their parents as they go out into the world at large. In this case, the young woman had carried on, within herself, the reflexes of a perfectionistic father as well as an overly compliant mother—who also had a little bit of redeeming trickster in her.

With the help of her mother's imp, she was on her way to get out from under perfectionism and judgment to claim her trickster and buoyant young feminine spirit. This shows the positive effect of the lighthearted puella, not the naive, unknowing puella who is taken unawares, as in the previous dream, but the more conscious puella. We develop this positive spirit through play and inner work such as art and fantasy, which give us the freedom and intuition to have fresh perspectives on life and see possibilities in difficult situations. Through her dream and active imagination, this woman became aware of her father's unconscious aggression, like a silent alligator lying in wait for a mistake, which she could elude with her playful spirit. Her puella helped her go her own way and dance out from under the heavy, harsh trap of aggression and catering to aggression. The imp had given her—and us—a new rule: Don't let the alligator catch your eye. Dance by!

## Fighting Aggression with One's Own Authority

Women have been so accustomed to retreating from aggression that sometimes we don't see what happens when we do assume authority. Different problems result from women taking charge than from male authority. If a woman happens to be large or tall, she reminds men—and other women—of the powerful mother they knew when they were small and helpless, so if she is assertive she may be seen as overbearing. On the other hand, if she is petite or short, she can be discounted or overlooked by others. If she is small and beautiful, she is put in the place where men may prefer her—in the "sex object" box, e.g., "You're so cute when you're mad."

Women sometimes become accustomed to using subterfuge, citing authority outside ourselves, and giving reasons for things, because we haven't been given authority itself, or haven't risked taking it. And it is a risk, as it is for a man to take his authority. But a man has a better chance of succeeding and being liked and respected for it, whereas a woman runs a greater risk of failing, or if she succeeds, of being disliked or categorized in a disrespectful way, and of being isolated by her power.

A woman who was very diplomatic and flexible found that while she was able to relate to her strong husband and negotiate with her colleagues in a competitive workplace, she was not getting truly fair treatment in the long run. She had been struggling uphill in her marriage and at work for years when she had the following dream:

> **The Mugger and the Stick.** My aunt and I are in a tunnel. A mugger is there. Should we go forward or back? If we go back, my aunt can't run fast enough; the man can run faster. So we go forward a short distance. Both of them—my aunt and the man—have sticks. Then I, too, have a stick. There's a tussle. My aunt and I say, "Let's just go through!" He says, "Fine."

As a figure who accompanies her in the dream, the aunt represents qualities that she should make more conscious in her life. She described her aunt as having "a mean streak." This is a negative, shadowy quality in herself that she doesn't want to admit. Because it is unconscious, this figure—that "mean" side of her—can't be mobilized to be helpful, can't run fast enough in the dream to escape being pursued by others' aggression.

In certain situations, though, one needs to counter another's aggression with one's own. In the dream (and probably in real life) her aunt had something useful—a stick, archetypal symbol of authority. When, like the aunt, the dreamer takes her stick, claims her authority, and decides to go forward to confront authority with authority, the mugger—who also has a stick—yields!

This was an important dream for this woman. Years of insight in analysis hadn't enabled her to become very assertive outwardly. She was introverted and needed to mobilize her inner fantasy world to help her implement her conscious insights. As she told this dream, one could sense some of the energy and bearing of Toshiro Mifune, as the samurai warrior, going through the tunnel in the dream. There was no doubt that this dream experience was as powerful—or more powerful—than an actual experience in real life. In the dream—in her innermost being—she had met the challenge. She no longer needed to project her own unknown aggressive side onto a big man and play the opposite, which had left her feeling vulnerable (pursued by a mugger).

And in actuality, the dream, on its own and as a culmination of other inner and outer work, did have a profound effect, as dreams sometimes do. She was now on her way toward claiming her own authority. A short while after the dream she reported a change in herself, especially at the office. Instead of automatically saying yes, or fibbing about something she didn't want to do, she found herself spontaneously saying such things as, "I can't do that—personally or professionally."

In the next section, Untangling from the Mother's Anger and Aggression, a long dream shows the intense closeness and terrible anger that can exist between mother and daughter, especially when the daughter is so dominated by the mother that she identifies with her mother's neediness at the expense of her own needs; then she must sort out appropriate guilt and compassion. Another dream exposes the bottled-up aggression of a daughter who can't counter her mother's authority with her own.

## Untangling from the Mother's Anger and Aggression

The closeness of the bond between mother and daughter, their common identity and empathic understanding, inevitably brings its opposite—great disappointment and anger over their differences, separateness, and individuality. The mother may use unconscious forms of control and aggression to impose her will or to establish closeness—or distance—and the daughter might use reciprocal means. The mother may try to enlist her daughter's natural sympathy for her feelings, such as wanting the daughter to side with her in any argument or keep a secret. This may cast the daughter into the dilemma of either forgetting her own feelings if she empathizes with her mother, or feeling guilty and hard-hearted if she doesn't. At this point, the mother may try to control her daughter with critical remarks, angry silences, threats, and even physical or verbal abuse.

Since a daughter identifies with her mother, she also chafes at differences. The daughter may want her mother to change: to be the model for her of who she herself would like to be, i.e., not be so fat; to conform to her cultural ideal of a mother to be proud of, i.e., not drink so much; or to fulfill her inner image of the all-accepting Great Mother she wishes her mother somehow could be, i.e., infinitely accepting. This can hurt a mother greatly because she wants so much to be a good mother, expects herself to be able to do it without conflict, and wants to do it better than her mother. Also, her daughter's rejection may echo her own mother's rejection.

A mother often depends on a daughter—more than she would a son—to stay close to her and give her emotional support. She may unconsciously expect or demand, in subtle ways, that the daughter—even as a young girl—be "always there," as if the daughter were her own mother, and this may be especially true when the mother becomes elderly with special needs for care and caring from her family. This aspect of the mother-daughter relationship requires perspective and caution as well as compassion on a daughter's part. In some cases, if the mother's needs aren't met, she may explode at the daughter with anger, blinding in its intensity. This is because it is unconscious anger. The daughter must sort out the legitimacy and the illegitimacy of these needs or demands. Most important, the daughter must do the hard work of handling her own hurt feelings or retaliatory anger, which she often turns inward as equally intense guilt. A daughter may find that just as it is dangerous to confront aggression directly in real life, it also feels dangerous to confront it directly in her inner arena. The following nightmare portrays this.

## Handling Personal vs. Archetypal Aggression

A woman had been trying in vain for many years to relate more satisfactorily with her mother, but more often than not their encounters left her flailing in turbulent waters, angry at her mother's criticism and demands, but also pulled down into the vortex of feeling intensely sorry for her mother. Her turmoil had increased as her mother became older and needed her more. This dream helped the daughter sort out these things. It also showed her what she might do so that she didn't have to perpetuate the same problem automatically with her own children.

> *Poison Darts.* An irresponsible young man is on a platform above my mother and me. My mother reads something aloud to him, accusing him of neglect— leaving my dog Rosie outside for twelve hours without water or affection. He denies that he has done anything so negligent, but I know he's been somewhat irresponsible.
>
> My mother is up in a vast high place throwing poison darts down at me. I try to get them from her and throw them out a skylight, but as soon as I dump one set, she has another! Suddenly there is an opponent between us there in the vast high place. It's a man, larger-than-life, with reddish, matted hair. He's unkempt and dirty, as if he hasn't been taken care of. He and I leap back and forth through the air; he's blocking the way so I can't get rid of the darts, and can't get down either.
>
> Finally I escape, and hide in a crowd of French-speaking women who are kind to me. We pull our hats down, so if the man enters he won't recognize us. We're in a circle and can see whoever enters. The women nod, "That's good. Keep an eye on things."
>
> The scene changes. There's a celebration with tropical fruit, singing and dancing. We're celebrating that I've made it and my mother has made it, too.

It was immediately obvious to this woman that the poison darts are the endless criticisms that she receives from her mother, that do, indeed, seem to sting with venom sometimes. Why are they so angry and cruel, and impossible for her to handle?

What stands between the mother and daughter is the unkempt figure with reddish hair. The dreamer had a sudden insight that this was a personification of her mother's own feeling of being neglected and her mother's fiery thoughts about how she was mistreated. But it is crucial to note that this is not just everyday anger about lack of affection: it is larger-than-life. It is on an archetypal level and more than a daughter can deal with. The daughter can only escape at this point.

The dreamer realized that the angry, unkempt figure—what stood between them—was her mother's own terrible grief and rage at the loss of her own mother when she was two years old: an image of Great Neglect indeed. All these years the mother must have been unconsciously blaming her daughter, with archetypal intensity sometimes, for somehow not filling her great need for mothering which, of course, no daughter can do. And all along the daughter had sensed her mother's great sensitivity— seen now in the figure of Great Neglect—blocking her way so she didn't feel she should ever throw darts back and return her mother's criticism. To perceive this figure was useful to her in interactions with her mother. It proved even more useful when she realized that the figure was also her own inner figure, tyrannizing herself with self-blame in her relations with not only her mother but other people, too.

The hardest thing to do in dreams is to see figures not just as depictions of people you know, but also as depictions of your own inner figures, which they always are. It was difficult, but this woman tried to imagine the dream figures as sides of herself so she could see her own part in the struggle with aggression. Looked at this way, the dream told her that she, like her mother, was caught in a vast high place from which she "can't get down either." Her own inner unkempt figure held her there.

A daughter often unconsciously senses a mother's great needs and tries to answer them with all her compassion, and ends up in an inflated (high) position of rescuing from which she can't escape. The more she does, the more she is accused of not doing. Yet she cannot bring herself to leave. She is more aware of her mother's needs than her own. This explained a lot of what this woman had been experiencing with her mother and elsewhere.

How does a woman know if she has this problem? It is likely if her mother always looms large as an intense presence in her life, and she feels that she must be responsive, e.g., she answers her mother's phone calls no matter how late at night or early in the morning; her mother's dramatic concerns always make her own seem bland. In this case, her task is to take the initiative from her mother and dare to be center stage in her own life.

How can you respond in real life if your mother accuses you of neglect, as does the mother in this dream, who claims that the dog Rosie was left without water or care? To sort this out, you can look at specific personal realities, rather than seeing reality only through the hazy lens of a mother's archetypal feelings and archetypal image of Great Neglect. This dreamer asked herself if she was a truly neglectful person. Did she leave her dog Rosie twelve hours without water—or her mother without proper care? No. If so, it would be grievous neglect. Did she leave Rosie without affection for great lengths of time? Yes, just as her mother had often left her without much affection, and just as she sometimes left her mother without much affection. And that could hurt, but was bearable and redeemable.

If a mother has always been confused about these distinctions, like this mother was, a daughter is left confused, too. With its poetic imagery, this dream helps sort out ordinary human neglect or grievous mistakes as different from archetypal cruelty or gross neglect. Even though a mother may feel that a particular slight or imperfection on a daughter's part "could kill her," a daughter can escape from believing this—that she can make or heal her mother's old wounds.

And in her life, this dreamer developed a perspective on a similar feeling, an echo of her mother's reaction—that *any* neglect was unbearable. She empathized with her mother's wound, but it was not hers. She had her own wounds, her own experiences of Great Neglect as all of us have in life. Nevertheless, she knew that she was much more resilient than her mother in this regard: She'd had no great loss in her *own* early life.

Knowing more consciously about her mother's wound and rage, admitting her collusion with her mother's tyrannical need, and acknowledging her own wounds and neglectfulness brought the dreamer some perspective so that her mother's darts in the future might sometimes bounce off. Yet the dream essentially says that the fiery figure is too strong an adversary, and she still needs to be wary about provoking her mother.

Archetypal feelings need archetypal healing, and this was accomplished somewhat in the dream by the ritual circle of kindly women, hats pulled down, keeping a low profile in the presence of the tyrant who might intrude at any time! Hidden, but alert. In the dream, she thinks she is merely getting lost in a crowd, but she finds herself in this group of kind women, in fact, a sacred circle, a mystery, a deeper sense of feminine protectiveness within herself. This is the wisdom of the heart that knows how to keep counsel and be quiet and vigilant around Great Neglect. In everyday terms, it is having kind respect for another's terrible wounds.

This leads us to the dream's conclusion that the mother and daughter are both in the same boat—enough to celebrate their mutual escape from the figure and enjoy some bounty. Where does this happy prospect come in? This suggests that a daughter can break the spell and manage to dump some arrows, and, within circumscribed areas, lighten the whole situation for both herself and her mother. This woman, however, has been given warning to remain careful of the threatening figure, larger-than-life, who can make his appearance any time.

How can a dream like this directly affect your life? The day before this dream occurred, the daughter—a mother herself—had had a flareup with her own twenty-year-old son, and had been afraid she'd sounded "just like my mother." However, the morning after the dream, before she had even thought much about the dream she'd just had, the anger at her son disappeared. That is, she did not echo her mother's fiery thoughts about how her son ought to treat her, but instead could tune in better to her own true feelings and also to his.

What happened was that the experience of the dream itself had helped her unconsciously sort out her feelings and allowed her feelings to shift. She had stepped down from her high place, her righteous anger. The dream had broken into her unwitting pattern of assuming that her son had to meet some great need of hers and it was a welcome relief for them both.

## Confronting the Mother's Authority with One's Own

Although mothers traditionally have felt entitled to some power in the home and especially in regard to their children, nevertheless, they have generally felt uneasy about wielding authority, and their aggression and control have an unconscious quality. Since her mother is a model for her, a daughter may find it difficult to take her own authority consciously, and this is further complicated if her mother seems too strong—or too weak—for her to emulate. The following case is a daughter whose mother was so strong that she found it difficult to grasp her own autonomy.

A reserved, mild-mannered woman, Abbie had a dream the night after a disturbing family gathering in which Abbie's mother, in a moment of jealous rage, had lashed out at her grandchild, Abbie's small son, terrifying him, while Abbie and her husband had stood by helplessly. Then the grandmother had looked to Abbie for support for her actions! At least Abbie had declined to back up her mother, but Abbie hadn't done much for her boy except to distract him afterwards. She felt bad that she couldn't help her own child escape from his grandmother's wrath. What also troubled Abbie was the fact that this incident left her boy with the impression that his grandmother, not she herself as his mother, was the authority in the house.

> ***Don't Know How to Use the Gun.*** **We're outdoors in the fields. A man is escaping from a policeman. I have a gun, but don't know how to use it. The policeman takes a fast car to chase him. I want to let the man escape, and he does. Our two lumbering trucks go after him. I try to get the ammunition out of my gun, but I don't know how to do either thing—take the bullets out or cock the gun to use it. I have no thought of stopping the man or helping the policeman either.**

This dream clarified for Abbie her mixed reaction to her mother's aggression. She didn't know how to use her gun (her own aggression) to stop the policeman (the authority/grand-mother chasing the child). Nor did she know how to take the bullets out (defuse her own anger). The two lumbering trucks (her and her husband's slow unconscious reactions) were no match for the policeman's fast car (the authority's/grandmother's quick reactions).

This dream made Abbie more sharply aware of the issues. It shows how complicated the situation becomes when authority in the family is faulty—unclear, unfair, or abusive. You hesitate to go against constituted authority, yet you want the victims to escape. You may be reduced to being only a bystander: helpless and guilty, neither stopping belligerent authority nor helping the victim.

Abbie realized that she had become immobilized as if she were a child again herself, instead of being a mother protecting her offspring. When young herself, she couldn't take much power, had been helpless and placating. She had dealt with authority by denying her anger in some way or distracting herself. Now she was caught between the old and new ways; she was in a better position to know her anger and take her authority (she had a gun), but was not yet capable of using it as assertion (couldn't cock and shoot the gun). These were areas for her to begin exploring—her options as a mother to take her power to protect her child.

While the previous sections have dealt with ways to counter others' aggression, the last section depicts how women might handle their own inner aggression. Women have been so bombarded with cultural messages to be good girls, to be passive, and to conform that we have internalized the taboo on our own aggression and even find it hard to feel assertive. The first step, then, is to feel and know our own assertion and aggression. Two dreams show women struggling with their own primitive aggression and transforming that kind of energy into a means of self-protection and feminine forms of assertion.

## Encountering Inner Feminine Figures of Aggression

Our families and society condemn expressions of aggression and allow only narrow ranges of assertion in girls and women. We are often left with the same outlets as our mothers, with the same consequences: to be passive-aggressive and manipulative, to be self-blaming and depressed, perfectionistic, and critical. Our own anger and aggression are driven underground so that eventually we don't even know when we are feeling angry or being aggressive. This leaves our own aggression very shadowy and vaguely unsettling, or at times terrifying when it bursts out.

Although inner feminine figures are featured throughout this book, mention should be made that the staging of the inner drama of aggression in our dreams often involves male figures, too, and the development of a woman's masculine side. Animus, or masculine, figures can be aggressive or helpful. Especially in women who have been mistreated, at first male figures in dreams can be threatening—sinister authorities, Ku Klux Klansmen, Nazis, a motorcycle gang, rapists, murderers, robbers, and bullies—but these may gradually change and become less frightening over time. *Helpful animus* figures also appear in women's dreams to deal with threats and aggression. Although one might assume that in dreams women would call upon strong men to do battle for them—and sometimes they do call upon a policeman, a protective older brother, or a John Wayne–type man—instead, women often enlist companions, advisers, or healers to help them deal with aggression themselves. These positive inner figures take a great variety of forms. Some are men whom the dreamers trust in real life: a male analyst, teacher, or boyfriend. Some are well-known figures. One woman dreamed of Don Quixote, who seemed to her a brave man of integrity, though foolhardy. Another woman, who couldn't stand her ground with her angry husband, dreamed that she got the backing of exactly the kind of man she needed, a famous baseball slugger, that is, someone who hits the ball back, connects well with his assertion.

Sometimes special men give women courage in the face of

danger. A rabbi, with spiritual power against Nazi captors, appeared in a dream which then gave the dreamer the courage to escape her real-life bondage. A Native American medicine man advised a woman how to protect herself against hostile forces. A boyfriend healed a woman's physical wounds with his numinous music. When one woman faced a perilous situation in her dreams, her male companion suddenly made a joke and the resulting laughter—a shift in perspective—dissolved the dangerous atmosphere.

Some women have been so mistreated or abused by men in their lives, and so deeply distrust men, that they don't have ordinary male helpers in their dreams. However, in perilous situations, they sometimes rely on unusual animus figures: One woman dreamed of a friendly alien from outer space who knew how to handle danger. Another dreamed again and again of her special guide in the form of a "tree man" who had emerged like a spirit from a tree; he looked like an ordinary man—except that he was green. At first some women don't have animus figures at all, but have helpful animals at their side, such as a dog or tiger. Early male figures may be threatening, ineffectual, or ambiguously helpful, and may evolve very slowly into constructive allies. In any case, as a woman develops, her animus does, too, and can become a special guide with wisdom, spiritual or healing powers, or can be a companion at her side, more like herself, a twin—who is her own masculine side.

When a woman dreams of female figures involved in aggression, they can represent internalized conflicts within herself, or her own struggles with aggression itself, played out as different images of herself. These often reflect early situations of feeling threat or safety with her mother, her ambivalent relations and identification with various women models or peers, and other experiences of conflict or aggression in her life. These figures take myriad forms, some of which you will find throughout this book. Aggressive female figures include the terrifying witch, a fierce mother, taunting girlfriends.

Of course, a woman herself, the "I" in a dream, as the chief protagonist handles aggressive situations herself in her unique feminine way, and often is rescuing her own vulnerable inner child. Women figures who sometimes appear in dreams to help counter threat, aggression, or danger come in many forms: a powerful goddess or saint whose presence neutralizes peril; a flamboyant, lewd old woman who completely interrupts a heavy atmosphere of dread; a group of supportive women; a warm Italian neighbor woman from a dreamer's childhood; a confident little girl who takes a dreamer's hand and leads her to safety; a bold woman friend who holds a knife to an aggressor; a sister who has the ingenuity to escape; a cautious twinlike figure who bides her time until the situation changes; a woman aikido instructor at a dreamer's side who knows how to deflect danger. Ultimately, all of the figures contending in a woman's internal dramas help her resolve the question of how to deal with her own aggression.

The following two dreams involving female images show us what fresh solutions to aggression might arise from our feminine side. In the first, the dreamer confronts an aggressive female figure; in the second, the dreamer herself is a primitive female figure whose potential aggressiveness needed special handling to be redeemed.

## Confronting Raw Aggression Within

Since we haven't had much opportunity to be aggressive effectively and to develop consciously differentiated kinds of aggressive responses to various situations, the raw aggression in our dreams can take the form of a physical struggle of terrifying proportions. When this is a struggle with an inner female figure, it may well have its roots in the earliest years with the mother and the great intimacy as well as the terrible anger that can exist between mother and daughter or, sometimes, between sisters.

This particular dreamer had been a shy daughter whose very intellectual, self-centered mother would suddenly strike out at her, as if disdainful of any vulnerability. An unexpressed, great unconscious resentment and thwarted aggression built up within her. But she had a dream and fantasy experience which helped her gain more authority in her life by confronting her own inner aggressive figure.

The dream occurred when the dreamer was in an unusual and somewhat frightening setting. For the first time, she was camping alone in the woods. Before she fell asleep, she wondered whether she could defend herself if she were attacked. Later, she awoke from a nightmare.

> *An Awful Woman Attacks Me.* **An awful woman with an intense look suddenly attacks me. She comes right at me where I'm soft and vulnerable: She's going to tear my guts apart. She's so strong and vicious that nothing can stop her. She's thin, with wild hair and dark clothes flying, like a child's version of a witch.**

When she woke up, she decided to confront the figure in a fantasy—actively confronting the unconscious by using active imagination. With her eyes wide open in the dark tent, she began:

> *Active Imagination.* **I see the awful woman who was attacking me in the dream. The way I fight back, I'm just as awful as the woman is. I have to be. I'm scared of the figure. So I tear her apart. I'm vicious. I put my hands in her mouth and rip her face, do the worst things I can think of. I have to, or she's going to kill me. Finally she stops tormenting me.**

Then the woman could go back to sleep.

She had had this nightmare before; a man had been with her in those dreams, but even he could not protect her. It was her own inner figure, representing the viciousness within her mother, and also deep within herself, whom she had to encounter, to wrestle with. She had to wrest from fierce, wild instinct her own conscious strength to protect herself as well as subdue her own viciousness when necessary.

Such archetypal aggression had to be met in a fundamental, archetypal way. It also had to be healed. The next night camping she followed her impulse to do a dance to invoke the protective spirits before she went to bed—a safe temenos for herself.

According to her last report, many years after the event, the nightmare had not recurred.

## Transforming Anger and Aggression Within a Safe Temenos

Since we are its victims, aggression itself seems so negative to us that the early images that arise from our unconscious—of our own anger and aggression—are likely to be very primitive, such as insects and snakes. These represent archetypal aggression that needs transformation into more human and useful forms.

Late one evening after a fine day together, a woman—Jan—suddenly "stung" her partner with some pent-up irritation about a problem. The sudden attack escalated to an upsetting fight. Too tired to resolve it at the time, they decided to discuss it in the morning. That night Jan had a dream.

> *The Mudwasp*. I'm a mudwasp, going to lay eggs. I'm impatient to lay the eggs, but I have to make a nest first. I realize it with an air of resignation—something I *have* to do first.
>
> It's a natural process: I excrete a substance out the point of my wasp tail. It's a whitish substance that comes out and I go round and round, like a spiral, building up a nest.

Jan's first thought upon waking was that she had indeed suddenly "stung" her lover, not preparing a time or place for her anger to be received or be effective in changing things. She had not been extremely deliberate and careful, as usual, but had been spontaneous. Jan had been wanting to recognize when she was angry and be more spontaneous, yet that turned out to be as much of a problem as holding it in!

The main emotion in the dream was impatience—wanting to get it out—and that's what brooding on anger is like, feeling like bursting and wanting to let off steam. The dream, though, says that she has to pause to prepare the nest—a safe container first, in this case, a spiral (a symbol of the development of the Self), a transformative white fluid out of her own substance.

The dreamer recalled an incident as a little girl. She had been talking with her aunt when she became vaguely aware of playing with something in her hand. Jan looked down and saw a live wasp in her hand, and it hadn't stung her! Looking back, she wondered if the reason was that her aunt was someone with whom Jan felt very safe. Wasps only sting defensively. She thought then that perhaps it's mainly anxiety in herself or others that brings forth stinging. Anxiety, in the guise of impatience, makes one either sting or be stung. If Jan wanted to become more aware of her anger, then she might find impatience and anxiety the first signs of anger she could notice.

Jan realized that her irritation had made her anxious and therefore impatient, and she might well have paused, if she could, to prepare a safe enough place and time—when she and her partner were not so tired—to resolve a problem and get what she needed. Beginning to deal with anger and aggression is often very difficult.

One question from the dream puzzled her. The wasp clearly meant aggression because of its stinger, but why "laying eggs"? It occurred to her that the dream referred not just to the safe nest that another person needed to receive her anger, but also the safe place she herself needed when criticized. She was in a writers' group and had let herself open to criticism—laid her eggs (her poems)—before she felt safe. Although she had rushed forth impatiently in her anxiety, perhaps she needed plenty of brooding time—inward preparation—as well as outward expression of her fear to the group so they could help her feel safe.

It took an outsider to point out to Jan that perhaps the wasp in the dream was also a pun on the acronym WASP, the initials of White Anglo-Saxon Protestant. Some people know they pun in their dreams and this dreamer was one of these. She laughed and said, "Perhaps that's one reason why WASP has really stuck, because the word fits! That's the way I was raised: One quietly absorbs anger, then suddenly stings with a barbed remark."

This cultural consciousness gave Jan a perspective. She needn't be confined to the ways her own culture happened to handle aggression. Stinging is not a very effective expression of aggression. There might be slight satisfaction, perhaps, in letting out some anger, getting even, warning others, but it usually just makes the other person feel hurt and want to retaliate. It doesn't do what more conscious kinds of assertion can do—help get one's way in the world—which is the purpose of aggression. There are more effective ways to express anger and be assertive, which may involve preparing a safe container first.

If we look at the deeper message of this dream, it echoes the larger lesson of the Swallowing the Needle dream that began this chapter. In that dream, a woman redirected her attention from the aggressive qualities of needling to the threaded quality of the needle, which suggested that she should shift her energy from the game of dominance in her life to the pursuit of her individual constructive feminine endeavors. Similarly, in this dream about the mudwasp, at first the dreamer concentrated on the offensive and defensive tactics of aggression, but she made the same mistake she made in life: focusing on aggression rather than on assertion, the pursuit of her own love, her own work, her writing.

What other possibilities does the dream reveal? Looking closely at the dream, we see it is a particular kind of wasp, a mudwasp, incidentally capable of aggression but preoccupied in the dream with laying eggs and protecting them. Mud refers to unconscious anger, and here it is transformed into a pure (whitish) fluid that forms around a center (round and round, like a spiral) symbolic of the development of the Self—the greatest strength and ally for a woman. The humble mudwasp, then, with her capability of aggression but her devotion to creativity, is an instructive image for us of the feminine way—to become strong and productive through our devotion to what is truly important to us.

# 4

# The Shadow:
# The Hidden Side

"Who knows what evil lurks in the hearts of men? The shadow knows." This introduction to the popular 1940s radio show, "The Shadow," has a ring of truth to it. We sometimes glimpse, lurking in the dark corners of our awareness, mysteries that are part of the human condition. We see and feel certain socially unacceptable things we would rather not acknowledge or experience. The term "shadow" usually refers to those negative qualities, all the bad things that don't fit our conscious picture of ourselves that we banish from the daylight of ego consciousness.

## Personal, Cultural, and Archetypal Shadow

This chapter begins with a discussion of three kinds of shadow: *the personal shadow*—individual traits or weaknesses that we are reluctant to accept as parts of ourselves and which we often project, disparagingly, onto others; *the cultural shadow*—general characteristics or deficiencies shared by a group or culture but consciously or unconsciously denied by members of the group and its institutions, usually projected onto another group in the form of prejudiced attitudes, stereotypes, or scapegoating; and *the archetypal shadow*—global qualities of humankind, the dark unknowns that lie deep in the psyche, that we perceive only vaguely, if at all, as irrational, overpowering, or destructive forces in the universe.

These "shadow" qualities reveal themselves in our dreams so that we can recognize and reclaim them as our own. If we don't face our shadows, they can work against us. Most shadow qualities are negative and so most of the dreams in this chapter deal with revealing and coming to terms with this negative shadow. However, many people also have positive qualities of which they are dimly aware and which they are forbidden to accept or afraid to use: the "positive shadow." Women, especially, have been taught by the wider culture to disown our many positive qualities, such as assertiveness, an independent or outspoken nature, a risk-taking, creative, or adventurous spirit. Therefore, the last section of this chapter is devoted to dreams about the positive shadow.

## The Elusive Personal Shadow

Your personal shadow consists of the impulses, feelings, thoughts, and images which you find so unacceptable, awkward, or embarrassing that you deny their existence completely or are only partially aware of them. These are your own individual, personal weaknesses. They might include worries about such things as social inadequacies, or sexual and aggressive feelings that seem inappropriate.

Our personal shadow is exposed in our family life and other intimate relationships. Through many years of relating closely, sooner or later we reveal who we are, good and bad. One reason relations with our own family seem so painful is that our family can see our faults, our shadow. And we also see their shadows, which is why they seem so extremely flawed. Similarly, in everyday interactions with people at work, year after year, we come to know ourselves and others too well to deny the reality of our personal faults in working together. The need for power and political maneuvering at the workplace, for instance, can be shadow qualities, however smoothly presented.

How can you know your shadow, since by definition it is more or less unconscious? The shadow may be more obvious at certain times: when entering close personal or work relationships, and also when ending them with mutual recriminations or dark thoughts about personal failings. You can detect your shadow in what you worry about revealing in a new relationship or new career. What do you want to cover up or gloss over about yourself? What are your worst fantasies of what someone might think about you? Your shadow also may come to light during spontaneous moments when you are joking, angry, or drinking.

What happens if we don't try to know and understand our shadow? It may make itself known to us and to others in an embarrassing slip of the tongue when we're relaxed; in an irritable mood when we're under stress; or in cruelty toward others when we're tired, intoxicated, or goaded. Sometimes we so strictly refuse to acknowledge our shadow impulses that they emerge as uncomfortable physical symptoms, such as indigestion or muscle tension.

We cheat ourselves by not knowing our shadow. People who are "too good," who cast no shadow, are two-dimensional. They don't have substance, and don't feel real to themselves or to others. Often, they try even harder to be better so they can feel satisfied with themselves and so others will like them, but that just deepens the problem. They become more guilty about themselves and more self-righteous about others who don't live up to their own impossible standards.

We are secretly delighted—or at least intrigued—by "bad" people. We talk endlessly about a member of the family or a colleague who is rebellious, who gets away with things, or gets a comeuppance. We like books and movies about faulty heroes who finally redeem themselves. In the shadow lies the psychological truth behind our interest in the detective story. Everyone could be the murderer; everyone is suspect—even the ones who appear good. And we are only satisfied when the murderer is found and brought to justice, because the shadow should be caught.

A welcome effect of owning up to our shadow is being able to shed the blithe naivete of the young girl, the puella, and the awkward self-consciousness of youth. Our young idealism—about how good we and others are or should be—gets buffeted enough to yield to dappled realities. Usually we avoid looking inward at our faults, but it is the mature, realistic person who can finally say: This is the way I am!

But the shadow is very tricky. It is well hidden and we have mighty resistance to knowing it. Friends and colleagues shy away from telling us about our shadow, unless we admit it ourselves first; that's why we can't tolerate the thought of others talking about us "behind our back."

What are indirect ways to find the shadow? Often it is easier to see the negative shadow in other people than in ourselves. In fact, this may be the first step in seeing our own. We often have negative reactions to someone who reflects part of our own image, which we don't like to admit to, and which we, indeed, *dis*own. We may dislike or feel oversensitive to someone who shows an exaggerated amount of our own forbidden characteristics: a pushy person, for example, or the class showoff. The intensity of our response to the other person—anger, repugnance, envy—measures how strong and hidden that shadow is in ourselves. If our shadow is very repressed, so that we don't know it at all, we find it difficult to believe such perfidy exists in anyone. *We* would not be capable of such a thing!

Dreams are the royal road to knowing the shadow. If a dream offers up an obscure person from the past, then the figure probably represents your own shadow. In a dream, if a shadowy quality appears in someone you know well, then it is probably the person's own shadow that your sleuthful unconscious is picking up. In any case, it is always useful to "bring the shadow home" and see how it applies to yourself. Sometimes, however, you will see that the shadow is not so much personal as it is cultural, so we will turn to that subject next.

## Cultural Shadow

Usually our use of the term "culture" refers broadly to Western culture in general, since it is the most pervasive influence in our society. However, any group or system to which you belong (family, workplace, region of a country) or any social identity you have (gender, class, race, ethnicity, religion, or sexual orientation) can have its own distinctive social-psychological "culture"—common myths, symbols, stories, history, beliefs, customs, style of social relations, and codes of behavior. Whatever qualities or behavior are left out can fall into the "cultural shadow": family secrets about alcoholism, the harsh unspoken codes of a junior-high-school clique of girls, ethnic jokes, racial prejudice, homophobia, men's hidden weakness or informal power networks.

The brighter the sun, the darker the shadow that is cast. The more pristine, powerful, respectable, or righteous group members are, the more of themselves they must relegate to darkness. These shadowy things operate underground, beyond conscious control, until they become so extreme that they provoke outside attention, such as outside intervention in family abuse or the exposure of covert operations of a "shadow government."

Just as individuals need to integrate their negative shadow to become whole, so a culture must integrate its negative shadow to thrive. Often this involves the inclusion of its members who are subject to shadow projections and prejudice.

At a fairly conscious level, Western culture, like many other cultures, rejects individual behavior that may be inconvenient for the institutions of society, such as: uncontrolled sex and aggression; the free expression of strong feelings; disorderliness or defiance of authority by those not deemed entitled to it.

At a less conscious level, in the United States, with our puritan heritage and heroic male ideal, ordinary human failings and weaknesses are perceived as deviations from the norm (which is actually an ideal) and loom large as dirtiness, laziness, selfishness, ugliness, stupidity, dependency, and craziness. These cultural shadow qualities are often projected onto handy targets, often individuals or groups who look different from the cultural ideal of the strong white male, such as women, children, older people, racial and ethnic minorities, and those seen as impaired in any way. The culture of the majority is denying its own collective shadow, its own share of human qualities that seem negative, and projecting and exaggerating them.

How would you recognize your cultural shadow? You can start with the ways in which you and your family, or other identity group, consider yourselves superior to others; and, inevitably, you will project the inferior, shadowy counterpart onto others. Another question might be: What are you most afraid of a group discovering about you? How fat you are? Fear of public exposure or condemnation of your fatness could be your own personal shadow, but it's more likely to be your incorporation of society's irrational, shadowy attitude toward fatness, especially in women. It is therefore important for women to detect deeply ingrained, prejudiced images of women in the cultural shadow. One source of such information is dreams.

THE CULTURAL SHADOW IN DREAMS.    How can you recognize when a dream is about the cultural shadow? Any *group* in a dream is likely to refer to the cultural shadow, as does any *member of a distinctive group* different from the dreamer, such as someone from another race or country. Bear in mind that dreams by even the most sophisticated and tolerant people have embarrassingly stereotypic and prejudiced shadow images, because the unconscious uses concrete images to express things. For example, in the white middle class of the United States, the cultural shadow is often represented in dreams as parts of the wider culture that are "foreign" or remote from its own cultural experience: the "bad" part of town, various minorities, bag ladies, and bums. Some of these, of course, are projections of one's own personal shadow, too.

Women's dream images of their own cultural shadow take such forms as shame about being naked in public, anxiety about performing before an audience, or terror at being stoned by a group of people. Often such images are an indication of our fears of rejection, which come from our internalization of the general culture's unconscious shadow projections onto women.

For her own dream images, then, a woman uses the handy brush and palette that her culture provides her as shadow projections. But a woman's images of *herself* and her shadow also need to be understood against the wider backdrop of society's shadow projections onto women in general. For society has painted its own colors onto the Woman, layer upon layer through the millennia.

CULTURAL SHADOW PROJECTIONS ONTO WOMEN.    Women, like other minorities, have a *negative shadow* thrust upon them by the culture. Those in power project onto others—perceive out there in them—whatever they don't want or can't accept in themselves.

So men project onto women qualities they aren't allowed: emotionality, weakness, and passivity as well as men's own very negative shadowy feelings about those human qualities. Those in power also attribute to others qualities advantageous for them to relegate to others, such as women's supposedly endless capacity to enjoy the repetitive, never-ending maintenance work of house-wife, mother, and clerical worker. At the same time, those in power don't truly respect the actual capabilities that such work requires.

Sometimes men will admire women as alluring sex objects with sexual desires that match what they themselves want in a woman: for instance, they imagine she is passive, that she secretly wants to be raped. Or, on the other hand, they may assign her their own forbidden feelings, then denigrate her for them. Their own feelings of attraction and desire are projected onto the seductive siren; their detached lust onto the whore; their perfor-mance anxiety onto the reluctance or "frigidity" of their partner; their own yearning for closeness and their own loving nature onto the "lovesick," "overly emotional," "cloying" woman.

Heavy sanctions forbid men to be vulnerable, or at least to show it, so that their own shy, tender, playful, childlike feelings become projected onto women and then disparaged as "child-ishness." Men's fear and awe of closeness, love, and commitment may be projected onto women whom they envision as either elusive tender maidens to be pursued, or the opposite, marriage-hungry women too quick to fall in love and thus to be avoided.

Women are expected to bear the burden not only of the culture's projection of its negative shadow onto them but its *positive shadow,* too. Men, children, older parents, and also other women—all exert unconscious pressures on women to fill in the qualities missing in the majority culture, such as patience, kindness, compliancy. These are impossible standards to live up to, so women—no matter how hard they try—feel that they are not good enough to fulfill the positive shadow: the Superwoman. This positive shadow problem—trying to fit the Superwoman image—combines with the negative shadow problem—trying to avoid denigration for "feminine" characteristics. The result is that women often feel exhausted and worthless.

Women have been turning to therapy for help with depression and feelings of worthlessness. But, as feminist therapists have pointed out, if a traditional therapist is unaware of cultural projections onto women, therapy can exacerbate a woman's problems by blaming her for her own lack of confidence or achievement and promoting eternal self-improvement so she can somehow feel happy with her lot! What looks like depression to a therapist may be simply exhaustion, such as that found in an overworked mother with young children.

One task, then, for women is to recognize the cultural shadow that has been projected onto them by others in their personal history, daily life, and in the man-made world at large. Women's groups can be particularly helpful because women can talk about their common situation in an atmosphere free of the usual projections from parents, men, and children. Because the best way to work on a problem is in a similar—but safe—situation, a supportive group may be a good place to correct and heal a cultural problem.

Once a woman discovers her own personal or cultural shadow, it may emerge as a useful source of energy rather than functioning autonomously behind her back. For instance, her righteous anger—when freed up—can be used assertively for herself or for society. In addition, knowing her own shadow gives a woman some immunity to the daily bombardment of cultural shadow projections. For example, if a woman consciously comes to terms with her own "fatness," she will be in a better position to handle society's shadow about fatness in women.

## Archetypal Shadow

Beneath the personal and the cultural shadows lies the archetypal shadow buried in the deeper layers of the unconscious and reflected in universal myths and symbols, dreams, and strong feelings. This shadow brings a sense of foreboding about something sinister, alarm about being out of control, anxiety about hidden things becoming exposed, repulsion and horror about terrible unknowns. Archetypal shadow may be expressed in our culture in images such as the vulture, the devil, the evil child, sinister ritual, the witch, the grotesque, the enemy, nuclear arsenals; that is, in threatening images that are distortions of unassimilated, deep, harsh truths known to the Self. These images are more intensely frightening and more global than the personal and cultural shadows. Archetypal shadow verges on the destruction of the Self; images extend toward cosmic dimensions of destructiveness that can overwhelm the individual or annihilate human society.

These rarely acknowledged images may account for the popularity of horror movies, such as *Psycho, Alien,* and *Nosferatu.* Recent science fiction movies, such as *Star Wars,* have complex negative and positive shadow figures: Luke Skywalker's father, Darth Vader, who is not entirely evil, and Luke's shadowy guide, Ben Obi-wan Kenobi, an ambiguously positive figure of the Self. Other science fiction movies show very positive, very unknown, shadow forces and figures of the Self: *E.T., Close Encounters of the Third Kind,* and *The Abyss.*

## Differentiating Personal, Cultural, and Archetypal Shadow

Let us examine how the human qualities of self-interest, selfishness, and aggressiveness are experienced in the different realms of the shadow: personal, cultural, and archetypal. If you deny selfish qualities in yourself, you might experience them in the *personal shadow* realm as vague, unconscious guilt about wanting things for yourself—even when it is appropriate. You might be subject to attacks of jealousy of your siblings, or you might find yourself envious underneath of friends and colleagues. In your dreams you might have suspicious feelings and images such as a gas leak in the house, irritating insects, a rat, a robber. However, the more you perceive your own selfish and aggressive qualities, claim them as aspects of your own personality, and handle them consciously, the more you can distinguish ordinary self-interest from too much aggression.

Knowing your personal shadow, you will be less preoccupied with the shadow in other people, and project less onto them. Also, in your own self-defense, you will be less accepting of other's irrational projections onto you. You will become more perceptive of the truth about others' personal selfishness and aggression ("It takes one to know one"), and this will make you more immune to those qualities in their more threatening forms—in the cultural and archetypal shadow.

In the realm of the *cultural shadow,* selfishness and aggression might surface as feelings of victimization—embarrassment, shame, or fear about being labelled as a member of an outgroup that is seen by the majority group as too assertive or not entitled to any assertion. In its projected form the cultural shadow could be righteous superiority toward a minority—or disdain toward the majority culture—for being too self-interested. Another example would be an idealistic group's general aversion and avoidance of a colleague who violates its norms of selflessness. Although the colleague might, in fact, be quite self-serving, subcultural shadow projections by the group members can distort their perceptions so that their colleague isn't seen as a whole but mainly in terms of that trait, which is exaggerated. In addition, any general labelling or scapegoating of others by this group around the issue of selfishness might not be accurate and would probably fall into the group's shadow.

In dreams, typical cultural shadow images of selfishness and aggression might be: a large person overeating, marks on a person's face, a bad smell in the air, being a member of a minority generally seen as aggressive or selfish, being chased by a gang as its target, or else being the one who scapegoats others.

The *archetypal shadow* is more unconscious, irrational, and symbolic in form. Feelings are diffuse and intense, such as anxiety about threats to one's own greed and power, terror about losing one's special status or belongings, or rage at others' rapaciousness. Dream images might be a tempting devil, a brutal murderer, pollution, plotting witches, monsters, terrorists, fascist forces.

It is useful to recognize all three kinds of shadow—the personal, the cultural, and the archetypal—because they often intermesh. If you close the door to one kind of shadow, it may come in through another door. For instance, if you repress the personal or cultural shadow, it can fall into the swamp of the archetypal shadow, so that your neighbor's faults or your own culture's shortcomings are perceived as "evil" or another country is seen as "an evil empire." Once something has fallen into the archetypal realm like this, we then feel compulsively drawn toward handling it by archetypal, irrational means: destruction, redemption, absolute avoidance, fascinated identification, or compulsion toward confrontation, ways that might be unnecessary or dangerous.

CLAIMING THE PERSONAL SHADOW TO NEUTRALIZE CULTURAL SHADOW. Conscious knowledge of any one kind of shadow can help you with the others. This example shows how knowledge of the personal shadow protected a woman—who inadvertently stumbled into the public eye—from cultural shadow projections. A young woman, Fran, was anxious and cried all weekend, fearful of what might happen if a picture, taken of her without her consent, were to be published in the local newspaper. She had been photographed in a socially compromising position—angrily confronting someone in the community. Although Fran didn't feel personally ashamed of what she'd done, she was afraid of what others, who were prejudiced, might think of her, especially because she was a member of a minority. She worried about how it might reflect upon her community position. Could she even lose her job? Fran was distraught enough, finally, to try active imagination (fantasy work) on her own, even though she didn't think anything could help. She concentrated on her feelings of fear and despair until an image came.

> ***Active Imagination: A Handful of Shit.*** **A group of people are dumping a whole truckload of manure over me, as if they're going to tar and feather me. I ask for something to help, and look down at my closed fist. There I am, holding a piece of shit in my hand, and that somehow saves me from harm.**

When Fran opened her eyes after the fantasy, she found that she was free from her uncontrollable crying. It was hard to believe, but this inner work, experiencing these symbolic representations of inner and outer truths, had lifted her anguish and fear in what is called "symbolic healing." She didn't need to understand them in a more intellectual way. She had deeply acknowledged her own "shit," that is, her own personal shadow—her own anger, and deep-seated fears of rejection. Clarifying her own shadow kept her more free from the "shit" of others, kept her from accepting their cultural shadow projected on her as a scapegoat. Of course, this was only half the task. Fran had handled the inner task, but the outer one remained to be done. When the newspaper office opened on Monday morning, she was settled enough inside to meet with the editor and protect herself.

Often the three different kinds of shadow are all present and intertwined. On occasion, though, in real life or dream analysis, you might try to distinguish between them. When you dream of negative women figures, you should check whether you're accepting cultural shadow projections onto women. In analyzing dreams about your family, you should ask yourself whether you are projecting shadowy archetypal fears—or hopes—onto family members. This is especially likely to happen when there are intense images, such as the bad or good mother.

The dreams that follow show all three kinds of shadow, sometimes in the same dream, but most feature the personal shadow.

## Dreams Exposing the Negative Shadow

### One's Own Shadow

In daily life, you may catch only a fleeting notion of your own shadow's existence in your avoidance of certain topics or your vague feelings of guilt, self-doubt, discontent, or discord. You may suddenly notice vague worries and feelings in a flush of embarrassment, in an awkward moment of nervous laughter, in a burst of tears, in a flare of anger. When a dream uncovers your shadow, you must be firm of mind enough to get past your resistance to understanding the dream's message and taking it to heart. This is a humbling experience, but it can also be healing and give you integrity.

This first dream shows how useful finding your own personal shadow can be, for by admitting your dark side, you can take better care of yourself and others.

> *A Rat in a Trap.* **I smell something bad. It's a rat or mouse in my kitchen, caught in a trap, though still alive, writhing. I kill it or dispose of it. I take care of it somehow.**

The dreamer, Peg, wondered, What's *my* rat—my shadow? Rats are sneaky, selfish, and stealthy. Peg's first association concerned her old boyfriend and her relief that he was not coming to town as he had planned. Suddenly it came to her—what she had caught herself at. She had been unconsciously planning to have sex with him even though she was currently in a monogamous relationship with someone else. Peg had uncovered the shadow many people have in their double standard toward affairs: It feels so innocent and understandable when you do it yourself, but so awful when your partner does it! This dream corrected that and called Peg a "dirty rat" if she did such a thing to her own partner. So the feeling of "I smell a rat" usually indicates the shadow in yourself or in someone else.

Dreams have many meanings, like layers of an onion, each true. You might wonder why the rat was writhing and needed to be killed, and why it was found in the kitchen—the place of nurturance. Peg had been unable to shake a flu for a long time; perhaps the dream could tell her what was wrong in her current life. Could the dream be a poetic metaphor for Peg's current relationship? It occurred to Peg that, indeed, she had been writhing in a trap and had to bring herself, sooner or later, to do the ruthless, but merciful act, of ending the relationship. She had been unconsciously drawn toward an affair because of her anger and dissatisfaction with her mate. This was something Peg had known, and yet had not known. The dream, with its strong imagery, snapped it into focus.

Even though the shadow brings unwelcome realizations—that we are not so fine as we think ourselves to be—finding it often releases lots of energy that has been languishing in the unconscious. In her next dreams, Peg danced in meadows with beautiful flowers in full bloom. Undoubtedly, the work on this dream—making her shadow more conscious—contributed to her flu clearing up soon afterward, too.

When a dream brings up your shadow, or a friend points out a fault, the natural impulse is to deny it and defend yourself, "I'm not that bad," or to shrug your shoulders, "That's just the way I am," or else take a breath and try to be better than you really are. These are mistakes. The shadow needs to be acknowledged and given its place. You must invite it to the dinner table, this dubious guest, civilize it as best you can, and see what it has to offer. You cannot leave it outside the door raising a rumpus or sneaking around and causing worry.

When Peg had another dream and found that "her shadow was showing," her first reaction was to assume she should get rid of it as soon as possible. That is what society had said all these years. It took someone else, as it often does, to catch the shadow and help her integrate it.

> *The Drowning Man.* I was in the water rescuing a drowning man. I took hold of him and started to pull him to shore, but he was very big and heavy. Then I found out what was making him so heavy: his pants pockets were loaded down with coins! I finally dragged him to shore and pulled him up onto the beach.

Peg mentioned the dream to her analyst, saying she was embarrassed about it, that she already knew that she was greedy about money and "probably shouldn't be so mercenary." The analyst, however, said yes, that's true, but the man was *drowning* and needed to be brought to shore. Peg's mercenary nature was unconscious, and that was the problem: She must bring it to consciousness! So it came to light that although Peg was indeed very concerned about security and was very careful of money in small ways, she had not really "taken hold" consciously, as in the dream she "took hold" of the drowning man. This dream said she was ready to do so. Consequently, instead of worrying about money, while at the same time neglecting it, she personally had to "take hold."

Then, in meeting her reluctance to "take hold" of her finances, Peg uncovered something in addition to her personal shadow—the cultural shadow, society's projection onto women of inadequacy in handling financial affairs, which unconsciously made her doubt her ability to do so. As a single woman, Peg had always thought vaguely that she must depend on her father to advise her about money or that a man would someday enter her life and do it for her.

Peg decided to handle her own finances, even when taking advice, so she decided to put aside some spare time and learn about money: take a year's newsletter on financial investment, interview a few advisors, select a retirement plan, etc. Peg purposely limited her studies to a year, and planned to look only at long-term investments. She knew that, with her mercenary nature, she could easily get addicted to monitoring things, and she did not want to have her happiness rise and fall every day according to financial ups and downs. Money was still partly unconscious for her, too important to her, and she could project security and the Self onto money, as so many do.

Peg kept to this schedule and learned enough about investments to take care of her future wisely, neither becoming too involved in financial matters nor reverting to her old ignorance.

Our intense and prolonged experience in the family, with all its members vying for attention and power, with its alliances, secrets, and resentments, has a profound effect on our expectations of ourselves and other people in society. These are often unconscious expectations shared by the family, and thus we can speak of a "family unconscious" and a "family shadow." Some of our strongest shadow feelings are revealed in our relations with our siblings. For example, we build up an unconscious claim to the kind of position, whether beneficial or detrimental, we occupied in our family and we expect to have a similar position in other social settings. We slip into these expectations unconsciously because they are familiar.

Dreams can reveal unconscious positions and attitudes, specifically, those typical of sibling order: the oldest, middle, youngest, the only child without siblings, or a twin.

As a case in point, the oldest child is in a position to carry strong envy. The world changes for the oldest, who is bound to feel unfairly displaced by younger siblings, who appear to get part of what seems to belong rightfully to the eldest—the whole pie. This contrasts with the experience of the younger ones, who are born into a world where others already exist—they each expect only one slice. The oldest are usually told to suppress their negative feelings because the others are younger. This is a classic situation for a shadow problem of jealousy, which a person needs to sniff out later.

> *The Aerosol Can.* **I had an aerosol can and I had to dispose of it so it wouldn't pollute the atmosphere. I couldn't put it in the ground or it'd seep up, nor in the ocean either, for the same reason.**

The dreamer, an older woman, woke up to a shadow problem she didn't know she had. Her immediate insight was that her jealous feelings, as an oldest sibling, were more poisonous when they were covered up. Then she tried to visualize the aerosol can. Printed on it were the words: "Lemon-scented." She said, "I thought my jealousy was nice and lemon-scented, but I have to admit that the cover-up is more deadly and insidious than the original stink. Real anger can have a bad smell, but it can be better tolerated than the poisonous cover-up."

The "cover-up," or denial, of envy causes it to slip out in little ways. Shadowy dark feelings that are unconscious make everybody uneasy because they are subtly in the air and no one knows where they come from although everybody feels their effect underneath.

One question to ask in regard to any dream is "why is it occurring now?" This often uncovers its relevance for current life. This dreamer had been co-leading a group with someone who talked on and on, leaving no time for her to present her own material. Until the dream, she hadn't been aware how angry and envious she felt toward him. "I just didn't know anything about jealousy. As the oldest child, I was taught that it wasn't Christian to be jealous of the others."

To recognize your envy of the "siblings" in your environment is not enough. You can't just unleash your jealousy. In some way, the oldest child—and we all—must handle the shadow by ultimately yielding to the more objective perspective that others are also entitled to a fair share of attention or attainment. Without this understanding, we bruise ourselves bumping up against the hard reality of others' counter-expectations out in the world of peers—some of whom are eldest, too!

In this case, there were two group leaders, each unconsciously expecting to be center stage in the group and therefore feeling poisonous toward each other for claiming dominance. The dreamer and her co-leader needed all their consciousness to claim their own shadows instead of resenting them in one another. Only then could they realize their mutual problem, laugh at their dilemma, and take steps toward competing more openly for center stage or sharing it.

Sometimes an archetypal event in the outer world stirs up a person's inner shadow world. Any summons to appear for examination or judgment usually evokes some fear about the forces of law and order—the Great Father archetype. In this case, a woman, Betsy, received a dreaded letter in the mail: a summons for a tax audit by the Internal Revenue Service. The next morning she had this dream about personal and archetypal shadows:

> *Manure.* I'm opening a fifty-pound bag of manure. But I'm opening it at the wrong end, and I'm afraid it'll all spill out upside down.

As Betsy began to work on the dream in her analysis, the first thought that came to her about the bag of manure was that she "wanted to get it all out and get it over with so it could fertilize the grass." What was the "manure" in her life that she needed to get out? Shadowy thoughts spilled out—all the things Betsy felt guilty about in her personal life: neglecting an elderly relative, feeling angry at her lover. . . . As Betsy continued further into her own personal audit, she sensed some dark secret and became anxious that she "would be found out." Then she remembered being molested by a relative, time and again, as a very young girl and being told never to tell anyone. Beneath that was yet a deeper secret—that she believed that she was not loved by her parents.

However, Betsy's first impulsive thought about the bag of manure—"to get it all out and get it over with so it could fertilize the grass"—doesn't work with manure any more than it does with secrets in real life. It's just an illusion, a quick fix. Too much raw manure dumped on grass doesn't fertilize it, but burns it. So, too, a torrent of anguish and anger spilling out is just the first step toward growth. Her dark secrets needed to be worked out, one by one, over time with the people in her life and in her analysis.

What about the tax audit itself? Betsy worried about all the little things that they might detect, and one thing in particular, something she foolishly had not reported. She said that the dream seemed like a warning: Don't panic and spill it all out to the IRS just to get it over with! That is, she might have an impulse to let the shadow slip out, be found out. For an IRS letter can carry archetypal force, as if it is an imperious summons from the all-powerful impersonal throne of All-knowing Judgment to confess everything to the patriarchal God, or "be found out" in an inquiry. However, Betsy could not get rid of all her life's guilt by confessing tax guilt to the IRS!

This dream served as a warning that Betsy had to sort out "what was God's and what was Caesar's." Her real personal guilt about the people in her current life had to be handled in light of her ethics and psychology; her morbid guilt and anxiety about her early childhood would have to be worked out in analysis; her current fears about her tax audit (which, due to her circumspection, actually turned out all right) as well as her future plans for reporting taxes had to be discussed with her tax accountant. Then Betsy could make a fresh start—growing green grass with seasoned fertilizer—in the different realms in her life.

* * *

Sometimes the shadow is so far from consciousness and so frightening that the door must not be opened until one is ready to face it. One may be opening the door to the whole swamp of the unconscious and can be flooded with archetypal anxiety. In a tide of enthusiasm, as in group workshops, a person can be swept up into "uncovering it all," the deeper the better, but a person's real vulnerability must be taken into account.

Deeper is not always better. After all, defenses serve a purpose. In your curiosity, if you tear off a scab you may leave a raw wound if it is too early. The natural process of healing takes time. Once you have grown a protective coating for a deep wound, then you are safe and can look.

A woman, Carolyn, had the following dream:

> **Spooks.** It's like sitting in an audience watching a movie. The scene is a beach at night. There's an evil child, blood all over, and slashed bodies.
>
> I'm sitting near an open door, a closet, and I hasten to close and lock it. But there's a young woman named *Verité* sitting near me wanting me to open the door again. We argue about it and I have to fight her physically to keep the door locked for now. Then we're reconciled and we hug.
>
> A voice says, "You're fighting to keep something secret about a woman." People come to the beach. There are dead people there, zombies, looking at us menacingly. I throw a thick liquid at them and it anesthetizes some of them; but the others, whom I can't reach with the liquid, either run or remain to menace us. I need something else for them.

Carolyn's first thought was that she herself was the "evil child." She was reminded of a dream the previous month:

> [Earlier dream] *Mother Doesn't Remember Unpleasant Things.* My mother is watching a horror movie and turns her face away, saying, "I don't remember un-

**pleasant things," but the daughter, watching her, knows that the mother *does* remember! It's as if both mother and daughter have vague memories of terrible things happening in the daughter's first years.**

This is how a child catches the projection of archetypal evil. When there is a dark secret in a family, a child feels at fault—feels like the evil child. Carolyn said, "When I start to go to sleep at night, then the spooks come out."

What is the secret? The Spook dream has some clues. The fight with Verité, Truth—to keep the door closed to an awful secret about a woman—seemed to the dreamer her unconscious need at the time to keep believing that her mother was good, so she could keep a "good mother" in her memory and feel safe. In outer reality, it was maintaining her mother's prohibition against talking about certain things, keeping the "family unconscious" intact—in this case, the capacity to mistreat a child. Verité was fighting her to make her reveal the truth, but she wasn't ready yet.

What is the liquid that pacifies? Carolyn said it was alcohol, that she drinks beer or wine to relax. But, as in the dream, it only works once in a while to dispel the images, like spooks, that have haunted her all her life. As it says in the dream, not all could be anesthetized, that is, remain in the unconscious. The truth is restless, the ghosts are restless and want to reveal themselves and be laid to rest.

Since Verité, the Truth, didn't win out in the dream, Carolyn didn't try to find out more details at this time. She was not ready. Years later, when she herself could turn her face toward the truth, Carolyn found that she had been physically abused by her mother when she was an infant and small child, and then sexually molested by her father when she was about four, and that she had probably experienced those incidents "like in a movie," in a trance state or dissociated state, as children under five often do. The "zombies" in the dream were the images Carolyn had retained of her parents at the time. Her mother had been on a tranquilizer those early years and seemed strangely absent, like a zombie, yet sometimes suddenly intense as she lashed out in unconscious anger. Her father, during the molestation, had not seemed like his usual self, but strangely detached and unreal, probably in an unconscious state of compulsion himself, perhaps a re-living of a molestation he had been subjected to as a young child.

How did the dream apply to Carolyn's life at the time of the dream? Why did the dream come up at the time it did? Carolyn wondered if her own shadow—what she was afraid to let out of "the closet" in her current life—was her lesbianism. She felt great anxiety about it. Carolyn's real life struggle with Verité, then, whether to let this truth be known, undoubtedly raised the spectre deep inside her of a more frightening archetypal shadow that had been projected onto her as a physically abused infant and sexually molested young child, and her early image of herself as an "evil child." No wonder the dreamer had a struggle with Verité in the dream! And no wonder it was terrifying to Carolyn to imagine coming out of the closet as a lesbian, for any cultural disapproval would touch her deep personal and archetypal wound.

Carolyn respected what the dream implied: She was too anxious at this time to explore the exact nature of her early wounds and heal them; she was too anxious, still, to be open about her lifestyle. First, she needed to differentiate her real fears and her archetypal fears. Carolyn said she felt some pressure from herself and others to be open, but she said, "Those who feel invulnerable don't know cruelty." So she needed to go down the road a while longer, alongside her "good mother" who couldn't yet hear unpleasant things, before she could face the cruel truth of her early years and face the various reactions to her lifestyle that she might expect in her contemporary world with its ranges of rejection and acceptance.

In all these dreams, opening the door to your own negative shadow, frightening and humbling as it may seem—knowing your own sneaky rat, lemon-scented rivalry, your family's spooks, and your own secrets—can help you soften your heart toward yourself and others, as kindred spirits in human foibles, and can also help you keep a cautious eye on the shadow in order to protect yourself and others.

## Other People's Shadow

Dreams can point out the existence of some quality in another person that we didn't notice consciously, perhaps because we didn't want to believe it was true, perhaps because we were blind to the existence of that quality within ourselves. Therefore, dreams can warn us to beware of someone else's shadow, and, at the same time, alert us to our own. As in everyday life, where it is easier to see the shadow in someone else than in ourselves, when our dreams show us someone else's shadow, we are more likely to welcome the insight than when our dreams present us with our own dark side. In some of these dreams, the dreamers saw others' shadows; in some, they also discovered their own.

ANOTHER PERSON'S SHADOW.   An administrator had finished all the interviews for a sensitive public position and had made her decision about whom to hire. Others agreed with her choice of a certain man who was very bright, bold, and generally regarded as a superstar. But she decided to sleep on such an important decision before telling him in the morning. That night she had a dream:

> *The Suspicious Minister.* **I was watching the applicant, who was walking along the sidewalk with a minister. The minister cast a suspicious look at him and turned slightly so I could see his look.**

She was puzzled because the dream cast doubt on the applicant. Then she remembered that in the interview he had skimmed over some trouble that had occurred during his work with a community group. Later, at the office, she checked with the other administrators. Yes, they thought he was the best choice by far, but come to think of it, for some reason they didn't actually want to work with him themselves! So the superstar was not chosen, and a very trustworthy man with a low profile, who had been overlooked, was chosen instead, and proved to be invaluable in the work. Later events confirmed what the unconscious had forewarned about the superstar: He proved to be a problem in another job.

A PARENT'S SHADOW. The following is another example of the unconscious revealing other people's shadows, in this case, the dreamer's parent's shadow. It shows how a family can collude in hiding the shadow of a powerful and beloved family member. At the time of the dream, it revealed one meaning to the dreamer. But within it lay hidden another meaning that was only discovered years later.

> *A Moose on the Rampage.* I'm out walking with my mother across a field. Suddenly we see a moose on the rampage. It has kicked someone, who's now on the ground moaning. My mother and I have to do something!
>
> I say, "I'll go get an ambulance." My mother says, "I'll get the guy who's hurt." I think that I'd be scared to go get him because the moose is still there. But there she goes again, my mother, with her Pollyanna attitude: She can get him because she's immune. I pretend not to be scared, too, but I tell her, "You have to get someone's gun. Don't go in there and get your own lungs broken!"

By concentrating on the image of the moose, the dreamer—Tanya—smoked out the shadow hidden there. She said, "It's a male on the rampage, massive, huge, wounded, and very dangerous. Moose are crotchety animals and shouldn't be provoked. He's an older male." Then the intuitive thought came to her, "It's my father; that's his shadow: crotchety and fearsome."

The counterpart to the moose—the wounded man—is the father's own woundedness and his potential to pass this on by wounding others. Tanya's father, like many men, hid his woundedness with anger. The father's woundedness is his deeper shadow which the mother knew about; therefore, his rampages didn't scare her as much as they did Tanya, who saw only the denial on her mother's part. Yet Tanya also knew a truth—that rampages are alarming and possibly dangerous to be around.

What can a daughter do with this kind of knowledge? How can she and her family handle a father's shadow? Tanya said, "Just as in the dream, ordinarily my mother is immune to my father's bad moods. She's blithe; she thinks everything will be all right. She's the Great Absorber. I pretend to be blithe, too, but it's different for me." She tried to gain perspective on their difference by considering their respective generations' attitudes: how her mother grew up in another era when women were supposed to accept everything and take care of everybody else, blind to aggression and their own needs and woundedness; how in the 1970s, women became disillusioned, and then, in the 1980s, started protecting themselves, doing things for themselves, not just thinking of others and pretending that all is well.

When a mother denies shadowy things in a family—in this case, the father's aggression as well as the mother's own fears and self-interest—then a daughter may pretend as well but also compensate for the denial by becoming fearful. Within a daughter, both sides exist: the "mother side" denying threats, upholding the mother's view, supporting her in not exposing the father; and the "daughter side," afraid, ashamed of her preoccupation with the threats but tempted to stop pretending and acknowledge the truth.

In Tanya's dream, these two sides took form as a mother and daughter confronting a situation, "having it out" in the unconscious. The daughter figure stands up to the mother figure and apparently prevails in her worries and warnings about taking a gun to protect them from realistic danger. Yet, at the same time, the daughter figure in the dream appropriately adopts the legacy of her mother's armor: "I pretend not to be scared, too." In this case, pretending is conscious and adaptive. Some denial is a necessary defense when one must take action in a dangerous situation.

At the time, what Tanya concluded from this dream was that she must be alert to her own unconscious tendencies both to exaggerate or minimize dangers.

Years later in therapy, a much deeper archetypal shadow hidden in the moose dream emerged: the negative side of the Great Father archetype—the end of order and protection in the universe for her. She remembered when she had been violently assaulted on the street as a child and barely had been able to fight off the attempted rape. Tanya had been very frightened by the violence of the attack and her sense of safety in the world had been shaken, but her biggest problem was her family's denial of its impact on her. She remained in the position of confusion between vague feelings of being betrayed (by being left alone with all her fears) and vague feelings of guilt about being so fearful.

This confusion had kept Tanya unduly fearful of the world. She unconsciously perceived her father's aggressive shadow as a "moose on a rampage," a very violent image, when his shadow was far less assaultive than that. Finally, reliving the childhood assault in active imagination and acknowledging these old fears in analysis, Tanya gained some release from this substratum of anxiety in her unconscious. She was better equipped, then, inwardly to sort out what was dangerous in the world and what was not, and to act accordingly. She also took a course in self-defense to defend herself better outwardly.

FAMILY AND CULTURAL SHADOW.  When we confront the needs of those less fortunate, whether we respond with compassion, denial, futility, or callousness, we inevitably meet the shadow. This makes us uncomfortable underneath. We rush by homeless people, or give a hasty gift with a twinge of guilt at how little it is. We are tempted to defend ourselves against uneasy feelings by attributing—rightly or wrongly—handy personal or cultural shadow qualities to others: They're too demanding or belong to a group that, for some general reason, is not as "deserving" as others. Conversely, when we are in the position of asking for something, we have another set of strong shadow projections onto potential benefactors and are afraid of their appraisal of us. This fact—that unequal situations provoke shadow projections onto each other—is one reason why self-help groups can be much more satisfying psychologically than interaction with authority figures. There is a commonality of experience which leads to more empathy and correct perceptions.

Similarly, the intense shadow projections in a family can be brought to light by a willingness among its members to discover the commonality of personal shadows. Since members of a family often share the same hurts, we have the potential to empathize deeply with each other. In addition, knowing our unconscious family style, or cultural heritage, can be a help in learning what qualities our family tradition has left out—the family or cultural shadow. In our deepest projections onto each other, we may also touch upon the archetypal shadow.

One of the times in our life when we are likely to meet the above situations all at once is in middle age, when we may be called upon to care for elderly parents, or in infirmity or old age when we ourselves are being cared for. This situation can bring each of us in contact with our own shadowy feelings of vulnerability at all levels.

A woman, called Kathy here, had this dream the night she talked on the telephone with her mother, who had asked for money. Kathy had felt torn between responding to the "desperate" sound in her mother's voice and sending her money, and not responding because she knew her mother didn't need it that much. She sensed, instinctively, that by agreeing she might, somehow, be promising much more than money, which made her feel apprehensive.

> **The Two Bums.** There is snow outside. Two big men—bums—and I walk through the streets of Boston. We see an old round-shaped mansion and want to go in. We inquire of the couple next door. I tell them that the bums are from Harvard, so they give the bums a key to the mansion. . . .
>
> Then I feel guilty about the deception and I'm afraid the bums could burn the place down if they started a fire inside and tried to live there. So I confess to the couple next door that I just made that up about Harvard, and tell them that they'd better be careful and get the keys back from the bums when they return, and they do. . . .
>
> [The scene shifts.] As she leaves, a woman hands me a small book, a German primer, as a gift.

At first, Kathy thought the dream was about her mother's personal shadow—deceptive, helpless, demanding—and, possibly, her mother's archetypal rage (start a fire) if Kathy promised her complete security (a round-shaped mansion), but didn't follow through. There probably was some truth in this. Kathy thought her dream showed how bad she really felt, and how much she unconsciously reverberated to her mother's tone of "desperation" in the telephone call. She thought the dream exaggerated her reaction so she could see her mother's shadow as well as see her own shadowy guilt about not being more generous with her mother.

Then it became apparent to Kathy that the dream was about her own personal shadow—her own bums, her unconscious scrambling to have others take care of her emotional needs, give her the key to security and happiness, with the inevitable resentment (burn the place down) which that entails. She had trouble being empathic—or firm—with her mother's "bums" because she didn't know how to handle her own "bums"! If you can't say yes or no to your own neediness you don't know how to say yes and no to another person's neediness.

Cultural and archetypal perspectives can also help clarify how a mother and daughter share a common cultural shadow or archetypal expectations. The fact of the matter was that—in this family's particular German-American tradition of emotional restraint and independence—Kathy's mother had not been warmly generous when Kathy needed it; now Kathy didn't feel warmly generous back. Her mother was reaping what she had sown. Nor could Kathy give her mother the "old round-shaped mansion," the archetypal sense of deep security, the early feminine Self, missing in her mother's early life as well as in her old age. The reality of the negative side of the archetypal Great Mother is symbolized by the setting of the dream—the "snow outside." A daughter just cannot provide the positive or negative Great Mother. Yet, within limits, she can give her elderly mother some personal mothering and care. Kathy realized that her mother could use *some* money and she could provide it. Her mother also needed this tangible sign of support, and the daughter could give it if she herself knew her own limits.

Often a small detail in a dream is crucial, especially if it is a distinctive detail—a signal that the unconscious wants to say something very specific. A clue to Kathy's understanding of this dream and its subjective impact on her was "the small book, the German primer." The primer, an elementary text, meant to her the simple fundamentals of the family's particular German-American community. The duty and obligations were clear. Even though relationships may be reserved and "cool" emotionally, a daughter nevertheless gives some concrete help to elderly parents, who will aggressively ask for things sometimes, but will be generally self-reliant and emotionally independent, just as a daughter is expected to be. Beneath this individualism and matter-of-fact manner lay another fundamental truth: the deep sense of solidarity and attachment in the family. This was manifest only at times of dire need or in the generous spirit of certain family activities, such as the *gemütlichkeit* of family celebrations. It was generally hidden, and unconscious, but nevertheless very real.

This is an instance of bringing the "cultural unconscious," the unspoken customs and underlying truths of a family culture, into consciousness. The cultural unconscious contains much wisdom and much foolishness; it needs an individual's conscious mind—reading the small book—to find its wisdom. This opened the way for her to feel comfortable about giving her mother some money, and she did so.

More important, the dream also revealed what the cultural heritage had left out: the cultural shadow—the bums—the disparaged ones who must beg for comfort. It was not just her mother's personal "desperation," but her own, too. It was their common cultural tradition: not to ask for help, or if asked, to appear more cool than generous in response.

This realization brought a change of heart in her. She felt more released to follow her own maternal impulses. These led her beyond the unconscious confines of her stark patriarchal background. She found it within herself to give her mother some emotional support—out of fellow feeling for the shadowy bums, the homeless ones who wanted to live in a mansion and needed to "start a fire" to keep warm.

## Dreams Revealing the Positive Shadow

Women find it hard to claim—much less proclaim—positive qualities or achievements. To be proud of ourselves is culturally unacceptable, as it is for many oppressed people. And even when we get together as women and yearn for positive models among us, we often relate to each other through empathy, weakness, and fellow-suffering. We are still shy about our positive sides, afraid to break the taboo and show our strengths, our hopes, our accomplishments.

Mothers feel a mandate to teach their daughters how to be "successful" in society, and often, alas, do so within the same narrow confines the mothers have known and with the same limited images of womanhood: to be pleasing, to be thin, *never* to be selfish, and to be fulfilled through others or through illusion. So that a mother, with the best intention of trying to shape her daughter to be acceptable, may actually make her daughter feel criticized, devalued, or, worse still, a failure.

Positive shadow figures within dreams can alert us to our own innate possibilities, unacknowledged by our personal mothers or our culture. The positive personal shadow is most obvious when we dream about people we admire. For instance, a very introverted woman dreamed of a friend "who has an essential sweetness." She said, "I don't like the usual 'sweetness,' but hers is the real thing." This is the reserved woman's own positive shadow, her own genuine generosity, ready to emerge now that she is in her sixties and more confident of herself, free to embrace her own extraverted side. The positive cultural shadow may appear in dreams in such guises as a *group of helpful women,* or a *special woman*—representing likeable qualities from an ethnic or racial heritage or other background that is seen as positive or fortunate.

Since many women have not had good personal and cultural models, their unconscious is drawn to positive archetypal images, such as goddess figures, to compensate for what is missing in real life. On rare occasion, we glimpse the positive archetypal shadow in our dreams. The forms this might take are images of unity, paradise, Shangri-la, an ideal religious group or utopian community, a great leader, a goddess of strength, calmness, or love. The archetypal feelings are those of well-being, optimism, idealism, cosmic harmony, hopefulness, illumination, or inspiration. These contrast with the negative forms—chaos, Hell, nuclear devastation, the Devil, despair.

Dreams of the positive shadow come to women who need a glimpse of light in the darkness of their lives. The dreamers represented here needed a strong jolt of something positive to awaken them to possibilities and hope. Perhaps that is the reason why some of these dreams in this last section have intense, archetypal images which could truly touch the dreamers' pain or longings and help move them forward.

## Flying High with Inspiration

A woman making a momentous decision to embark upon a new career dreamed of the positive shadow in archetypal images.

> *The Horse and the Elevator.* I'm riding a horse and we go right into a building and straight into the elevator. A guard says, *"You can't do that!* You can't take a horse up an elevator." I call, *"Oh yes I can!"*
>
> The elevator goes up and up and up until we reach the top. I'm still on horseback. We come out onto some fields with a golden glow, like the high meadows in France that are infused with a special golden light—the kind the Impressionists painted.

What is this strangely fascinating image of a horse ascending in an elevator? Those of us who have been astride a horse as a girl or woman know that surge of energy, the thrill of energy beyond our own, and the fine art of relating to it—letting it loose or holding it in with a gentle, firm rein. We know our unconscious animal energy.

Rising up in an elevator carries this dynamic image one step further. This horse in the elevator suggests Pegasus, the winged horse, archetypal symbol of flying beyond our usual human energy, buoyed aloft by the unconscious. Pegasus is inspiration, imagination, hope. He appears when a woman is lost in the grayness of everyday life, casting her Self into shadow, and she is in need of some inflation, some buoyancy of spirit. She may be too aware of her own limitations, or she may need to burst beyond the confines of society's ideas of her limitations and not let them stand in her way. She needs to mount her winged horse, her soaring hopes rising from deep within. Then she must summon "all the king's horses," that is, gather her utmost strength from the center of her unconscious for her journey.

The horse represents to us useful strength—fiery, enduring, and free, yet bridled and sensitive to the touch of our will as if we were one. This returns us to our earliest experience of riding on our mother's hip when we were "one," and the primordial knowledge of oneness in nature. For the predecessors of Pegasus were the Mare-headed Goddess and the Muse Goddess whose moon-shaped hoof could strike springs of water from the earth.[1] It is no wonder that Jean Auel's book *The Valley of Horses*[2] has caught our modern imagination with its image of a strong, prehistoric woman taming and riding a horse, discovering the thrill of that elevation of emotions, the fiery, light spirit we know through the horse, and for which the horse has been sacred from prehistoric times.

This modern dream of Pegasus helped a woman say, *"Oh yes I can,"* from deep within herself at a crucial time in her life. Now an elder stateswoman in her chosen field, she said, "So I did change, and it was good! Everyone at the time thought I was crazy to leave a good job . . . but after this dream I knew I had the reins in my own hands. I could do it."

In fact, it was something she must do, must attempt, despite the doubts and prohibitions symbolized in her dream by the guard. She must follow her tremendous inner energy—on horseback—upward to the promise, the soul-choice, the golden glow in her dream. It was a hazardous undertaking. Others thought it foolhardy because of the serious physical problems she had always had, but it would have been more deadening to have remained in her gray world. Just as the negative shadow can sap one's life energy, so, too, can the positive shadow if it is not given its due. It is as if something in us cries out to be who we are, what we can be, and that Something itself gives us strength—or is our demon if denied.

## A Long and Painful Search for the Positive Shadow

The following series of dreams depict one woman's long search for her positive shadow. Kate grew up in a world of such darkness—deprivation, alcoholism, violence, and desertion—that she hardly dared hope for light. At the time of the first dream, she was approaching her forties. She was very much afraid of the aging process and growing old. The first dream shows her inwardly leaving her mother's dark realm (alcoholism and grasping at youthfulness) for the lighter realm of her grandmother and the Wise Old Woman, albeit a negative version of her.

> *The Old Lady with the Broom.* I drive my car up the hill; it's a strain to make it. Then I walk up to my old apartment building. My place is only an empty room now because I've moved out. I'm overdue to be gone, just picking up a few things.
>
> An old lady is sweeping the sidewalk. She lifts the broom and swats at me disapprovingly because I'm still there. She says, "It's *you* again!" She's cackling and confident, a wacky old bird. I feign indignation: "I'm still here. I've a right to get my newspaper and mail." The old lady's not impressed.
>
> Somehow I'm not supposed to get rid of her yet either. I want to befriend her. There are three doors to the apartment building. I ask her, "Which one is yours?"
>
> But then we see a redhead. It's the landlady who lives on the ground floor. [It's the landlady I once had. She drank. A real fascist in a bathrobe ringing our doorbells, out-of-control, with angry energy . . . like my mother.] The old lady with the broom doesn't want the redheaded landlady to see us talking.

What the dream shows is a woman struggling uphill to finally move out of the empty room—the daughter position under the rule of her mother and her own inner landlady, both of whom are dramatic, irrational, angry, and powerful. And it shows her drawn to a new and archetypal figure, a somewhat negative version of the Wise Old Woman—an old woman who sweeps things clean, who has a witchy cackle of confidence, who knows about dark things, and with whom she has a bantering camaraderie.

In the dream, she wants to know which door is the old lady's. How can she find access to the one who sweeps things clean, her own Wise Old Woman? This relationship has been clandestine, but she is starting to shift loyalties within her to this new authority, one usually forbidden to her.

How are children taught to avoid positive people or deny positive qualities in themselves? One common way is for parents to make children feel guilty or rejected for liking someone who is positive. When such children have been deprived so that they don't expect much anyway, they can be left with an indelible impression that they are not *entitled* to someone positive. This is apparently what happened to Kate. As a girl, when she had preferred her grandmother, an energetic woman who treated her a little better than her mother did, she was accused of betrayal. So the grandmother and her positive qualities—being supportive and being a "go-getter"—became forbidden and shadowy, and those qualities became suppressed in Kate's girlhood.

Kate's intuition told her that the dream was about her aging. "I've left my youth, but I don't want to give it up and take the old one's place!" Like her mother she was very concerned about growing old, losing her attractiveness and her security. In contrast, Kate said, "My grandmother was a go-getter and she believed in me. But later she became very old and disappointed in life."

It is as if Kate thinks she has only two choices in life: either being like her mother, an alcoholic clinging to her looks, or being like her grandmother, once active but then depressed at the end. Deep in the unconscious, Kate seems to have the choice of either remaining the helpless girl, the archetypal puella in her forlorn

Cinderella-in-the-ashes aspect, subject to irrational attack from her inner negative mother, or else of aligning herself with the archetypal witch, her inner independence gained from her grandmother, but forbidden and thus in the darker layers of the unconscious. Of course, her task eventually is to encounter the archetypes of both the puella and the witch to discover what positive value each can offer her.

Yet it is always important for a woman to find, if possible, something of value passed down to her from her own mother. Kate's mother had been so critical of her that Kate, in return, felt only critical of her mother and the qualities they shared—a reckless, free spirit that could be brutal, and a depressed, suicidal side that drank. The first stirrings of the positive shadow can come from confronting the reality and the depths of the negative mother complex and salvaging some positive side from those negative qualities: from recklessness, perhaps the capacity to take risks; from free spirit, play and individuality; from depression, perhaps sadness, the gateway to feminine softness. At this point Kate said that she still didn't know if she could settle down and commit herself to a relationship or to work, but she wished she could feel "feminine" and "soft" toward her partner.

The next dream shows that in order to emerge from this kind of puella—passive, resentful, and under the dominance of the negative mother—a woman needs first to go to the father world. The puella often needs to confront the masculine "other" and gain such qualities as separateness or active assertion to handle the intensity of the mother realm. However, in Kate's next dream this Cinderella did not find a Prince to rescue her and take her away to happiness. Instead, she found an image of the harsh patriarchal culture that still kept her captive. The dream prompted her to do active fantasy work, where she found the quality of separateness within herself to break free from the oppression of her past.

This horrifying dream came the night after The Old Lady with the Broom. In the dream, Kate *witnessed* what happened, that is, she acknowledged her own past that was still part of her. For indeed, she stirred the old murky waters when she dared reach for the light. In fact, for some people the old darkness is so painful that they cannot bear to see it again, and they wisely decide to let things remain as they are.

> *The Footbinding.* I'm watching. The master of a well-to-do house puts a girl—alive—into his freezer. It's just temporary, as a punishment, as he's old-fashioned.
>
> There's a lamp over the freezer. What if the lamp falls? It does fall, and there's a fire, a conflagration. Does anyone know? She'll die!
>
> The man opens the freezer as though it's a treasure chest. Where's the girl? Under the food. One large foot is wrapped up. He readjusts it as if it's a treasure. Is there an inspector around and he's trying to hide the foot?
>
> I'm in a hospital and I see a young man with his feet smashed. They're a foot shorter than they would have been if they hadn't been deformed. He sits up in bed and the sheet is whipped off. His feet have been deformed badly like Japanese [sic] footbinding, not the toes bound but the foot bent over and pressed flat at the side. He picks up his leg and puts it over his ear to show how he'd been forced into that position in order to be put in the freezer.

Kate said that the deformed feet referred to her puella, who isn't living up to her potential, a condition that society—the father world—had brutally forced upon women. She felt compelled to change this. (It is puzzling that, in the dream, the girl becomes a man with bound feet, but this probably serves to highlight how much her own strong masculine side has also been bound up.)

This dream has many other images of importance to women in general, such as that of the giant Procrustes.

THE PROCRUSTEAN SOLUTION. Women need to be especially aware of the "Procrustean solution" to problems. In mythology the giant Procrustes cut off his captives' legs if they were too long to fit their beds or stretched them if they were too short. To lie in a "Procrustean bed," then, means to conform to arbitrary standards that are enforced with harsh disregard for natural growth and individual differences.

For the modern woman, the giant Procrustes represents senseless cultural attitudes that loom large and force women into painful and absurd equivalents of the dream's "footbinding" and "the leg put over the ear." Modern examples of such extreme practices include obtaining a face lift for a woman who is "too old," stooping over if she is "too tall," wearing uncomfortably high heels, and doing all the other myriad things women feel forced to do to fit a mold instead of accepting—and feeling accepted for—their uniqueness and their natural physical development through the years.

The "master of the well-to-do house" in the dream refers to those with patriarchal power—a father or others—who promise power and rewards, but actually oppress a woman, put her in the freezer, and keep her cut off from her warm feminine feelings. This hope for reward can keep a woman an eternal girl, a daughter who can't depend on her own good feet, her own groundedness in reality. She remains her father's girl who can't go out into the world and seek her fortune as a grown woman or bear the realities of aging and death.

The image of a treasure or a treasure chest is crucial in dreams. It usually refers to what is truly valuable, the Self, which must be kept safe. In stories and myths, the task of the hero or heroine is to find the lost treasure or rescue the jewel from the giant or fierce monster and bring it home. Here, however, the dream exposes the terrible truth that a woman can be captive in another's treasure chest—a freezer. Somehow, Kate had been conditioned to find her fulfillment by becoming the image of what her mother groomed her for, and what her father and others value—an image so tempting for a beautiful woman to try to fulfill, and so tragic, as in the case of Marilyn Monroe. Ultimately, for her (as will be seen in her work on the dream), the real treasure is the Self—the truth of her own self-worth as an individual, her intrinsic lovability, which she can find by wresting her own fire from the father world.

ICE AND FIRE.   The dream images of ice-and-fire (the freezer and the fire) help us understand people we know who are extreme in this way: icy and remote or fiercely angry and passionate. We are sometimes drawn to such people, especially actors or artists, because we hope to spark those extremes of feeling in ourselves and glimpse the dark drama and spiritedness of human life, while remaining as safe as possible ourselves within a more familiar world of moderation and the avoidance of the negative extremes. Because people generally value ease, safety, and the positive aspects of life, it is difficult at first to understand people whose lives are dominated by ice and fire. Such people find it easier to accept the negative than the positive, strange as that may seem. They may readily receive a criticism but rebuff a compliment. The reason is that criticism is familiar; they are numb to criticism. It merely joins the rest of the negativity that has been relegated to cold storage so that they can survive without flinching all the time, whereas something positive is disturbingly unfamiliar, and found in the shadow. The positive shadow can therefore open up a great hurt, a great anger, a great hope, hence the deep fear of it.

The dream suggests that the truth for Kate will emerge from the collision of ice and fire, with fire predominating over ice —the conflagration of anger, hurt, and knowledge as she recognizes her oppression and begins to melt her inner coldness in her passionate search for something more in her life. As anyone knows who has come in from the cold and thawed out numb hands, warming must be done slowly. For a woman who has been "out in the cold" for too long, it will take patience and endurance to bear the slow pain of coming to life again. This she needs to know, and so do others around her who would rush to rescue her. If a therapist or friend is too warm, she will recoil, as if burnt. In people with bleak backgrounds like this, the Self is hidden but close to the deepest hurts, in a precarious position like the lamp in the dream. They can be overwhelmed by the conflagration of anger and blinding insight. "Leave me alone!" may then be an absolutely right response for them.

Instead of the Self, we find still in the dream, as yet, the puella—the young girl—now angry at the benefactor/oppressor for keeping her helpless. And furious at the fall into helplessness. The falling of the lamp implies a fall from an equilibrium or false

Self centered not in herself but in her identification with masculine power, passion, and a masculine viewpoint. So the fall can be a release into her own life. For a puella, a harsh fall is inevitable. It can shake her loose from being a victim in someone else's realm, and can give her the impetus to pick herself off the floor, stand on her own feet, and start to move independently, or else regress into helplessness again.

Kate was shaken up enough by the dream and angry enough that she could do the fantasy work of concentrating on the frightening feelings in the dream. In her active imagination, the word "father" came to her spontaneously and she found herself putting a fence around him, with herself outside. What she had found within herself was the traditional masculine way to handle intense feeling—to draw lines and keep a safe distance. This is what she greatly needed in her repertoire, not just intense feeling. In fact, intense feeling requires at least some of its complementary opposite, objectivity, in order to work in a beneficial way. Thus Kate began the step-by-step movement to find her own Self, find a way to use her fire as fuel for her own development.

Kate had another dream the week afterward.

> **Amends.** A woman I know asks, with tears in her eyes, **"When will you make amends to me?"** I said, **"Amends are the fourth step. I haven't begun the first."** I was angry at her and thought, **"You're the last I'd make amends to!"** but I didn't say it.

The woman "with tears in her eyes" is a woman Kate knows in real life who strikes her as a good father figure, someone with a paternal quality to her. Kate said the woman is an articulate feminist who uses her intellect. However, the dream tells us that Kate is not at all ready to accept this positive figure, her own potential, emerging Wise Old Woman who can be moved to tears. Kate needs this strength to confront the realities of past behavior, to acknowledge vulnerability, and to gain control over daily life.

However, Kate is still rejecting any parental figure in the same, old, angry way that served her well as protection from her parents earlier in life. In fact, up to this time in her therapy, in disbelief, or perhaps alarm, she had often angrily rebuffed any analytic interpretation, other attempts to understand her and her dreams, as well as overtures of encouragement, empathy, or hope. This dream says that she has to go through many steps first before she can be reconciled with her analyst, and her own inner guide.

Evidently this dream did mark a small opening of the door to her more positive side, for, during the week following the dream, Kate said she felt good, and she made her first warm gesture toward her analyst. Months later she felt a wave of love for her partner, whose warmth she had not been able to reciprocate or value as much as she had wished. And she decided to forge ahead in her training for a particular profession.

For Kate, then, these were the intermediate steps—to know the witch and the landlady, to protest that her feet have been bound, to want to move ahead but not to lose her old power, to soften her anger—in her inner shift toward the positive shadow.

Some time later, on the night Kate graduated from a professional training course, she dreamed about potentially positive images of women, tainted again with her old fear of the positive shadow. She was aware of how "evil" her mother seemed to her, and at this time of hope and transition into a new role, the dream made her worry whether she herself had a positive enough side to use her training to heal, or did she have such a terrible shadow that she could do possible harm?

For as soon as the dream, described below, brought her a Wise Old Woman figure in a culturally religious form, she feared for her individual way. And in the dream, as soon as she claimed her own wisdom, it evoked her fear of a frightening archetypal image of a collective, religious initiation that could destroy her identity. Among other things, this could be her own personal awe of positive commitment.

The dream has a wider significance serving as a warning about entering a "healing art" or a profession serving the public. If you don't have enough personal grounding, or your new profession doesn't have enough tradition or ethics, you may face various dangers: losing your individual standpoint, becoming subjugated to group power as a pawn, or becoming inflated by group membership to misuse your own power.

*Have You Always Been This Wise?* A friend of mine and I are in the house with her mother, who is a religious person. The mother asks us, "Do you pray?" My friend answers, "Yes," but I'm unwilling to say that, so I keep my integrity and pacify her by answering, "Not in your way." She says, "Jesus can take away your sins."

I'm at a dinner party in a study hall, where we are paired off in desks side by side. The woman beside me asks, "Have you always been this wise?" It's flattery, but I take it in! I feel in the mood to tell how good I am.

Out of the corner of my eye I see a procession of the mother and the others all dressed in white chiffon, all with feminine, seductive grace. There's a tall figure on stilts in a black cape, with a round head like a moon with translucent light. There's a young, helpless girl with three women dancing around her in a ritual.

I know this is a set-up to get me, a religious initiation for me! The mother comes up to me, "We can cleanse you of your sins." She reaches out and I fall over backwards, then run back and forth, acting crazy, laughing maniacally to scare them all away. They chuckle, "Oh yes, people are hysterical before they're cleansed. We've seen sinners this way before."

I race out the front door. The daughter runs after me. She calls, "My mother will help you." I turn and say, "Get away from me." I left my purse, identification, and money back there; maybe the woman beside me when I was eating and studying will bring them to me.

Kate believed that the dream was about her fear of getting older, of "just being who you are instead of your *fantasy* of what you could be." She had always relied upon her captivatingly sexy good looks in life, but her completed training was a chance to shift from her life as a puella, a "helpless girl," to a "wise woman" for her future years. And the dream came, as a dream often does, at a time of transition—her graduation from training—to do the necessary work of initiating her into a new life.

The dream portrays the inner process of a woman struggling with a strong, negative mother complex. Just as she is about to graduate—to grasp the golden ring in her life and accept recognition and claim her wisdom—she has sudden qualms about not deserving it, and sees a compliment only as "flattery," rather than confirmation of her feminine Self. Furthermore, if she dares to accept her status, she might fear inflation and vulnerability as the center of attention for a circle of women. Could she fall under the spell of feminine power, be converted to do evil, or be robbed of her identity? She wondered if she had any integrity, whether she could possibly have a good future herself.

This was a pivotal dream for Kate in recognizing her fear of the positive shadow. In her next analytic session she had a fantasy: She and her grandmother walked out of the house, leaving her mother and all her negativity. Her grandmother then hugged and comforted her, despite her grandmother's own disappointment in life.

Then at last came positive dreams: a dream in which Kate felt new compassion for her brother, a dream where she felt great joy to see her grandmother still alive, and a dream in which her mother finally protected her. In real life, for the first time in almost forty years Kate found herself spontaneously confronting her mother about her mother's drinking, and that led to a genuine conversation and better feelings between them.

These four dreams, then, show how the positive shadow can emerge to deal with the negative mother and negative father forces. From her personal memories of the past, Kate retrieved some positive aspects of her father, her mother, and her grandmother, claimed them as her own, and affirmed her own separateness. Kate wasn't ready yet to accept her own wisdom, and could not trust being initiated by a group of older women. But she did expect the woman at her side, an inner figure close to consciousness, to help her.

It is indeed a difficult, painful journey for many women to claim their positive qualities in our society, and it is a great disappointment when some stumble and fall along the way. For Kate, who had always walked along the shore of a stormy ocean, the undertow—her fear of the positive shadow—was too strong a pull backward; a few months after this series of dreams she quit analysis. Perhaps she had to remain alone awhile in her old familiar world of the negative and absorb what had happened, rather than venture any further on a new path. Maybe she needed more acknowledgment of her true dark nature, her desire for power, and her concern about "evil." Kate may have needed more of the bantering witch in her analyst and less of the Jungian optimism that reminded her of religious zeal. Perhaps after all it was "not her way" and she continued along an old path. However, Kate did have a fundamental commitment to growth and it is likely that the unconscious will eventually help her find her way. We can slide into old patterns until the next time that life shakes us up and then we must try again to mobilize our innermost strength to resume the journey. Perhaps Kate will find another path with the good inner woman at her side who recognized her wisdom, who first asked her, "Have you always been this wise?"

# 5

# Relationship:
# The Discerning Heart

All the relationships that encircle women are important to them—relationships with family, children, close friends, therapist, teachers, and, in the center of the circle, at times in our life, the intimate one, our mate. The heroic journey for women is taking the risk to love, day after day.

A woman's journey is a moonlit way, a hazardous, rock-strewn path that winds along the ocean. We let ourselves be drawn into the vortex of dark and turbulent waters, committing ourselves to know our deepest emotions and instincts—passionate or delicate, angry or joyful, nurturing or selfish. Leading a life of involvement with another has terrible challenges and no sure reward except the involvement itself, our daring to be ourselves as women and living life wholeheartedly.

The discerning heart learns to trust its true feelings, whatever they are; knows itself and its individuality; has the sense and the sensitivity to know another's receptivity—when, and to whom, to show its feelings. It also respects the other's individuality, the boundaries, the spaces between two people. A discriminating heart also understands the sacrifices in relationship: It waits out the fallow times or the times when one person draws ahead and the other falls behind; and it accepts and makes known when it is worthless to continue.

Along the heart's journey, we learn to use compassion well. First we have to experience empathy—the basic instinct of "feeling with" other people. This can lead to compassion—accepting others' deepest feelings, reaching out, and helping. However, our instinct to help others must be balanced by awareness: When should we reach out, and when should we keep our own counsel? We need to learn that too much closeness can be exhausting and lead to anger. We must learn that sometimes we can't meet other people's needs: Sometimes they don't want it; sometimes they don't need protection from those hardships they can handle themselves; and sometimes they need to feel their own strength and independence. Some people simply need quiet time alone to clarify their own thoughts and feelings, to follow the deeper course of their own natures, and to go alone into the darker layers of their psyches. Then we must exercise not the quick compassion that reaches out, but a quiet compassion that stands close by.

Relationship includes both *closeness*—empathy, warmth, dependency, a sense of union, sexuality,[1] and oneness—and *separateness*—individuality, differentness, and a sense of separate selves. To commit ourselves to relationship, we take the risk to care about another and to let ourselves depend on someone in return. Being "dependent"—depending emotionally on someone—is not a bad thing in itself, patriarchal values to the contrary. It is just a great risk, compounded by the fact that men have usually been socialized to be independent, often fear dependency, and sometimes resent the one they love because they depend on her for love. Some women who have been badly burned in relationships, or who have been taught to disparage dependency in themselves, also fear and resent being dependent.

Sometimes being in a relationship means facing the fact that the relationship is "not enough" and challenging those things that diminish relationship itself, such as addictions—alcohol, television, work—when those addictions take center stage and push the relationship too far into the wings. And, at the other extreme, separateness is, ultimately, preservation of ourselves and other people. Just as we need more differentiated compassion, so we need more differentiated distance in our relatedness (the silences, the absences, the gulfs, the clashes, the ever-differentness and unknownness of the other) for full "wisdom of the heart."

## Expectations, Choices, and Pitfalls

Women in our culture traditionally have, until recently, placed most of their sense of personal worth in affiliation, not achievement, that is, in husband and family and not in work outside the home. Today, though, many women choose both intimate relationship and achievement, a choice which brings its own problems. Whatever their relative emphasis in life, though, relationships are risky for contemporary women.

A woman's great capacity for relationship can be a pitfall. Relationship is usually very important to a woman because of her close identity with her mother, and the sense of continuity—or discontinuity—with her mother that follows her throughout life. If she had a close relationship with her "mother" (be she mother, sister, grandmother, nursemaid, or a nurturing father), she may expect her mate to be someone who is always there, in an attempt to re-create the old intimacy she knew, causing inevitable disappointment with an adult partner who is not. If her "mother" was negative, however, the same tone of voice in her partner can throw her back into early murky feelings of confusion and low self esteem, and she may be more likely to welcome a partner who doesn't repeat the closeness of the usual mother-daughter pattern, or to appreciate a partner who has the ability to move gently toward her vulnerable inner longings.

This unconscious expectation that her mate will be similar to her earliest close relationship—that her partner will be wonderful or terrible—places a special burden on adult relationship. Women in our culture generally tend to be more willing to sacrifice for the relationship than men. A major task for many women becomes how to enlist men's involvement for more intimacy on their part, and how to have less self-sacrifice on our part so that we don't wear out our goodwill. Sometimes this means recovering our inmost feminine wholeness and self-sufficiency: to be center stage in our own life, to have a sense of separateness, to have independent pursuits.

In contrast, in close relationships between women, whether in friendship or love, both are likely to be highly involved in the relationship and prone to self-sacrificing, so there is more equality and mutuality, but the problem then becomes too tight a twosome—whether cozy or entangling. With our softer boundaries, we can lose our separate sense of ourselves and become isolated from other people outside the relationship and forgo independent pursuits.

What, then, can a woman do to protect her integrity in a relationship but also maintain true intimacy? She must try to carry forward into her life what she knows in her bones: that intimacy is consonant with her deepest nature, that it is possible, and can be worth the tremendous effort it takes. And she must be aware of the tasks of each stage of relationship. In the passionate beginnings, a woman explores the roots and limits of passion. As the relationship develops, she learns pacing while suffering inevitable disappointments and reconciliations; she makes difficult choices to continue or to end it. A relationship requires time and hard work, as she sorts out her true nature from the images and roles projected onto her as well as her projections onto others. In these tasks, dreams can be a help to her.

The subject of relationship also includes aloneness. Some women feel alone within relationships; others live all or parts of their lives alone by choice or by circumstance; and almost all women are destined to be alone as older widows. What follows in these pages, then—about suffering, basic centeredness in oneself, and relating to inner figures—pertains to these "alone" times, too. How can women live their lives fully and if necessary overcome the cultural stigma they often experience from being without a partner? Women *can* live full lives alone. Many do so, some living without physical intimacy, some maintaining close and enduring relationships with others with whom they don't necessarily live. While this chapter centers around the intimate other, most women also have vital friendships and continuing family bonds throughout life, and much of what follows applies to these friendships and bonds as well.

## Love and Its Beginnings

### Eros

Eros is the spirit of love. In its broadest sense, "Eros" refers to the sense of relatedness, warmth, fellow-feeling, and intimacy that we can feel continuously throughout our life. The feelings of love come from the very beginning—our earliest impulses to touch, to smile, to be together. The archetypal pattern of love unfolds into adult life where it is represented by such images as a goddess of love, a couple in union, or the most familiar one, the ancient image of Eros—the cupid from Greece or the more powerful figure with bow and arrow from India. This archetypal figure of Eros expresses the mysterious, emotional, sensual, and sexual passion of lovers. As the ancient story goes, whoever happens to be hit by the golden arrow of Eros is thrown into the madness, the torment, the ecstasy of love; whoever is hit by the lead-tipped arrow is indifferent. There is great uncertainty about when it will happen or what will happen. This quality of love—being so deep an instinct and archetype that it comes unbidden—comes from our depths and is beyond our conscious control. It seems as if we are suddenly favored, or doomed to fall from grace with the gods.

Love, as archetype, will always remain mysterious and unknowable—the powerful emotional force that unexpectedly draws us to someone quite different from our conscious ideals, or accounts for the unbearable anguish of losing someone we have loved. Besides the cupid or goddess of love, there are other archetypal images of love. The great longing for love—and its fulfillment or great loss—is expressed in the archetypal images and feelings we associate with the symbol of the heart, stars, the mermaid, the distant lover, or Romeo and Juliet. The deep bond of mature love that can form between people—especially over a long period of time—is experienced in archetypal feelings of an unfathomable sense of fulfillment, wholeness, or transcendent oneness in being together, often expressed in symbols of union—

Eastern figures of a king and queen hand-in-hand or Rodin's statue *The Kiss*. The archetypal, deeply unconscious quality of this love is shown in Shakespeare's Antony and Cleopatra and in other poetic imagery of the coming together of water, earth, fire, air, and stars—emotion, sexuality, passion, and spirit—such as crossing or bridging the waters, entrance and emergence from the waters, the joining of continents, the constellation of earth and moon.

Of course, at times, we must become conscious enough to sort out unconscious projections, possessiveness, illusions, and willful egotism from love—a deep wish for the well-being of another person as that person truly is. Yet, in letting ourselves be open to love, in spite of its painfulness and faultiness, we open up to the great energy and creative resources of the unconscious. The way to know love is not to judge it too much intellectually, by dissecting it and putting it into boxes of words—as if "the more conscious the better"—but to respect its reality in the watery realm of emotions for which we have few words.

We can search in our history, but we will not find much about the fulfillment of love in our patriarchal legacy of Greek gods[2] of power and sexuality, the Age of Chivalry and its ideal of romantic love and honor, or the Freudian psychology of childhood sexuality and penis envy. American psychology—so extraverted and practical—has developed workshops and books for couples: how to express feelings, how to fight fairly, how to satisfy each other sexually, how to show affection and love, how to be assertive. These are very useful but leave something missing about the unconscious subtleties that underlie love and sustain the bond between two people, between soul-mates.

Perhaps women can begin to fill in this gap by looking at their instincts, their archetypal roots, their subjective experience as women, to go beneath the layers of patriarchal culture emphasizing possession ("my husband," "his wife," "my child") and current society's general values. We find echoes of ourselves here and there coming down from women in earlier times—in statues of early goddesses, ancient writings, rituals, fairy tales, and ballads. We can hear responding chords within ourselves when we look at contemporary women's art, poetry, novels, drama, and dance. We can gather together and tell our stories to each other. And we can look at our dreams.

To understand how deeply emotional and unconscious love is, and how it is best honored in its natural form so that it continues to flow in all its richness from the watery depths, let us look at the ancient archetypal image of the mermaid. What meaning did the mermaid traditionally have and what does it hold for contemporary women? We will examine a woman's dream about mermaids and then a dream about oceans—both dreams about women remaining true to themselves and their feelings.

## The Mermaid Archetype

The Mermaid may seem strange to us, at first, as an archetypal image of woman and love. What she represents, though, is a woman at ease in the great waters of life, in the flow of emotion and sexuality. For a long time we have felt estranged from the ancient Mermaid in us, and those mermaid images which have come down through time—though intriguing—make us uneasy. One reason is that through the centuries the Mermaid has been seen through the eyes of men: their anima image of emotional impulses, their soulful yearnings and their erotic fantasy, as well as their object of infatuation and dread. For men, mermaids have taken many forms: supernatural sea maidens who lure them under water or rescue them from drowning; full-breasted mermaids with sinuous tails reclining on rocks and tempting sailors to their destruction; or sirens who sing songs of fatal attraction to Odysseus lashed to the mast. These images don't thrill the modern woman.

Is a story of pain and sacrifice all we have left of our heritage from the Mermaid: Hans Christian Andersen's *Little Mermaid* who falls in love with the prince, takes human shape to be near him at the cost of being struck mute, then is left with bleeding legs and a broken heart when he marries a human? Today she expresses a sad truth about the problem that occurs if we lose the connection to our unconscious depths; if we simply join the man in his realm rather than introduce him to ours; if we must give words for things; if we must justify what is real but ineffable; if we must *explain* our feelings.

We must reclaim the truth in the Mermaid for ourselves: that is, shift—from how she looks to men—to how she feels to us. Dreams show that the Mermaid, in her earlier form, is still alive in the nether regions of a woman's unconscious. With her supple tail, bare breasts, and her home in the ocean, the ancient symbol of the feminine, the Mermaid symbolizes a woman's connection to the Great Mother, archetype of change and changelessness, the womb of life and love, the numinous source of healing, the place of return in death. A woman knows this through her personal mother and her natural continuity with earliest childhood memories of immersion in emotion: the watery depths of oneness with the mother and within herself, the still waters, stormy seas, and rocky shores of early tenderness and sensuality that later become adult love and sexuality.

The mermaid symbolizes that, throughout life, love springs anew from its origins deep in the unconscious. Our capacity for love is unconscious, cannot be captured in words, explained, or justified. Our love and sexuality are as real—yet unknown and secret—a part of our very body and experience as the Mermaid's mysterious tail under the sea. To remain true to ourselves we must respect our unconscious nature and let the mermaid move freely, for if we try to direct our meanderings too much, we lose the connection to our deepest feelings.

The woman's archetypal Mermaid began as an ancient sea goddess from a mysterious realm of great splendor under the sea. She was a love goddess, early Aphrodite born of the sea, sitting on a rock in a healthy narcissism with comb and mirror in hand, dating back to pre-patriarchal times—before the Greek distinctions between human and divine, mortality and immortality, the earth and the underworld—when people were closer to the unconscious, the fluidity and rhythm of life and death, the mystery of birth, and birth of the soul, when the Hereafter wasn't a separate underworld but water and islands where one traveled. The spirit of the sea goddess is alive in the earliest figures of Aphrodite, Artemis, and Ariadne, and in the young woman, confident within herself and by herself. The early sea goddess held symbols of sacred power. These have come down to us through the ages as the mirror, which symbolizes a woman's deep self-reflection and self-absorption, and the comb, which represents her careful discrimination of thoughts and feelings. This sea goddess also expresses another quality of a woman. In her naked full-breastedness, exposed to others and open to their attraction, she shows her capacities for love and devotion.

The sea goddess and the mermaid harken back even further to the sea serpent whose undulations with its long tail were believed to cause the waves in water. From earliest times, life and wisdom have been associated with water. Ancient creation stories found the origin of life in the ocean, mother of all creation. And Jung discovered that the image of a fish or a serpent in the ocean represents active life and wisdom stirring in the depths of our unconscious psyche. The sea goddess conveys to us today our capacity to be at home in the great sea of unconscious archetypal feelings, to enter into life fully, love fully, with naturalness and awe for the oneness of life, oneness within ourselves, oneness with others.

If we look at more contemporary folklore, we see that the sea goddess became a Mermaid who came up on land. She was under a spell, so she couldn't speak or sleep, and she was still attuned to the sound of the sea in her ears. Because she became separated from the sea, she became more conscious, but perhaps too highly conscious for her own good, losing her connection to the sacred depths. In some folk stories, the mermaid rescues the drowning sailor, who seeks her but cannot live in her realm, brings him onto land, and tries to join him there. The mermaid longs for love and human companionship, but faces the sad fate of inarticulateness and loss because she is between the worlds of goddess and human. The Mermaid archetype, then, represents a dilemma.

Can a woman retain her inner sea goddess—remain herself and risk love—and succeed? Perhaps the drowning sailor must join her in her own world. That is, just as a woman's inner sailor, her own conscious side, must know how to survive in the sea of love, in outer life, a man, too, must learn how he can dissolve in the sea of love and still survive. The modern movie *Splash* suggests this shift in a man. In the surprise ending, the man so loves the mermaid that he forsakes his terrain and accompanies her when she returns to the sea. However, such solutions—his world or hers—pose the further question of how a woman and man can live in each other's realms. These "either-or" solutions feel unsatisfactory, but are necessary steps along the way. We must develop respect for the real differences between us: the gods and goddesses in us, the conscious and unconscious in us. Then we can hope to move between both realms of earth and sea, love each other not just in the pain of one-sided sacrifice and silence but more in the fullness of our own integrity in the midst of outer realities.

If the mermaid chooses to come ashore to walk—to be in a relationship—great sacrifice may be asked of her, as shown in the mermaid stories of our patriarchal societies. Relationship does require some sacrifice, but the dilemma for modern women is that certain relationships may require too great a sacrifice. What does a woman need in another person? The way for someone to pull a woman from her dreamy mermaid self-containedness is to reach her with the intensity of one's own feelings of caring and commitment, enter the sea oneself, join her, sometimes bring her out, and sometimes stay there with her! That is what contemporary men must learn to do.

The Mermaid archetype in a woman today can constrain her by keeping her in thrall to unrequited love; or free her into her inner feminine realm and very core of passion.

A DREAM OF MERMAIDS. A young woman, Judy, dreamed about mermaids the week before she met someone who eventually became her lover and her first real partner in life. It was as if this encounter with her inner Mermaid prepared her to make a commitment to love. The mermaids appeared in the final segment of this series of dream fragments:

> **Glass Mermaids. I'm on a plane to India. As we take off, I'm panicky, but a friend takes my hand and I feel better.**
>
> **A sick woman patient has lain in bed all night freezing cold. Did the doctor forget her? I wonder if**

the bottle of medicine is spoiled, but the doctor says, "It's fine, give it to her." But I still wonder, what if it's the wrong solution? The patient needs to go to the hospital. There someone asks me, "How's your boyfriend?" There's a locker room or sauna with women undressed and men looking sexual, and I admire a woman's body.

You [the analyst] are teaching a seminar in a room with locked cabinets all around, and you're trying to do individual therapy with everyone. You really want to talk with me—I'm the teacher's pet—but it's messy with all those people trying to get your attention. So I give up on the seminar and leave you to deal with them, having them take turns. I ask you, "Can I get my journal from your locked cabinet?" You give me the key, and I go away.

Outside my friend is at the river. She's getting into an inflatable boat to float to sea for three days. She has no provisions; she's just in her shorts. I ask, "Will you be okay?" She's vague. I walk with her as she wades into the water.

I'm staying with my grandmother. I look over and see a series of statues of little mermaids, all different colors of glass—one of each color: pink, purple, rose pink, olive green, emerald green. Freeform figures. Beautiful colored glass in the room.

This dream is about a woman's unconscious fears about falling in love and mobilizing the innermost core of her being. This is not apparent from the dream itself, but only emerges from the dreamer's own associations to the dream (which is true of most dreams) and the knowledge of what followed in her life.

Flying off to a remote place like India in a dream suggests going to a very foreign place in your psyche, a new place for you. Judy's association was even more specific and meaningful. She had gone to India once as a very introverted, self-possessed young woman and had been jolted "by how much I could be changed by an outer experience." This suggests that her panic now was at the thought that she could fall in love and be as deeply moved by another person as she had been with her unrequited first love. Judy said that in the dream she was panicky when the plane took off, but the reassuring hand of her own inner guide in the dream affirmed her basic integrity so she could venture forth, knowing that "the voyage can be made in my own internal way."

Where does this panic come from? The next scene—of the sick patient—holds the clue. The sick patient is her own body, abandoned too long, frozen. She (as dream ego) is worried about taking good care of it, worried that the doctor (her extraverted analyst, or her own careless inner authority) will impose a doubtful solution on her.

In her associations to the careless doctor who gives the sick patient spoiled medicine, Judy spoke about doctors "who have surface warmth, but treat you without caring for you." She recounted a traumatic incident as a little girl, crying in fear, when a pediatrician gave her an injection as her mother helped the doctor hold her down, instead of comforting her or waiting until she felt ready. The result was a lifetime phobia about shots. Engraved in her psyche from that incident was the belief that she was ultimately helpless against someone using force against her body and the fear that her mother would abandon her at such times, to follow male authority, even when it was wrong. This was a critical incident, for the way a girl's body is handled by her family sets her expectation, her fears, and her hopes of the way she will be treated sexually later as a woman.

The locker room scene presents a parallel dilemma. Judy said, "When I think of sex with men, I want to retreat to a safe place." This statement in addition to her dream image of "admiring the woman's body" hint at an appreciation of women's unique sexual energy; or a potential attraction to women—who might seem more safe than men; and/or an affirmation of pride in her own body. She is expressing a woman's deepest body instinct—to protect herself from being abruptly penetrated as she had been by the doctor with the needle and her college boyfriends with their hasty penises. She said the important barrier to sexual yielding for her was "if they don't establish first that they care enough."

Men's rape fantasies to the contrary, in real life a woman must find her way to yield, and must not be forced. She needs a partner to walk beside her as she finds her way, sometimes running ahead of her, persuading her to leap past barriers and catch up, sometimes lagging behind while she moves ahead, but being ever attuned to her as a real person, not a thing.

Why, then, do women themselves sometimes dream of wanting to be overpowered sexually or even raped? These are *exaggerated images*—as unconscious images often are, in order to break through to consciousness—and usually express a woman's own neglected sexual desires. She might want a reluctant partner to be more eager about sex. She might have a deep desire to let her own sexual impulses overwhelm her, break forth and gain dominance over her passivity, her qualms, her reluctance. So images of rape in women's fantasies or dreams don't need to be interpreted *concretely* as an actual desire to be assaulted sexually, dominated, or degraded, but can usually be interpreted *metaphorically* as a desire for something missing in a woman herself or her partner in their internal dramas of yielding to sexuality.

Also, rape dreams sometimes re enact early sexual trauma in a woman's life, and thus represent the resulting anxiety about assault, sexual fears, helplessness, and guilt. Just as in real life, where a survivor of sexual assault can become either overly inhibited, or—to defend against overwhelming feelings of helplessness—become overly seductive or fascinated with sex, so, too, in the dream world there can be various pictures of extreme, defensive reactions. These should be understood as the psyche's attempt to handle the trauma internally and bring it to the attention of the conscious mind.

Returning to Judy's dream, the next episode in the dream shows her competing for her analyst's attention in a seminar and wanting to know that she is special as "the teacher's pet." Knowing you are special—respected and loved as an individual—is an important issue in analysis, as it is in life, but her dream ego leaves this issue (leaves the analyst to let others take their turns) to pursue something more important for her as an introverted feeling woman: She is given her own key to her locked cabinet—her own unconscious flow of feeling. Judy said, "It's a direct connection to the safe container, into the ocean, a passive very unconscious thing." That is, she gains release from dependency on her analyst—the good parent—to claim autonomy for her own inner journey.

Next in the dream comes the departure to "float to sea for three days." Whenever you have three days for a journey, it refers to the mythic time period found in stories—from ancient times through modern folklore—for an inner symbolic journey of transformation. This is a perilous trip. How hard it is to open up one's heart and sexuality, be out of control, and yet trust one's instincts. Sometimes it's exactly right to do something that looks foolhardy. And what she found in this journey into the Great Mother realm was her grandmother, a guide in the tradition of women and the archetype of the Mermaid.

The dreamer remembered Andersen's Little Mermaid, who changed herself for her prince, who, though he was kind to her, never loved her and married someone else. Judy said, "She was mute, devoted, hideously passive. It made me angry." So the mermaid story Judy grew up with represented the fear of falling in love, which meant making too great a sacrifice of one's true nature for another person, being silenced and handicapped, then subject to desertion. This story expressed an important theme in Judy's life. In her relationships, she had been under the spell of an unconscious Mermaid archetype.

An archetype which is very unconscious seems to offer only two extreme choices, as does the mermaid: to be too self-contained alone on the rock, having just emerged from a state of oneness with the sea, or else too devoted, sacrificing unduly for relationship. This dreamer had identified with this archetype too much in her history of unrequited love. When an archetype grips your unconscious—and you don't know it—it cannot help you. This archetype had been too closely bound to the innocence of a young girl's feeling of oneness and devotion to her parents—an archetypal love that allowed her to flourish as a girl, but that eventually had to be relinquished. In a sense, she accomplished this task in the course of the dream. She moved from needing to be special to the analyst to finding something more important— her own key to her flow of feelings. This dream made her more conscious of her mermaid and ushered in a new era in her life of feeling safe enough to be herself in a committed relationship.

If we can develop an awareness of the Mermaid within us, she can become a good inner ally. We can sense the Mermaid at those times when we are in danger of losing her—losing our wholeness, our connection with our deepest instinctive feelings, our own free form. We preserve the essence of the Mermaid when we remain true to ourselves and our feminine feeling, whether alone or in relationship; then we can hope to transcend the polarity of being self-sufficient or self-sacrificing.

Judy's dream cherishes the mermaids and redeems them. Judy said, "The dream is about the fear of letting the heart go." Then she described the mermaids in her dream: "unreal green, bottle green, emerald, rose pink . . . all different colors, tactile, lovely." These beautiful colors are the rainbow of her feelings as she dares to care about another person. The mermaids are "free-form" figures but feminine. She understood that she needed to have all her emotions and wholeness to plunge into love. And shortly, she did find someone who could return her full measure of emotions.

The fact that the mermaids in her dream are glass suggests the delicacy of young love, reminiscent of *The Glass Menagerie*, where a shy woman treasures her fragile fantasy world, and hardly dares venture forth into the real world of relating to men. Glass is magical. It is liquid transformed into solid beauty. It is an image of introverted feeling, molten within and brittle outside. This is the paradox for an introverted young woman, so near her feeling and yet so far from expressing it, seeing it through a glass shield. In this introverted way, the moment of feeling-flow is preserved and endures, as in the formation of glass, and becomes a capacity for great devotion and loyalty. In contrast, for an extraverted young woman, the mermaid is felt in the swish of the tail, the wild ebb and flow of passion in her body and soul as she is drawn toward someone, loses herself in the other person and curves back onto herself, then is drawn forward again in the tidal waves of feeling.

Judy's dream emphasizes that there are times and places for the mermaid side of us in modern life, but we are more than just the contemplative, full-breasted mermaid. A modern woman must renounce the mermaid—at times in her life—to get ahead in patriarchal society. There are times and places to leave the seashore and become the full-force "animus" woman who has to deny her emotions, her flexible spine, her compassionate breasts. She must go out and adopt the hard-paced walk of the student, housewife, or working woman in order to handle words, examinations, schedules, overload, and deadlines. And she must emerge from the silencing strategies that society imposed on her from long ago and speak her mind. This is as important as the mermaid, and complements her vulnerability and helplessness. We are land creatures, after all!

At times, to win a relationship in the world as it is, a woman must edge out the forlorn mermaid in herself and become the princess who wins the prince. Then she is daring to be the special one in society who wins the prize. And she is daring to be special to a particular man, to be the "anima" woman who reflects back to a man his own image of the woman he wants, who resonates with special qualities that he discovers and appreciates in her, hopefully without losing the mirror to herself, the substance of her own treasure from the bottom of the sea.

In denying her mermaid, though, a woman often takes a certain risk in our society. The danger is that she may unconsciously become a man's idea of the siren. If she doesn't have enough healthy narcissism, and doesn't differentiate her own thoughts and feelings (doesn't comb her long hair), she may lose her role as an independent feminine guide for herself and her partner, a guide to the deeper ocean of feelings they could share. Her whole array of colors—her array of emotional relatedness—can easily become concentrated on the intensity of sexual passion alone. This passion can appear hot, but she may remain emotionally detached, cool as glass, and strangely unattainable or dangerous to others. Then she has unconsciously become the mermaid's shadowy sister, the siren of the sea, the enchantress who casts spells and lures men to drowning in the sea of their sexual entanglement with her and her wild hair.

Why is the mermaid mute in folklore? It could be that the sea goddesses became mute through time, just as the heroines in fairy tales were silenced by later generations[3]—patriarchal and Christian—to deny the ancient feminine powers revered by our forebears. It is also poetically true that muteness expresses the ineffable quality of love, the mystery of emotions.

This dream holds a further clue. The mermaids shone in an array of subtle and vivid colors. The subtle soft hues of the rainbow register the delicacy of a woman's love and devotion; the more vivid colors express the more intense energy—the aurora borealis—of her passion, fear, and anger. These can be known in sheer emotion, in color. They cannot be put into words.

In the presence of a rainbow, in the presence of the aurora borealis, one is mute. Only feeling silence can do them honor. It is the same with the devotion and sacrifice in love that endures through the years. The deepest bonds of love between a couple are real, though they have no name and no explanation.

## Inner Polarization

The previous dream explored a modern woman's dilemma, her inner polarities in the struggle to be true to herself in entering a meaningful relationship. This theme again emerges in the next dream, which also involves water imagery—a river and two oceans—suggesting that this dreamer, too, is in the realm of the archetypal unconscious and must become aware of her yearnings for love which go back to her early history. This woman, also, had always been disappointed in her search for "the right man."

> *The Panama Canal Zone.* I'm taking a trip and dive into the river. I leave my clothes behind. I talk with Tom and find he's leaving. Then a young fellow refers to Mike as an idol. . . .
>
> I'm dressing in the other room and find the old clothes I'd worn. A woman recognizes that I've been in the Panama Canal Zone, and I reply, "How did you know!"

This is an inner journey: plunging into the stream of life, leaving behind old clothes—your old view of yourself. In this journey, the dreamer meets two kinds of men in her life. One is Tom, who is softhearted, generous, protective, but seems too "sappy" to her, sapped of his vitality and worth because he is too self-effacing. The other is Mike, confident and dominant, wielding power over women. She had always wondered why other women found him attractive, for she had always had an aversion to him as somewhat of a bully. He was, however, an extreme version of the kind of man to whom she was unconsciously attracted, whom she had "idolized." He dared to think himself important to others, something she and the other women found hard to do themselves, a position denied them in their backgrounds, so they thought they could only have it vicariously through him.

But this is a trap. The more a woman gives up her importance to another, the emptier she feels—and the more important the other person must be so she can identify with the other's importance, until they are quite polarized. This is what happens when a victim "identifies with the aggressor," whether the victim is a prisoner with a guard or a child with an abuser. The victim gradually feels so worthless and helpless, and the other person looms so large in life with just those qualities the victim needs—power and control—that the other person can become all-important, irresistible, and even loved with fierce tenacity!

The Panama Canal Zone is a striking image of polarization between people and, specifically, the dreamer's projections onto men. She pictured the Isthmus of Panama as a narrow bridge of land linking the two great land masses—the separation in her mind of two kinds of men, one who is too self-effacing and the other too self-important. The isthmus is the crucial link between two hemispheres, symbolic of the coming together of the two great halves for wholeness, that is, the possibility of these polarized qualities being in one person. But the deeper symbolic meaning of the Canal Zone couldn't become clear to her if she only pictured the land masses, if she only looked at what was on the conscious horizon: men and their qualities.

When she shifted her attention to the waters, the emotional world, the more subtle and unconscious symbol of the Panama Canal became clear as a waterway, linking two great bodies of water, the warm Atlantic and the cold Pacific. In her deep intimacy with another person, the early watery world of the Great Mother was stirred in her. She yearned to yield and be safely buoyed by the warm waters of tenderness, yet feared drowning in the cold waters of indifference. So intimacy was not just something she yearned for; it also held some old dangers. In searching for her "other half," her mate, she had been suspended between the two worlds. When she found someone who was extremely warm and loving like Tom, she was indifferent. When she found someone like Mike, she suffered from *his* indifference.

It wasn't hard for her to see, then, that she had a Tom inside her, but it was harder to see the Mike in herself. She had a fleeting image of the terrible Hindu goddess Kali, and she recognized the Kali in herself: a flicker of ruthlessness that could be stirred up in her by certain men. If a man was too much of a bully, her anger was sooner or later stirred up in her own defense; if he was too much of a doormat, she felt a touch of ruthlessness in herself as an aggressor. Incidentally, when she had begun thinking about this dream in her therapy session, a twitch had begun in the pit of her elbow that hadn't gone away. What was so deeply disturbing to her about this dream? The twitch in her elbow seemed to her as if she were keeping herself from raising her arm in a clenched fist, her instinctive knowledge of her own Kali.

Thus, the real revelation of this dream was that in the innermost crannies of her heart, she was too self-effacing, too tender-hearted, too "sappy," or else too self-important, too indifferent, or too aggressive. The "canal" held the hope of transcending this inner polarization. It was the construction of a safe passage between two sides of herself, the first step in healing her psychological complex.

The intense magnetic attractions and repulsions between people that bring them together and draw them apart reflect the joining of their inner archetypal complexes, their hemispheres and oceans. The more conscious complexes reflect the great polarities between people that draw their hemispheres together or apart, like masculine and feminine. The deeper unconscious polarities represent the great bodies of water, the deep watery connections within and between them in the subtle realm of intimacy and distance. By understanding her own complexes and by plunging into her inner world to find these polarities in herself and recognize them in others, the dreamer gradually found that they became less extreme, less polarized; and eventually, after a long time, she found herself drawn to someone who was less extreme, someone who became her mate.

## The Anguish of Choice

In the last dream we saw the topography of relationship in the layout of the great land masses and oceans. In that dream, and the one before it, we saw an image often found in dreams, the river, which usually represents the course you take in life—entering its natural flow and making choices over time. Sometimes the deepest layers of the unconscious show the course life is taking, carved out deep in the psyche, like a river wending its way, cutting through the layers of a canyon. Akin to this kind of imagery is the "chart" in the following dream, probably a sea captain's chart, to find the dreamer's individual course through the waters for her own choices in life.

> *You're Behind, Valentines.* There are two women lying in a large bed, and I choose their room, number 202. The man next to me also did, but I put out my hand to stop him. I open the door to the room and say to him, "We're wanting the same thing, but you're behind."
>
> There's a woman with charts. I don't want the usual chart. I want the "other chart." There are valentines on a nearby table with hearts to cut out and mail. As I make valentines I think, "Now I'm wise enough to know who will cheat me in love and who can benefit me." But I can't bring myself to choose a valentine. And I think sadly, "I don't have a partner yet. That's what would make the difference."

In this dream, a woman was choosing a relationship with a woman, "wanting the same thing" men do in women—loving partners—which most men seem "far behind" in being. It seemed as if she were asking Fate (the woman with the charts) for "the other chart"—the different choice in life. The valentines reminded her of the excitement she had felt in school as a girl cutting out red paper hearts for her boyfriends, and how she would have to leave "far behind" all her valentines—her lifetime hopes of being with a man and fitting in with society—for a life that would seem to benefit her personally the most.

So her dream was mourning her loss, while keeping her choice firmly in mind. Any choice of a partner, any commitment in life, brings anguish at first, not the happiness we would expect. Great choices in life are anguishing because you have to leave behind all your other hopes, all the other things you love. You leave behind all your valentines.

But evidently she couldn't bring herself to make a choice of a woman partner in the abstract. It was too hard to do. Even though her old identity did not fit any more, her new one had not been realized, but would have to happen in its own time, with the quickening coming from the reality of loving a real person.

Until a new reality is born, you can't feel the sweep of life that new commitment brings—whether it is a person, a community, or a job. You are left for a while with only the loss. That is why most people find it difficult, if not impossible, to leave an old life: It seems too painful. In this case, the dream revealed an archetypal truth about the process of making a choice—that it involves loss—to prepare the dreamer for following her true course.

## The Larger-Than-Life Animus

A woman, Eva, had worked together for years with a colleague, John, and their friendship had deepened through time, but the constraints of his situation (he was separated but not divorced) had kept their passion from bursting forth. He seemed to Eva "the measure of a man" among the men she knew. He had been the "great man" of her life, and she felt equally respected as a woman. Then, after many years, they planned a long weekend together. When they finally met, the ease of knowing each other so well and the undercurrent of electricity between them suddenly changed to high-voltage tension. It was as if she were his Egypt and he, her Rome. At least, Eva imagined he felt this, the same as she did.

But to Eva's dismay, they suddenly became two ordinary people, self-conscious, awkward, and strangely barren emotionally. It wasn't at all the golden moment she had expected. Perhaps, with the barriers down, their inner reluctance had emerged. That night she had the following dream:

> *Man as Prow of the Ship.* **A well-built young man like John tries to escape with other slaves, but is caught and strapped to the prow of a ship going out to sea, a figurehead that's a composite of John, a horse, and an older man. As if it were in olden times, John had been caught and impressed into service by a bad captain. This captain goes out to sea for three years at a time; he hasn't much home life with his wife.**
>
> **There's another captain who takes shorter hauls out to sea. That suggests he has a good life back home. Later, this good captain comes by to rescue the young man. While the bad captain had been beating him up and kicking his face, the good captain had stood by, unable to stop it or show his concern. He had played cool, and bided his time to rescue him later.**

This dream warns about the archetypal forces behind high-voltage feelings. You can be possessed by the gods. The reason John had meant so much to Eva through the years was that he seemed more than a man to her. He seemed larger than life. Through him she knew her "other side," her deepest masculine side, her "animus," and she was enchanted! He was the prow of the ship, her guide to explore the unknown—Sagittarius with the fiery energy of the horse and the wisdom of the elders.

This was the archetypal role John had played for her as a figurehead of exploration, passion, and wisdom. And this was the role she unconsciously wanted him to stay in, hence, the bad captain in the dream who strapped him and kept the real man bound to an archetypal role.

But we are not good at being gods for long. This caused the tension between them. From enchantment they stumbled and fell into reality. Their coming together had brought forth their best, their most profound depths. But they were ordinary people, too. Only sometimes did John really spark fires in her, and the fires sometimes turned to ashes. He excited her intellectually—her ideas flowed forth and they often touched wisdom together—but they stumbled over barren ground in talking about their relationship. Would he be like the bad captain who had little time for his wife left ashore? Perhaps Eva was mistaken, after all, in John's actual ability to commit emotionally to a relationship together. Or perhaps her hopes were too high and only a god would do. This was the reality of their situation.

The dream shows Eva was vulnerable to falling under an archetypal spell: longing for a perfect love not possible in the real world. She would be bound to an unreachable animus, this figurehead who leads her on an endless search across the waters on a phantom ship condemned to sail forever and never touch shore.

Some women are especially vulnerable to this archetype of the phantom ship, the ghostly lover. Women who have been especially fascinated by their unreachable father or older brother, or who suffered an early loss of a beloved father, brother, or other important male figure, naturally cherish an idealized image of a special man, and may continue this pattern of cherishing an ideal into their adulthood. For them, to feel love is to feel longing. They long for a ghostly lover, someone who fits their larger-than-life image, rather than someone ordinary (as well as extraordinary) whom they can know as a real person. They are turning away from life, even though their inner life seems heightened by deep-felt love and, often, spiritual yearning. For there is a sad, deathlike, spiritual quality in this love, as seen in the myriad stories of phantom ships that never make port, ships that sail to the Great Beyond, and lovers who can be together only in death, can meet only in the watery grave of the unconscious.[4] The task for these women, then, is to try to seek these emotional and spiritual depths within themselves and within a real-life partnership.

A dream like this can have a sobering effect. The dream woke Eva up to the realities of her actual relationship with John. At the same time, it also revealed to her the inner meaning he held for her. It showed her how much he truly meant to her, not just as familiar John, strong and wise, but as someone who reflected back to her something musky and male—the strength and instincts of the horse. He brought her in touch with other inner figures that knew deep down about her own wisdom and folly, toughness and illusion.

Thus, the dream underscored Eva's first dismaying experience with John on the weekend—that big hopes and passion were probably not enough to overcome their situational constraints and their problems as ordinary people. It was painful. Could the good Captain come forward enough? The dream figures were all male. Where was the feminine, the compassionate, in their relationship? It would take time. It was hard to tell how it would turn out. The inner figures would need to "have it out," as they did in real life.

## The Great Female Self

Another woman who also needed to retain a stronger sense of herself in a new relationship had a dream that provided her with a strong inner female figure. This figure would help her keep her own center and make room for a new love in her life, while giving her a more conscious position in relation to her overpowering mother and her own mothering instinct. This was an exploration, in depth, of the archetypal Self and how Eros should relate to it.

> *Columbia: Gem of the Ocean.* There's a huge statue of a woman on top of the Columbian Building, larger than the building could support. She's in a gown, her robes flowing. A statuesque bearing!
>
> Three rings—glowing rainbows—surround her. I asked why. Someone said, "The sun, earth, and Venus

**all come together here in one place." It's a stellar diagram, like the New York transit system, one station on top of another. You can swoop through the air. It's important to know at which level you are, and not get disoriented.**

This Great Female is an early form of the Self, barely emerging from the awesome power of the Great Mother. Universal qualities are often represented by colossal female figures, like the Statue of Liberty or the weighty and confident goddess figures. Here, this figure, statuesque and flowing, shows the great importance and moving power of the Self. How should we relate to it? It is the matrix of us all, the great permanence that is the beginning and ending of all life. It is the great inspiration. All other archetypes emerge from this one and rotate around it; in this case, the great forces of the sun, the earth, and Venus.

This is a picture, then, of the dreamer's inner constellation of archetypes, depicted, as they often are, in the configuration of the stars and planets. The dream holds a great truth: the fundamental Self is central, and others—even Venus/love—are secondary to it.

This dream explores a proper relationship to this archetype and its satellites. As humans, we must bring them "down to earth" (the underground system in the Great City—New York), as well as let them inspire us, as when, in our imaginations, we dare to "swoop through the air" toward them. Then their presence can inspire us despite the risk of becoming identified with their power and losing our human orientation. The dream says straight out: "It's important to know at which level you are."

This dream followed a dream in which the woman was swept away in tidal waves. Here she is emerging from that watery world of childlike passivity and anxiety before the great forces of emotion—love—to come into her own as a mature woman. She knew that this dream figure meant a lot to her, but she was, at first, mistaken in not differentiating it from Venus. She said, "Columbia is the Gem of the Ocean, an idealistic place or idea, and she is a goddess, a mature woman, the Venus of love, emerging from the water, surrounded by the elements, amidst a map of it all." This misses what the dream is trying to tell her—what it says is "important to know."

First, a perspective is in order. In interpreting our own dreams, we often see only what the ego already knows, thus compounding our error and not benefiting from what the unconscious could tell us. This is the universal problem of the "arrogant ego." That's why it is necessary to notice the exact details of a dream or have someone else help interpret a dream. A dream is, by its very nature, *compensatory* to the ego position, telling us something the ego doesn't know or value enough and should know.

In this dream the great goddess figure is not, as she thought, Venus herself nor a mature woman—both of whom are at other levels. The Self is fundamental and central: The Venus of love is different from it and secondary to it; and a mature woman is only human, though she can feel the force of the goddess as she swoops nearby.

This Gem, this treasure, emerging from the waters of the unconscious, then, is the dreamer's knowledge and awe of the Self, reflected in her own inner center which should endure, not to be shaken out of place by the forces of sun, earth, and Love; but rather maintain its independence and lend its power to them. The dreamer needs this deep sense of confidence, calmness, and security in order to endure in the midst of the bright sun of the new male force in her life, and to hold on to her earthbound connection—in the midst of the pull of love for her new man.

This symbol came at the right time for her, at the time of love's blossoming. It would help her in relation to the forces of sun, earth, and Venus. At this crucial time, it was important for her to keep her own feminine center in relation to the sun— giving herself over to the dazzling warmth and power from her man whom she valued so highly. There was real love with her new mate and he was good for her, but she shouldn't lose herself too much, as she had done as a child in her fondness for her father.

This was a time when she also needed her great integrity to relate properly to the "earth" in the dream—the great value she placed on her own home, her own mother, and her own sexuality. Her mother was a Grand Matriarch who expected primary allegiance from her children. Married or not, all came for Sunday dinner. So the daughter needed all her own earth-forces to be true to her own sexuality, her own new home, and motherhood, rather than remain under the spell of her mother's authority summoning her "to stay home." She needed the courage of the Self, so closely aligned to the origin of Eros itself, but even stronger.

It had taken great courage for her to leave her first husband, someone her mother had chosen, more or less; and it would take more courage to stand by her own choice in a new mate—someone whom her mother strongly opposed. To help her do this, she especially needed Venus at her side. But it was the great statuesque figure, moving forward, inspiring her, who could see her through this time of love's blossoming and ripening.

As a person, this woman especially embodied feminine warmth, generosity, and sensuality. She had been given the great gift in life of being close to her own magnetic forces of the Great Mother, the early source of the Self and Eros. For this reason, it was vitally important for her to differentiate between Great Mother forces and Venus. As a woman capable of great love, close to her mother who was a matriarch, she needed to know the independence and primary importance of the Self *consciously* so that Venus could detach from it. This would prevent her from giving herself totally to a man, or expecting the same from him, which would be just copying her mother as another matriarch. That's what this dream is about: consciously differentiating kinds of Eros and giving each its rightful place—her own matriarch, her Venus of love, the sun of her animus/lover, and beyond them, the enduring Great Female Self—Columbia, Gem of the Ocean.

## Difficulties and Choices in Relationships

What issues do women encounter as they face the everyday realities of relationships while they try to stay true to their own individual, feminine way of loving? Many of the dreams in this section highlight women's problems and options as they start relationships and have to choose whether to continue or not. Other dreams address wider issues with which women have to contend throughout relationships, such as cultural projections or anima projections onto them.

## Inner Pattern/Outer Blossoming

The blooming of a fresh relationship promises the fullness of relationship to come. The first blossoming of all our hopes for relationship propels us forward to fulfill them, and we make great adjustments in our outer lives to fit together. But we may hardly realize that we have to make an equally profound settling of affairs in our inner life. We can't just reach out for the fruit of relationship, whether we're ripe or not inside. We must wait for the inner fruit to ripen in its own time.

Our extraverted culture leads us to believe that if we grasp an idea, or grab something and hold it in our hands, we have it as our own. We hope that, if we learn communication skills or if we reach certain goals, we will be satisfied, but instead we often *feel* empty-handed at the end and wonder what happened to the promise. This happens when we have forged ahead of our inner selves. For we need to tend our great inner tree: the generations of underbrush and deadwood, the roots, the budding, the branching out so we can see the tree's true silhouette. As each tree has concentric circles of growth from its inner pattern in response to the outer world of sun, earth, and rain, so, too, the individual unconscious has variations in its pattern of growth rings, glimpsed, sometimes, in our dreams.

The following dream came to a single woman, Sylvia, after a fast courtship that fit cultural images of the sequence of seduction, conquest, possession, and intense sexuality. After the first attraction, the suspense and relief of choosing and being chosen, the relationship had quickened into an intense, passionate bond. Sylvia had been rather passive for her nature, following the man's lead. They had just embarked upon a steady pattern of seeing each other when she had the following dream.

*Baking Layer by Layer.* There are two women in a room. One woman is giving the other a massage. I've received a massage, and I offer the masseuse one in return, but what I actually give her is a hug out on the street.

I notice her car nearby. She has packed her car, ready for a trip, but I'm upset that she has overlooked any care for her animals—her turtles and other animals.

I need to enter her house to take care of things. I'm at the back of the house on a wide brick walkway. There must be a similar wide brick stairway inside the house, too, but I can't get in the back door to the wide steps. Finally I do get in somehow, but I have to use a rickety wooden ladder to get between floors.

I go from "layer to layer," actually floor to floor. Women are baking for each "layer" or floor. I tell them I'm the owner, and they let me pass by. It occurs to me that it's important to keep each layer separate this way. However, I might use the wide brick stairway between layers if only I could get permission from Helen [the tough, manipulative manager where I used to work].

In the last scene of the dream I tell others, "Now I have a mansion *and* it has a plush red parlor *and* a place for a cook!"

The opening scene, as the stage setting for the whole dream, reminds the dreamer of her own feminine nature and gives her feminine images of what is missing in her new relationship. A woman massaging another is an image of sensuality and closeness—gentle, quiet, caring, and sensitive—reminiscent of the soft caresses and subtle kindness received as a child. This is probably the tenderness she desires as a woman, not just as a prelude to sex, but for itself. In fact, in return for the massage in the dream, she offers a hug on the street, thus bringing into everyday life the hug she knows from childhood: that feeling of warmth and closeness, that small everyday affirmation of liking each other and enjoying each other. This is the soft core of love that women usually know about, but men have too often left behind.

In contrast, if the opening scene had been a football game or a debate at the dinner table, it would have meant that Sylvia needed to understand competitiveness and aggression in her current relationship. Rather, she is being reminded of her own inner feminine nature.

As in most dreams, various characters portray different parts of the dreamer. The observing ego, the "I" in this dream, needs to react to these "characters" and resolve the problem posed by the stage play.

The "I" in the dream is "upset that she has overlooked any care for her turtles and other animals." Sylvia tried to understand why she would be upset at her gentle (masseuse) side, packing the car and forgetting the turtles. It occurred to Sylvia that her usual gentleness had quite disappeared as she rushed into this relationship. She had abandoned her turtles: her usual slow-moving, introverted instincts. As she contemplated the turtle—with its slow steps, its protective shell, its house on its back wherever it goes, and its longevity—she realized the long-range importance to her of having a quiet home, feeling safe, and following her own inner pace.

Sylvia became aware that she had begun to resent her boyfriend's "pressure." She said, "It's as if sex is more important to him than a person. At first everything worked like clockwork. I liked his assertiveness and possessiveness, but now I find myself pulling back in my shell, and that makes him worse. It's as if we don't fit together anymore." Her usual outer barriers, which had melted before their passion, had been replaced by inner reluctance.

The dream woke Sylvia up to the fact that she had been following her partner's lead in the relationship, and now she balked at the narrowness of the relationship they had created around sex. It was as if they had become addicted to sex, which went well between them, but like other addictions, produced a problem by eclipsing everything else because it was so quick and easy. Now the time had come for her to bring to the relationship her feminine knowledge—that a relationship must grow in the atmosphere of everyday life.

The dreamer had drifted, like many women in our culture do, into following a man's lead in relationship. A woman is conditioned by our culture and by her very nature to be responsive, and a man to be aggressive sexually. And the power inequities, the far greater number of single women than single men, also tend to force her into this position, at first, in a relationship. But when a relationship loses what a woman can truly bring to it, both man and woman are diminished, and the growth of the relationship is stunted.

Women need, then, some ways to compensate for this feeling of being overwhelmed by male culture. One way is for women to talk with other women about relationship—what we truly value; another way is to consult our inner women, as in this dream.

The rest of the dream is deep archetypal work, finding the way in the back door and the way between layers. The atmosphere in the dream felt "murky" to Sylvia. What was murky? Hardly admitting it, the couple had become wary of each other. Sylvia had begun to think of him as manipulative, and he had begun to have doubts about her. The dream had taken them from blossoming springtime to the first cool breezes of fall, the gray of their shadows. In talking over the dream, she saw his shadow first. "Perhaps he only wants me sexually, not as a whole person. Maybe it's his way of loving; I'm not sure."

The dream confronted Sylvia with her own shadow in the figure of Helen, the tough manipulative manager in herself. As Sylvia thought hard and sincerely about how she herself might be manipulative in the relationship, she realized that she wasn't wanting her lover as a whole person either. Her own shrewd Helen was wanting to catch him as a husband and father. Sylvia was approaching her later thirties and wanted a baby. She couldn't counter his aggression because her own aggressive side was so unconscious. Thus, her unknown aggression colluded with his, and it had begun to feel very murky.

The problem was that her own inner Helen was running the show. She allowed only a rickety ladder as a transition to the other layers, to reach the other inner levels and meanings in their relationship. In the dream, Helen has to yield, give permission to the dreamer to take the wide brick stairway—the spacious way, built piece by solid brick piece. In all honesty, Sylvia had to form some idea if her new love was indeed right for her as a potential husband and father. She would err going after him with the shrewd, devious side of herself, to grasp him without concern for his true nature and their true fit. The dream leaves the choice an open question. Perhaps there would be a wide stairway for them, and brick by brick, bit by bit, they could find out what they could have or couldn't have in their relationship.

The main image that gripped the dreamer and stayed with her from this dream was the image of women baking something "layer by layer." This spoke to her of a more instinctual, archetypal layer of women's wisdom about the alchemy of relationship and the slow development of Eros. At its deepest level, baking symbolizes the mysterious process of birth and growth, and was honored as long ago as 6,000 B.C. when there were sacred ovens in temples.[5] The art of old-fashioned baking had been passed down to Sylvia by her mother: dissolving the yeast in warm water, shaping the sticky dough, kneading it just enough, waiting for it to rise in a warm place, punching it down again, waiting for it to rise again, then waiting for it to bake in a hot oven and turn out light, or heavy. Each stage had its separate rising or falling. It needed patience and attentiveness, but the yeast—the active ingredient—did its magic at each stage if conditions were favorable. Yeast, like all living things, has its own pace. As observers we can't plan and make it happen, though we can be ready to do our part in the ineffable process, one that directs our own nature, too.

This reminded Sylvia of the slow, stylized courtship in high school and college that kept her from rushing ahead of herself. Each step was marked by a certain conclusion, and every boy and girl knew what it meant. Each step in intimacy followed a slow progression, and each step meant a conscious decision to move, or not to move, to the next step in intimacy and commitment to a life together: first catching each other's eye, holding hands (or not) after a certain length of time, the first kiss (or not) after a certain length of time . . . building relationship layer by layer. She wondered if it had been patterned after women's pace and was now lost.

The image of baking seems an old-fashioned feminine image, but perhaps a true one about the nature of authentic relationship and how it develops. In this culture, we are bombarded with extraverted masculine images of how people get together. In movies people feel erotically attracted to each other, fall instantly in love, and soar into the future together, or crash-land on infidelity. There are hardly any long, slow-paced romantic movies or musicals because people don't believe any more in the old images: the ardent suitor and reluctant innocent, or the conquest and happiness ever after. Perhaps women screenwriters and directors will be providing us with new women's images, full of the yeasty life, the risky stuff of real-life romance.

## Too Hot to Handle

Sometimes a dream gives warning that you should not enter a relationship or proceed with it. Sometimes you have inner work to be done first. In our extraverted, growth-oriented society, it is believed that you can "work things out" in relationship, or that, even if a relationship doesn't succeed, at least you can learn and grow from the experience. While this is true to some extent, this is actually using someone else to practice on, which can be wounding or even dangerous. The following is a case where her dream vividly warned a woman against acting out her inner conflicts by entering a destructive relationship.

A woman, Wendy, suddenly found herself strongly attracted to someone with whom she had worked for years. Based on past experience, Wendy had not wanted to get involved with anyone at work. Moreover, she distrusted this particular man. He was earthy, full of life, but also full of raw energy. He did what he wanted, was outspoken, angry, and—what astonished her in the stories he told—had few compunctions about "conning" people. As much as Wendy felt drawn to his warmth and spontaneity, she wondered if he might be too different from her, if he played by different rules, was too dangerous for her, perhaps too callous or cruel.

Wendy had the following dream:

> **Rattlesnake in a Glass Container.** We're on a little float that has some movement on the water, but the float knows to always stay in the inlet, not go into the ocean. . . .
>
> We take a room together in a hotel. I wonder if others know. It's lots of trouble to fill out the form for the hotel. Then I decide it's not necessary. I change to lighter clothes. . . .
>
> He left something in my room. There's a rattlesnake in the glass fish tank on the mantle. It hisses and snaps as I go by. There's also a dried-up seashell creature in there with very little water left in the tank. I haven't taken care of them, haven't given them any food. I ought to give them back or do something with them.

This dream immediately struck Wendy as a clear warning not to drift further into the ocean of archetypal or instinctual realms with this man, but to stay in the safe inlet of a limited relationship at their place of work. The dream alludes to some inner concern about entering a relationship with someone at work (trouble to fill out the form, I wonder if others will know), but in the dream Wendy at first dismisses these fears (not necessary; lighter clothes).

The consequence, the unconscious shows, is a powerful image: the dangerous rattlesnake. The unconscious dramatizes and exaggerates to shock you into paying attention to something. The image of the rattlesnake he left in her room, hissing and snapping in the glass container, shocked Wendy into recognizing how dangerous he might indeed be for her. She could be left with primitive, cold-blooded hostility at the end of such a relationship at the office. It was contained for now, safe behind glass, but as the dream says, Wendy had to give it back or handle it somehow.

Just as a snake in real life should not be confined in a glass cage but should be in a freer, wilder environment, so, too, it was unlikely that their relationship—given his qualities—could flourish when they both worked in the glass cage of the same quiet, conventional workplace.

The dream also warned Wendy that he stirred up tremendous fears in her unconscious. She knew immediately that this was not just his dark side, but her own deeply repressed side that she projected onto him: her own snake—her raw instinct, her own unconscious powers that she kept behind glass. Glass represents intellectual distance behind which one is safe from emotional impact. Wendy saw her own primitive, raw power to be cruel or even deadly.

In the image of the dried-up seashell creature which Wendy hadn't watered, the dream warned that, in the relationship, she could neglect her own introverted sense of safety. What should she do? Instead of an extraverted approach—entering a relationship that was likely to founder and then working on the problem of the snake between them in an outer way, Wendy chose instead to return to analysis and work on the snake problem there. She was attracted to his snake because she didn't know her own snake—her own sociopathic side—that could eventually know how to contend with his. Instead of trying to get in touch with her own deep instinctual nature through another person, then, which would have probably wreaked havoc with her outer life, Wendy chose instead to work it out in the inner realm.

This was the ethical imperative of the dream: "I ought to give them [the creatures] back or do something with them." And Wendy did tend her undersea creatures. She worked deeply on her dreams and on her relationship to her analyst in the ensuing years to become more aware of her own spontaneity and warmth as well as her own aggressiveness. This eventually yielded in her life some of the warmth and excitement that she had sought, a doomed prospect when she had sought it only through others.

## Knowing Your Aggressive Instincts

Times of transition and turmoil can be opportunities for insight and growth in inner and outer life. Dreams can be crucial at these times to show us what is happening in the unconscious. In this case, a dream helped a woman become aware of new ways for handling very primitive aggression so that she could avoid either being trapped herself as a victim during the termination of her old relationship, or—without being aware of it—being the one who trapped someone else in her new relationship.

> ***The Spider and the Web.*** **A fly is caught in a spider's web. It's a big fly that had been buzzing all over in the laundry room. It flew into the web, struggled, so entangled it got stuck. I watch a huge black spider creeping up to the fly.**

This dreamer, Maria, had been slow to defend herself during divorce proceedings, just as she had been during an emotionally abusive marriage. During the week of the dream, she had finally gotten angry, outraged, in fact, at her husband's latest deceptive proposal for a settlement and the fact that it was accompanied by threats of harassment if he didn't get his way. Maria was persistent enough to manage to see her busy lawyer immediately—not an easy task because the woman lawyer was the most aggressive one she could find! The lawyer had been teaching Maria how to be appropriately aggressive: to bargain and take initiative on her own behalf to counter her husband's plots, and gave her good advice on handling the latest threats.

At first look, it would seem that the dream recounts the story of the abusive marriage and divorce proceedings: Maria's being trapped as a victim in the web of her husband's aggressive designs. The dream would then express Maria's fear that the more she struggles, the more she will get stuck. And this was a true fear of hers, based on past experience. The dream points out the terrible helplessness when you face raw aggression that cannot be escaped.

However, dreams usually carry more meanings than the obvious one. Dreams about animals, especially, herald changes. A woman is getting in touch with basic instincts that she's ready to make more conscious. What had shifted recently in the dreamer's instincts? Instead of reacting with more helplessness the previous week, Maria had become more aggressive. She thought this dream might express her newly found aggression and vengeance. *She* was the spider turning the tables on her husband. To counter a spider, a woman must know her own spider. Maria had found a culturally acceptable way to do this, through her lawyer who could be an aggressive plotter, who passed on her skills to her client.

Shifting from one raw instinct to another, turning the tables, still leaves a person in the realm of raw instincts and caught in the same old polarity of aggression-victimization. It is noteworthy that in the dream Maria still largely identifies with the fly caught in the web. But what does she do with her compassion for the victim? That is what often keeps a woman from turning on her aggressor no matter how abused she is. She is afraid of harming the other person. She identifies with the other not just as an aggressor but also as a victim. Maria said, "He would be so helpless without me."

When you get out from under aggression, then you are faced with another set of problems: differentiating your own aggression without merely imitating your victimizer; and differentiating your compassion for a victim. Victims are not totally helpless; they do have a range of options with degrees of helplessness and strength.

Maria laid this problem to rest by reminding herself that her husband had a lawyer, too: Each would work within society's bounds and not as primitive insects. The legal system, with its procedures and regulations to contain the adversaries, provided an appropriate framework.

Since animal dreams are important, and this dream was so primitive, the analyst asked if there might be an additional meaning. Was there some other kind of plotting or possibility of being caught in a plot? The dream was especially concerned with the victim. Since Maria didn't have to worry about the participants in the legal proceedings, was she worried about a victim in some other part of her life? Maria had been separated for many years and was hoping to marry the man she had been living with. That week, however, he had shown some reluctance about moving ahead with their plans. In fact, he had pulled away that week, leaving her depressed. As Maria explored how she had reacted to his withdrawal, and honestly faced what was happening in her current relationship, she found the victim—and the most profound meaning of the dream's warning about a spider and a web.

Deep in her unconscious, Maria was plotting "to catch him," and she was rightly concerned about it: She'd been hoping, unconsciously, to become pregnant. The dream woke her up to the fact that she did not want to do that. They did want children someday, but she did not want to trap him like that! Or trap herself. Maria decided to use contraceptives, allowing them to find their own pace in weaving their lives and plans together, neither of them as a predator or a victim.

## Trusting One's Deepest Feelings

In the first passion of relationship, if we listen to our deepest feelings they can be true guides for us. In the close and intense atmosphere of a weekend conference, a woman found herself swept into an affair even though both she and the man were married. The next morning she woke with the following dream.

*The Giant, the Cauldron, and the Snakes.* Sticky black snakes are coiled around each other.

My mother, a child, and I are on a path. We come upon a woman brewing something in a cauldron outdoors: a slice of soft petrified wood with designs on it. She stirs it around and around to make medicine. Then we see two snakes in the pot with designs on them like copperheads or water moccasins. The child goes up to look, but I pull her face back from the pot; the snake, who looks asleep, has become almost white by now, but not quite harmless yet.

Back on the path, we look down into a valley and see a dirigible in the air, with a rope dropped to the valley below. Over at the side of the canyon a wooden arm swings out every so often in a mechanical motion. The wooden arm hits against a wooden brace on the rock canyon wall that makes it bounce back. It finally breaks the wooden brace and hits the rock. Suddenly, down in the valley, the straw inside a hut bursts into flame, and a family sprawls out of it.

A young man, a giant, comes up beside us. He immediately takes charge and lets out an enormous stream of unending urine and sprays all the burning straw until all is well. The young man and I talk closely. I said I'd been interested in someone else for a while, but he wants to be back with me.

THE GIANT. The dreamer knew deep in her heart when she woke up that the giant in the dream did the right thing (spraying urine) and that she and her lover needed to "put out the fire" of their relationship. The huge inflated dirigible—their great hopes, their high-sailing feelings when together, their vast liking of each other—could only end in harm to their families (the hut bursting into flames and the family sprawling out of it in the dream).

A giant in dreams, as in fairy tales, represents larger-than-life feelings or thoughts that are overblown because they are unconscious. Thus, in fairy tales, the hero or heroine needs to trick the giant, keep an eye on it, vanquish it, or get its cooperation. You need to have the giant do good work for you, instead of letting it fall into trouble by itself or letting it wreak havoc on its own. Giants can be dumb, impulsive, or temperamental like the unconscious. But giants also have pure feelings and simple straightforward solutions, like the unconscious does. They can be destructive or benevolent. In this case, the giant is helpful by unself-consciously putting out the fire with his enormous stream of urine.

Urinating in dreams usually refers to letting out pure feelings. One finally "relieves oneself" and it feels good. An interesting distinction can be made: defecating in a dream has a somewhat different meaning. It often refers to anger, blaming, or feeling guilty. Defecating itself is getting rid of something smelly, and it is a more conscious act that takes effort, so it naturally evokes feelings of pride, shame, or disgust. It has more of society's prohibitions against it, so in a dream one is often left besmirched or smearing others, as the case may be. Sometimes, though, it can have a positive meaning: finally getting rid of one's own anger or society's prohibitions.

In the dream, then, the giant, with his pure feelings, led the way, so the woman could wake up with the thought that such a flow of clear feelings could "put out the fire." The experience in the dream had shifted something inside her. She could know the fullness of her feelings yet also an acceptance, in a "just so" way, of the realities of their life situation. She found herself the next morning able to refrain from fanning the flames of their passion. Instead, she "relieved herself" by freely talking about her pure feelings for him, without awkwardness or guilt. Fortunately, he responded in kind, and they could quietly be together with their sense of mutual treasuring of what they meant to each other in their inner worlds, their knowledge of the heart, now that they had settled their resolves for the future. Those moments of having quietly known their feelings together so fully—without acting on them—proved sustaining through time. They knew what they meant to each other. If you know something well, if you see what the treasure is in your hands, sometimes you can give it up and still have it—inside, at least. But if it remains lost in the mists, you must reach for it endlessly.

In contrast to this ending, most affairs end in a desert land of awkwardness, denial, and true—or false—promises about continuing the relationship somehow. That is, feelings are left scattered about like the sheets on a rumpled bed. For if you cannot be true to your feelings, if you cannot acknowledge what happened (or didn't), if you can't respect what is or could be, if you don't acknowledge the tug of the dirigible sailing by, then you are left with disquiet: raw, torn-apart, half-expressed feelings. Not having known or accepted the pure flow of feeling within yourself or with your partner, you are left with unsettled, unrequited love or resentment. You avoid each other or else compulsively push to get together and prove "it" true. The true quality of the feelings are never expressed, never truly known, and they should be acknowledged.

For passion is rarely a small matter for a woman, although she may fool herself or become inured to its power or its misuse.

Her lion can be put in a cage, but it will always be restive; and it is worth treasuring—as is any moment of great beauty—when it moves freely, even though fleetingly, before it melts back into the underbrush.

THE CAULDRON AND THE SNAKES. What do the cauldron and the snakes at the beginning of the dream mean? The dreamer's conclusions about the whole dream only came after finding the meaning of these two images. But first, an important clue lay in a strange detail—the wooden arm—referring to a sexual incident in her childhood, which had left her feeling guilty, in a superstitious way—as if she shouldn't be entitled to her own sexuality in life. The unconscious part of the psyche is prone to superstitious fears, as seen in the fateful bargains, curses, and redemptions in fairy tales. Because of its superstitious quality, this kind of guilt can require archetypal healing. In this dream, the means of redeeming her forbidden sexuality was archetypal brewing in a fitting vessel: the cauldron.

In modern times the cauldron usually conjures up a vision of the three witches in *Macbeth* brewing evil: "Double, double, toil and trouble; / Fire burn, and cauldron bubble" (Act 4, Scene 1). But this is a diabolization of the feminine symbol of transformation, healing, and the nurturance of life. The Triple Goddess, the Three Fates, the Muses presided over this symbol of woman and the womb of life, this vessel of creation, continuously bubbling like the mysterious, ever-changing processes of life and death. This is the way of nature: incubation and change. This is the way of the unconscious: the slow distillation of feeling, the simmering of ideas, the brewing of dark thoughts, the waiting for inspiration.

Like our own mother's pot of soup (or coffee) on the stove, the cauldron was at the center of the hearth from earliest civilization. It was a sign of woman's caring and craft: cooking tough roots, washing clothes, boiling soap, and brewing medicine. As the sacred vessel of early priestesses for transformation—healing, trance-states, and blood rites—it was the original alchemical vessel, the lost Chalice, the communion cup of blood and wine. Although the cauldron symbolized life—and the continuity of life and death—for thousands of years throughout the world, it lost that meaning, and came to be remembered only as an evil receptacle for omens and sacrifice found in remnants of later cauldron cults of death and rebirth, and in our projections onto witches.

However, the psyche knows about nature and rediscovers old truths. The dreamer didn't know about the cauldron as a positive symbol, yet it came up fresh from her unconscious as benevolent witchcraft or shamanism: a woman brewing petrified wood into medicine, and transforming poisonous snakes into harmless ones.

The image "sticky black snakes coiled around each other," indistinguishable from one another, suggests an early symbiotic relationship with the mother, which can be wonderful but also terrible. The terrible part requires human alertness and sometimes special neutralization of toxicity. The dream, then, starts with the dreamer's entangled relationship with her mother and her desire to remain a child. Evidently her early entanglement with her mother is reverberating deep in her unconscious at this time, stirred up by her intense attraction to her lover and their sexual entanglement. However, you will notice that in the dream she also acts like an adult to warn the small child who goes up to look in the pot. That is, she is now more alert to misplaced innocence! Like the earliest priestesses who handled the awesome power of snakes, so, too, she must know snakes, and not be compelled forward in unconscious fascination, rush to unite with her lover's snake. She must wait. The inner processes—upheaval and change in symbiotic and sexual matters—take time. The snakes must undergo alchemical transformation to become white, symbolic of their deeper purpose of healing and wisdom.

When passion and instincts suddenly interrupt the ordinary pattern of life, a woman is shaken to her roots and it changes her afterward. The fire of sexuality had to be contained in this particular situation, yet this allowed deep inner changes. The snakes and cauldron in the dream meant a stirring of great energy in her nucleus, and prophesied that she herself would be changed in the vessel of life. Her sexuality was awakened, changed, and channelled so that she could have a transformation of feeling. Then, as depicted in the dream, she could have a perspective from the top of a canyon: a transcendent view but also a clearer vision of what was important in her life.

CULTURAL PROJECTIONS. At the beginning and ending of relationship, the time when we have great anticipations and disappointments, we are likely to find cultural projections: images unconsciously placed on women or men as a group. These are pictured in our dreams and give us a fresh look at the old half-truths or whole-cloth fabrications that have been accepted by the majority culture. Understanding of these projections frees an individual woman to pursue her relationship without, at least, the *unnecessary* complication of these projections remaining unconscious to pursue her. A woman has enough to do taking care of her own real problems in relationship without also taking on society's projections onto her, especially regarding things she can't do anything about.

A young woman, Robin, had the following dream which revealed one of these societal projections that she unconsciously carried.

> *Cat and Mouse.* I'm in a big Army barracks. It's a depressing, olive-drab building. I'm on an important mission when I see a cat and a female mouse. It's a big orange cat with no tail. I screamed when I saw it. It was creepy or frightening, and unnatural.

This dream came in the aftermath of a divorce, underscoring the fact that Robin's "important mission" was to get out of that relationship, just as in the dream the female mouse needed to escape. Now that Robin was safe, her feelings tumbled forth about how bad the marriage had been. Mainly, she felt relieved, but she also felt depressed.

The dream pictured a "depressing, olive-drab building." Why was she depressed? As Robin thought about the dream and her situation, it became clear that she now felt guilty and was haunted by the half-conscious thought that "a woman should make sure men feel all right." Robin had generally been warm-hearted and attentive to others in her life; however, in the divorce proceedings she had concentrated on her own needs and had been assertive and firm about a fair settlement.

More precisely, the problem was this: Robin's usual motherliness and more recent assertiveness were both instinctual and only partly conscious. The dream seemed to indicate she needed to become more conscious and selective about her instinctually helpful impulses or she'd end up a mouse. Had her new assertive instincts been right? Looking at her assertiveness by the light of day, she realized that it had been appropriate. At this point, it was important for her to protect herself and not extend herself any longer to her husband who couldn't reciprocate.

As in other dreams, the setting was a clue to the dream's meaning. The "olive-drab Army barracks" was obviously a male world, not her own, where she saw a cat that had been castrated (its tail cut off). It seemed such a terrible thing to Robin that she had woken up screaming out loud. Robin's association to the Army barracks suggested to her that castration anxiety might be an issue for *men* and concerned their own hierarchical standing among other men. Robin had been feeling guilty that the divorce would make her husband ashamed among other men at his "macho" work setting. The dream helped her realize that it was his own castration anxiety in his own world. It was not her doing. Robin knew that she had not wanted "to do him in." She might have had some unconscious anger and vengeance, but her main motive had been to escape.

The main idea that came out of this dream, useful for other women, is that we needn't necessarily take on men's concerns and projections about castration anxiety. Castration is not a woman's problem. Even though we are accused of wanting to castrate men whenever we are angry, assert ourselves, or demand fairness, we aren't usually seeking to castrate men—deprive them of their basic *instinctual* rights as men. Unless a woman is very angry and overbearing, the more likely truth is that she mainly wants to have ordinary rights as a person herself.

A man's concern about his standing among men is basically an issue with other men, not necessarily an issue with his woman partner, unless she is too casual about it, needlessly insensitive about placing him in a position where he'd lose some pride or feel ashamed in public among other men. Similarly, a man's concern about whether his penis is big enough for a woman is basically his own concern about performance and measuring up against other men, even though he may *think* it's very important to a woman. This is another instance of a man's "blaming the woman" instead of confronting his own feelings of vulnerability. In the male world of orderly relations, a man needs to know where he stands in hierarchical competition, aggression, and sexual assertion. He might act out the problem of his position among men by dominating "his woman" or seeking her reassurance, but ultimately he has to handle the problem himself with other men. The dream underscored this by showing Robin that empathizing too much with her ex-husband was distracting her from her own mission.

## Anima Projections onto Women

In relating to a man, a pervasive but subtle problem for a woman is a man's projection of his own feminine side, his inner image of a woman—the "anima"—onto her. A woman is sensing this projection when she thinks, "Even though he loves me, he doesn't love *me*—he doesn't know who I really am!"

Sooner or later in a relationship with a man, a woman must confront a man's anima image because it does, indeed, present quite a dilemma for her. She must find a way to respect his inner vision as something vital to him, and at the same time she must be authentic and find where she fits as a real person. For, by unconsciously colluding with his image, she diminishes or inflates herself.

When in love, a woman is responsive to a man and attuned to his innermost desires. She is quite naturally drawn to mirror back to him what qualities he wants to see in her, as he, in turn, often mirrors back her image of the masculine—the "animus." However, if a woman more consciously understands the anima projection, she is in a better position to retain her individuality and bring forth her true feminine nature rather than rely too much on his inner vision of her and her femininity.

When a woman is of great interest to a man she may inspire him to seek the elusive, enchanting anima in his inner world, or may spur him to try to know her as a real woman in his outer world. Only through an actual woman, however, can a man touch the actual differentness that is beyond what is in his imagination, can he affirm who he is as a man and who she is, and affirm their commonality as persons, too. Pursuing his own anima is important but is not enough. If he is fortunate, he can truly know the other in moments of transcendence: in love, in sexual union, in parenthood, and in the gradual process of aging together. During this process, his anima develops beyond an inner figure of sexual fantasy or naive romanticism to become his guide to feelings, relatedness, creativity, spirituality, wisdom, or whatever his feminine side represents, to complete him as a person. In rare instances, a man can become truly rounded in his inner world, as can be seen in the shaman's androgynous face.

A fundamental difference in male and female psychology helps us understand the place of the anima. A traditional man is usually so strongly identified with consciousness that the anima sometimes comes to represent the unconscious. That is, much that isn't conscious thought is seen as "feminine"—an impossible expectation indeed for an anima figure or an actual woman. Men have a fundamental need to be conscious, to be different, not to identify too closely with their mothers. So a man needs to affirm this differentness before he can feel much "sameness." Then he must feel sameness with other men, a man among men, before he can afford to relate to a woman. He relates to a woman, at first, as someone different before he finds their similarities. That is, he tends to see a woman before he sees a person.

On the other hand, women don't have such a fundamental need to identify with consciousness, to be different from their mothers; thus they can feel sameness first, can see a man as a person first, then someone who's different. Furthermore, since a woman is freer to retain some identification with the mother and the unconscious, her animus doesn't have to carry such a load, to represent all the unconscious. Nor, as traditional Jungian psychology would lead one to expect, is the animus a counterpart or mirror image of the anima in men. Sometimes there are various animus figures, and they don't necessarily represent the unconscious or consciousness either. Often they refer to "the other," qualities different from a particular woman's conscious attitude, often qualities seen as male ones in the culture, and these figures take their place, not necessarily the most prominent, among other important inner characters in her unconscious.

Turning, now, to the woman's dilemma: The usual way she experiences a man's anima projection is that she feels excited as she catches his eye and enlivened as she meets him at his depths. But then she begins to feel inadequate in comparison to his image of who she should be, or she feels restricted to a certain role: sexual partner, comforter and listener, innocent child, intellectual companion, creative inspirational muse, or spiritual guide. Moreover, since a man's anima is greatly affected by his mother, a woman may sense that he sees her only as a housewife-mother who is always there, anticipating his desires, picking up after him or else confining, abandoning, or criticizing him.

In fact, a common difficulty that a woman finds in a man's thinking about her is his separation of sexual and mothering qualities, as if a woman has only one or the other quality, not both. Consequently, a man may think he requires these in two separate women—lover and wife. A woman chafes at such limited anima perceptions of her, such silent violence to her wholeness as a woman. Additionally, both these visions are male-centric, centered around what a man wants from a woman, as if she doesn't also have an independent existence outside his realm, a direction of her own. She is not the one slice of the pie that a man happens to want; she is the whole pie and it's hers!

Women often feel uneasy about movie and television images because they exaggerate and perpetuate the underlying anima images that men have, and, in fact, set them as standards for us to model. Why can't we be more like Marilyn Monroe? Lately, however, this intrigues both men and women anew, as we seek to uncover the real person underneath the image. Large numbers of women enjoy movies or television shows where the usual roles are reversed: *A Captain in Paradise, Some Like It Hot, All That Glitters, Tootsie*. Refreshing new images are emerging in movies where the usual anima type has other qualities, too: Goldie Hawn plays a scatterbrained, sexy young blonde who is also surprisingly tough, clever, motherly, and compassionate. Meryl Streep plays a cool, elusive woman who also reveals other complex qualities of a real-life woman's character.

Because anima images are by their nature part of a man's unconscious, the cultural unconscious, and the unconscious responsive chord in a woman, they are difficult to discern. Therefore, dreams, which directly tap the unconscious, can help a woman see the anima more clearly.

The following dream came to a woman, Lori, who had finally gotten fed up with the limited roles relegated to her by men—in her personal life, in her academic work, and even in the literature by male authors in the social sciences. As the token woman in her academic setting, her insights and resentment had mounted as she reached a sense of frustration and futility about trying to be cooperative.

There were two precipitating incidents before the dream. A few days before, Lori had read a major article by a male psychologist on women's relationships with men and had been disappointed in what she had found. Although the author considered himself feminist, his views seemed mistaken and disturbing to her, she said, as if he were appropriating the feminine viewpoint in a web of theory and words, as if the masculine could still dominate and subjugate women's experience by putting into words, or boxes, what can only be known through empathy and fellow-feeling. She felt bombarded with his words, as if for this man labels served as substitutes for actual feelings. They substituted for listening to women and being affected by them. Once again, unwittingly, a man was telling women how to relate to men from the male-centric view.

The next thing that happened was that Lori spent the evening, the evening just before the dream, with a male academician whom she had always seen as enlightened and sympathetic about women's issues. But in the course of the evening he burst forth with apparent fellow-feeling and empathy to tell her, "I know exactly how it feels as a woman—to walk home on a dark street at night. . . . I know exactly how it feels as a woman to have a baby; I've felt it in my own body."

He was a brawny man who hadn't undergone the lifetime of uneasiness and caution that Lori had known as a female, and he certainly hadn't known pregnancy and the actual throes of childbirth. It seemed to Lori that he didn't want to hear her experience; in his imagination, he knew! He wanted to *tell* her what a woman's experience was. Lori was outraged. He, in turn, seemed dismayed, then furious at her reaction. Later, she wondered what had happened. He had good intentions and couldn't understand why she wasn't grateful, but it seemed to her he had fashioned a new form of male arrogance.

Only *accurate* empathy feels good to another person, and it requires a receptive, not a dominant, attitude. It is no comfort to another person to hear "I know how bad you feel" unless it comes from someone who's had the same experience or who admits it is only a similar experience.

As men, along with women, move into the arena of emotional responsiveness and deep communication and try to learn the language of the inner world and feelings, women feel pressured to name things that flow through our hands like water, and are only delicately caught, if at all. These things are best treasured in their own forms, known subjectively, acknowledged, and simply valued, or shared with quiet sensitivity. This is something most men need to learn. Emotions can't be pulled out of their more natural realm of personal and mutual experience to become objects: examined, judged, and intellectualized into sterile words. As if you could conquer water!

The issue, then, in this kind of misunderstanding is to find clarity and compassion. The fire of anger in the confrontation brought Lori some understanding about a man's unconscious anima in a dream that she had the next morning. Surprisingly, the dream also revealed to Lori another greater issue of her own.

*Hashish, the Moon, and the Mystery.* I'm in a foreign country. A local young man, who's attractive but disdainful, "puts the mark on me" because I happen to be near a hashish dealer. It's a case of mistaken identity. I think, "Oh no, this is what I was afraid of. What can I do? I have to remain alert!"

I go home on the bus and he gets off at the same place I do to walk home, just as I'd feared. I tell him,

"I don't have any hashish." But he doesn't want to believe me, and I'm afraid he'll do away with me. So I say, "I can show you I don't have any hashish on me: I could strip right here in the moonlight." But I think, "No, that's not necessary."

Instead, I have a plan. I engage him in conversation and tell him I'm interested in him. He might well believe me since he's a ladies' man for tourists, his ego inflated by women tourists eager for a man. I even engender some attraction and liking for him. My plan is to build his trust, then perhaps lead him to a spot where I can push him over a cliff or can somehow let him stumble over his own egotism.

The real problem, I see, is that he's only interested in the illusion, the hashish, and he would mistakenly take my life—the one thing I need—to possess his illusion. The only thing I do have in real life is access to the mystery. I'm not it—the mystery; I just carry it.

In this dream, Lori is sorting out how to relate to men's illusions, her feminine nature, and the feminine mysteries. In the dream she is afraid he might "do away with her." In real life, a woman often experiences this "being done away with" as being overlooked by a man, as if she isn't there, when she doesn't fit his inner picture, his anima. This is a repeated experience for a woman who is older or seen as unattractive. This can have a deadening effect on her, undermining her natural feelings of self-worth.

Returning to the dream, Lori can't produce what the man wants—the hashish. She doesn't have it, so, for survival, she pretends to be interested in sex; that is, she deliberately holds up to him the mirror of a handy anima image—the woman hungry for sex. It is no coincidence that the dream has a foreign setting. In actual foreign settings, men and women act out their fantasies. Anima (and animus) illusions exist in a faraway place, the unconscious. In fact, when people are on vacation in foreign settings and feel free to act out their fantasies, you can get glimpses of what is happening underground back home in everyday inner life. Vacations are an especially good time to notice your dreams because they are likely to be unusual and vivid.

The option Lori forgoes in the dream is to "strip," to reveal her true feminine in the light of the moon, in the soft light in which it can be seen. This might convince him that she doesn't have the hashish—she can't give him the illusion to which he is addicted—but instead show him her true self. However, to strip would have been risky, making Lori vulnerable, as in real life, where it might very well be misunderstood and dangerous to do. Perhaps, in the dream, she (the dream ego) should have taken the risk; it is hard to know. Maybe this inner feminine figure can't assert her own femininity enough, or perhaps she can't expose her innermost feminine self to someone she can't trust. For in the dream the man appears attractive but also disdainful. He represents Lori's experience of anima-possessed men. Of course, as is true of any dream figure, he is also a part of Lori—her own animus, her own "other side," that might scorn her true feminine self.

How did this dream relate, then, to the events of the previous evening? In real life, Lori, too, had stumbled on her pride, her hubris. Thus, she and the male academic had colluded and collided in their deadlock over his claim to know the experience of childbirth. In the dream, the only solution was that the disdainful man get rid of Lori or she get rid of him, which paralleled real life where the two people didn't want to see each other again. Lori's association to the dream was that the disdainful man "would kill the goose who lays the golden egg"! This association was a strange and intriguing one. It made her realize that, unconsciously, she was equating herself with being a Golden Goose, as if she, a real woman, were indeed sacred herself! So her outrage the night before had been that of a Sacred Goose: She was identifying with the power and mystery of childbirth, the Great Mother, and the golden egg—the Self. This was different from the genuine self-respect and pride of a woman; it was hubris, the pride of the gods. It was as if Lori had thought, "I'm sacred," instead of the more appropriate, "I'm not it—the mystery—I just carry it," as the dream said.

Thus the dreamer differentiated and truly valued her human

womanliness—knowing the physical experience and travail of carrying new life and giving birth—when she *was* near the divine without necessarily claiming it as her own. Claiming it was her hubris; and her outrage at him suggests that she was unconsciously projecting her hubris onto him, instead of experiencing rightful anger for his presumptuous knowledge of the physical burden, pain, and joy of real birth. Lori had no more dominion over the divine than he did over women's physical experience. Her special outrage, then, was that he stepped on sacred ground, which Lori had unconsciously reserved only for herself as if she were a goddess! The truth is that a man and a woman are equals in the realm of the spirit—when they stand in awe before the great mysteries of birth, death, and love.

## The Choice: To Sustain or End a Relationship

Sustaining a relationship is very hard work. The decision of whether to continue or end a relationship is very difficult. And the long process of ending a relationship is one of the hardest things in life to bear. We are little prepared for any of these. In this rough terrain of relationship, we are all pioneers—no matter how many years of analysis we have had, no matter how mature we are. We are up against tremendous forces and we know very little, really, about interpersonal relations. Much of the difficulty lies in the unconscious sphere, so our dreams, especially those about our instincts—with their special messengers, the animals— can help tell us what is happening.

### Helpful Instincts and Dream Animals

As noted in the first chapter, whenever an animal appears in a dream it brings an important message about our deep instinctual nature. Women have had to control impulses so much in adapting to society that we must return to our natural instincts to know ourselves. The problem is that when our instincts have been suppressed or neglected too long, they no longer come at our bidding: Even when we wish, we can no longer call them forth, nor can we stop them when they come unbidden and uncontrolled. Like the lion or the sloth, our animal nature suddenly takes over raw and wild and has to be tamed anew, this time hopefully retaining some of its necessary energy. Then, respecting our instinctive natures, we can become more truly human. In fairy tales, helpful animals—if treated with respect and kindness—help the heroine. So too in dreams our animals can be helpful if we pause to know them.

At the time of this dream, a woman's marriage was in serious trouble, and she had scheduled marriage counseling to see whether the marriage could be saved, or if not, if counseling could help them end it as well as they might. She was aware only of her heavy sadness until this dream told her how angry she and her husband had become.

> **Two Scorpions.** Two scorpions are trying to kill each other. It's as if they're under a spell of hostility, utterly intent on striking each other, rather than protecting themselves. They remind me of mechanical toys, which, once wound up and set in motion, must play it out until they wind down, as hostility finally does. They scurry around each other, circling, to kill or be killed. Each finally gets the other and they're both in the throes of death.

This dream dramatizes the fact that alongside sadness can also be very primitive destructiveness! Thinking of the scorpions' poisonous points, the dreamer said, "I have to admit that we're at the lowest point in our relationship. Underneath, I think, we must be under a 'spell of hostility' and can't stop ourselves from trying to destroy each other. It's very primitive—such destructive elements in nature—like scorpions. I think it's our ability to hurt each other very badly." People who know each other well, as couples do, know unconsciously just where it hurts and can strike out at each other—and strike back—instinctively, right to the mark.

The woman was reminded of her first marriage that had had a painful ending. She said, "Our last energies were put to hurting each other, not into self-preservation." She didn't want to do that again—remain in such a state of destructiveness. How could this be done? Mindful of her own scorpion and her husband's, she tried to avoid subtle stings of hostility. She took steps to de-escalate conflict. When she could, without undue hardship for herself or her husband, she got some respite for herself away from home. These helped them both while they waited for marriage counseling—a safe place to work on their problems.

When a relationship has been close and tender at one time, as it had been for this couple, there can be a great fall from the paradise of all the early hopes. But you can't stay in paradise forever. To indulge in one extreme, denying hard realities in life, inevitably brings about its turning into its opposite—in just as extreme a form. (The term that Jungians use for this is "enantio-dromia" [en-an'-tio-dro-mi'-a].) Thus, the natural consequence of your false sense of unremitting tenderness, trust, and well-being is the opposite—disillusionment, suspicion, hostility, and destructiveness.

As this marriage had progressed, they continued to deny their differences by focusing on the positive aspects of their marriage, as if it could be good if they tried hard, and it seemed to work for a long time. But finally all the irritations ignored too long, all their true vulnerability to great hurts accumulated and finally came back to haunt them.

As the woman thought about this dream, she remembered another animal from a dream a few nights before. This time it wasn't a deadly one but a goat—an animal which might help her!

**Goat on the Sofa.** I'm going to meet someone in order to go to Bianca, a fascinating inland town. But first I have to find a bathroom.

I go through a big impressive building with brass signs on the doors but no bathroom! The walls are made of beautiful marble—subtle greens and golds, semidark marble. There's a meeting of the Hospital Board with elegantly dressed men in waistcoats and women in felt hats. I notice a long line and ask, "Is this line for the bathroom?" They say, "No, it's to see the view from the skylight."

In the midst of the big room of elegant people is a white goat! A person is hitting the goat with a chair so the goat will show off to people and get up on a sofa. I tell the person that it's not necessary to hit her. Goats are smart, can't she see? I entice the goat up onto the sofa. She leaps up and I pet her neck. She wags her tail, makes a purring sound in her throat, smiles and laughs with me. The goats are part of the grounds. The woman says that they love to come in and be part of things. Then I finally find the bathroom and make a date to go to Bianca.

If you look back at this earlier dream in light of the subsequent scorpion dream, you can guess that things had become so deadly because the dreamer couldn't "find a bathroom," that is, she couldn't let out her negative feelings in the relationship, because of the marble walls of their civilized inhibitions and pretensions.

What such a relationship needed was the goat—the wayward spirit. As the woman said in the dream, "goats love to come in and be part of things." Indeed, goats are sociable by nature. In fact, the females seem symbolic to us of nurturance since they give milk, and the males are seen as pleasure-seeking and randy. The dream also demonstrates other qualities prominent in goats. They are freedom-loving and crafty; and they break free when they please. They lighten up the atmosphere with their devil-may-care attitude. Goats have a glint in their eye and they like to provoke. They're agile and can jump onto any precarious foothold just for fun and in order to stir up some excitement. They make us laugh. This is the positive side of the trickster.

If the trickster is suppressed too long, however, it can cause trouble. If your goat spirit is confined too much, it can easily be provoked. Then someone can "get your goat," make you nasty and ornery. It's better to let your goat run free now and then; it'll be mischievous and lighthearted, but will only cause a bit of trouble. This is quite different from the mechanical compulsiveness of the scorpions in the later dream.

This couple had fallen into an unremittingly heavy spirit. They'd forgotten how to laugh and let things move. It was probably too late, but what they needed was the goat spirit: to forget how it'd look and just let themselves jump up and down and yell, try absurd things, get into predicaments. It would help keep things fresh and enjoyable. And, if they were ever in the mood (which looked unlikely given the state of their relationship) they might take a chance to loosen up their affection and sexuality.

The idea that the woman got from the dream, then, was to let the wayward spirit out—shake things up, be a bit rowdy, get some perspective and humor. Perhaps she and her husband should appeal to the goat in each other, or they'd end up with only scorpion deadliness. There's no "nice" way to relate all the time. And this spirit did help some to alleviate unnecessary heaviness and hostility during the interim period before the final separation.

The next two dreams came from another woman, Jill, whose marriage was also shaky. Her dreams foretold a very different path from the previous woman's—a deep inner journey of her own. The first dream came just before her husband of many years, Ed, suddenly dropped the bombshell that he was moving out, and the dream gave her a course of action to take—to work on her own psyche.

This dream has interesting parallels to the Goat on the Sofa dream from the last woman: the need to go to the bathroom (let out feelings), difficulty in finding an adequate place, and the appearance of a helpful animal, in this case, a caterpillar, which first made her recoil in fear—at this very different part of herself.

Not all animals are seen as helpful at first. When an instinct is a shadowy side of ourselves or deep in the unconscious it may seem vaguely unsettling or frightening—just as a strange animal in nature, suddenly coming forth from the woods, would startle you. Yet an animal like this in a dream might have a special message for you, some deep wisdom about nature.

*The Caterpillar.* I'm with my husband, Ed, in the waiting room of our marital counselor. Ed goes and does warm-up exercises.

I go to the bathroom. It has old pink walls. I select a booth. I try to go, but nothing comes. I hear someone walk into the room and she sits down in a chair and reads. I'm upset at the lack of privacy.

A brown fuzzy caterpillar, pink with orange spots, crawls toward me to get on my arm. I scream. I want it to fall on the floor. I open my eyes. It's crawling toward me again.

As Jill talked about the caterpillar in the analytic consulting room, something "synchronistic" happened—a coincidence that was meaningful to her. A butterfly came fluttering in the office window. She looked up and saw it, and immediately she knew, intuitively, that she had to enter a dark, introverted "cocoon" phase herself and see what she would find. And this is what happened.

As the dream suggested, what Ed needed to do was "warm-ups"—learn how to be warmer to her. Jill had natural extraverted warmth but she had begun to feel as if her well had run dry after years of little return from him. According to his values, feelings and intimacy were superficial compared to what was important to him: the meeting of minds. This was important to Jill, too. In fact, originally she had been attracted to Ed—a very introverted man—because of his capacity for profound philosophy and spirituality. Through the years together, though, they had gradually become polarized, she in charge of warmth and sociability and he in charge of the intellect and inner truths.

This is a classic case of polarization, where each of you concentrates on your area of natural ability ("Why don't you do it, you do it so well") to the neglect of your less-developed ability, which is relegated to the other person. Consequently, each of you feels much more inferior in certain ways than is really true. You can see the truth of this when your partner is absent and you suddenly find yourself more capable in your partner's area of expertise. Ironically, the dynamic that originally drew you together as a couple—the attraction of opposite qualities—later becomes the issue that can push you apart. Each can feel one-sided, diminished, and cheated of the original promise—to learn each other's way. This is a problem you're most likely to encounter later in marriage, when gradually, through natural laziness, you have developed widening divisions of labor. The remedy is to do the hard work of developing the other side, even though you may feel awkward at first.

Being extraverted, Jill's natural inclination had always been to work things out in interaction, and they had both benefited from marriage counseling in the past, but she didn't sense it was the right thing to do at this time. Although in the dream Jill and Ed were "waiting to see a marriage counselor" this probably refers metaphorically to a later time of repairing and healing the marriage together. While they are waiting, the caterpillar comes. It must be dealt with first.

Although it looked initially frightening—Jill actually had been terrified in the dream—the caterpillar was moving inexorably toward her. She must accept the humble caterpillar—a creature who crawls into the cocoon of the unknown. She had to undergo her own inner journey and find the depth of spirit she had projected onto her husband—and emerge with more of her own butterfly. The butterfly is the universal symbol of natural development and change, symbol of innermost archetypal transformation, a symbol of the spiritual aspect of life that goes back to prehistoric times. This was the gift the Self promised her—if she'd start out as the caterpillar, which goes inevitably forward.

In the dream, Jill was upset about the lack of privacy, which suggested that she needed to be alone in order to let out her accumulated feelings and not be distracted by an intruder: her husband or even, at times, her analyst. In contrast to the previous dreamer who was proper and reserved, Jill was often outspoken, angry, and provocative with her husband. Her task, then, would be to go to her opposite pole—withdraw and contain herself.

Couples cannot afford to wound each other too much. They reach a point of no return. It becomes so painful to be near each other and they feel so hopeless that neither has the receptivity to register goodwill or any positive changes which might occur in the other. This is the time to separate: to de-escalate conflict, to lick wounds, to undergo self-examination. As Ed did, and as her dream suggested Jill should do, both must do their individual work.

Jill had to find her own most introverted feminine nature—go into the unknown cocoon and yield to her inner development. This meant that she had to go into her past and she also had to contend with her innermost figures in analytic work. Jill was frightened of the prospect, but she embarked on the journey, her dreams as her guide.

Couples who are deeply attuned to each other through the years are often "in synch" with each other in their inner timing. Evidently the time was ripe for Ed, too, because very shortly after this dream, they both decided to separate for a period of time, instead of trying to work things out together. Despite her fear of the caterpillar, the deepest unconscious, Jill found herself following the path this dream predicted. She found her direction, did the hard work of analysis, and made a retreat to the wilderness by herself. After a separation, they would come back together, each wiser, more accepting and appreciative of the other, for what would turn out to be a much more solid marriage.

As if to survey the course this inner work would take, two weeks after the last dream Jill had a dream where she was standing on a shoreline looking across the waters. She watched—with intense curiosity and fear—creatures of the sky and water, that is, images of her innermost thoughts and knowledge emerging from unconscious realms.

First, let us look at what birds and fish generally mean in dreams. Birds who fly in the air represent what is beyond conscious knowledge: autonomous thoughts that come to us in the form of creative inspirations or spiritual truths, hence the expression "a little bird told me," and hence the transformative significance of feathers and wings in fairy tales, myths, and religion. Birds in flight express the elation and excitement of our earliest creative thoughts or spiritual experiences, which suddenly and mysteriously appear, but, like birds, as suddenly fly away into the wind and disappear from consciousness, perhaps leaving us as untouched and unenlightened as we were before the experience. Birds, then, are messengers of new beginnings, and promise to guide us—if we are earnest like this dreamer—toward further development and more solid realization over time.

More remote from conscious knowledge are fish, which represent the movement of life, very primitive or very wise, deep down in the waters of our unconscious. The monstrous fish in this dream required the dreamer to do some powerful work at the bottom of the ocean in the ensuing months.

> **The Spectacular Swan and the Dinosaur-Fish.** I'm standing on the shoreline with a group of people. I look across the water and spot a bird cruising over the top of the water. It has a long neck. It's black, white, and gray. I wonder, "What kind of bird is it?" A *swan*! I watch it fly. Fascinated. In a whirl of feathers it turns upside-down. What an acrobat!
>
> I use my binoculars to see it close up. Something's swimming under the water; I see a shadow. It's huge, with fins. It has a silent, huge head. I wonder what it is. Others say it's a whale. I say, "No, it isn't. It's something bad." I look again. It's a dinosaur. I see it diving. It's dangerous. Down the shoreline some fish come to the surface and people say they're big, but not dangerous. I say, "No, those aren't like the one I saw—the shadow underneath. That was a dinosaur-fish."

Jill greatly admired swans. "When swimming they're stately, and when flying they're spectacular," she said. From her further associations, it emerged that the swan in the dream with its grand flight and acrobatics represented to her the convolutions of intricate, sophisticated thinking, and the soaring of truly mercurial, spiritual thought. She recalled that from childhood she had admired her father's intuitive thinking and his spiritual outlook, as she later admired similar "swanlike" qualities in her husband, Ed. Unconsciously, she felt that if she could be close to those who had these qualities, through identifying with them, somehow she would have these qualities, too, and she would be transformed.

Jill had fallen into an enchantment. This is echoed by her dream image of the swan—the great, regal bird of enchanted maiden-love and transformation. While Jill greatly admired Ed's qualities, they paled compared to the specialness she had known with her father. In any case, Ed didn't discuss things with her any more. They had polarized into opposite positions: He readily became exasperated with her for not matching him in deep conversation, making her feel "dumb," until she had finally given up making any effort even to discuss topics in which she was interested and well informed. She was left wistfully recalling earlier times basking in the golden glow of listening to her father. In this state of mind, you are content to admire the swan, rather than try your own wings.

As Jill contemplated this dream, the story of the Ugly Duckling came to her mind—one of her favorite stories from childhood. When a story has its origins in your early history and feels special to you, its theme may well play a central role in your life. Although Jill knew that she was intelligent, having done very well in school and in her profession, somehow she had always felt "dumb" compared to others and especially liked the story because "the underdog ends up good." This promises well—that she may yet find her own swan.

Most stories, especially those featuring animals, have a dark side as well as a light one. The dreamer considered swans "too perfect and stultifying." How might this pertain to her own shadow? The dignified, noble bearing of swans, as if they're serenely "beyond it all," was echoed in her subtle air of superiority as she described her admiration for her father—with whom she identified—in his grand flights of fancy and eloquent thought. The "upside-down" side of the swan is its viciousness. She said, "Swans are nasty and possessive." If you look at the dream, you can see that this is represented by the frightening big fish, the shadowy counterpart to the swan in the depths of the ocean: her own primitive, negative thoughts.

What Jill had to do was to get to know this big-headed,

amorphous monster, which represents undeveloped thinking and primitive impulses. It also suggests the devouring parent. The cost of basking in the sun, admiring your father's or husband's golden glow, is to feel helpless and envious. Jill had to develop her own inner depth in analysis and in her retreat during the separation. She had to give up her projections onto her father and husband as those who held the powerful secret of the swan. She had to separate from her father and the storybook world, and know her own deep-swimming fish, search for her own primitive self and her own soul. Eventually, because Jill was willing to give up her special status as an enchanted daughter, and because she and her husband could stop their polarization, they got their marriage back on a better footing.

# 6
# Sex: The Other Half of the Garden

Sex means many things to many women. It can be vitally important or incidental. Anticipation of sex can bring warmth, calm, excitement, dread, reluctance, indifference. Sometimes sex is mechanical, sometimes artfully playful, sometimes lusty and passionate. The stimulation can be expert and the orgasm perfect, or the experience can be awkward, painful, frustrating, and problematic. It can be emotionally barren, or the expression of deep love and the communion of souls.

For some women, sex brings up memories of intimacy and mutuality; for others, memories of being used—unwilling submission to an acquaintance or partner, violation by a molester, humiliation or brutality from a rapist.

Some women fantasize during sex with a partner or without one; some don't fantasize at all. Fantasies that satisfy a woman tend to be safe, but have an element of the unknown. They are sometimes surprisingly different from women's more conscious personal and cultural thoughts about what they'd actually countenance in real life. Fantasies can be ethereal and romantic or frankly erotic; coarse or sublimely poetic; proud or shameful; controlling or submissive; with a man or with a woman. Some people can only imagine sex with a stranger in an exotic setting; some, only with the loved one at home. Sometimes a fantasy is an abstract image; sometimes it is formless, more a mood or a feeling state than an image. In any case, fantasies sometimes reveal various unconscious feelings underlying our sexuality.

The unconscious is partly responsible for our feeling strongly drawn to someone, especially when the attraction is compelling and surprising to ourselves and our friends. Often we are attracted to someone with qualities opposite our own: dark, shadowy characteristics we fear, or positive ones we admire—extraversion or introversion, thinking or feeling.

Sex combines the apparent opposites of the animal and the human, the sacred and the ordinary, selfishness and sharing, tenderness and lust, assertion and yielding, and various kinds of sameness and differentness within ourselves and between partners. In coming together with another person, we can have the numinous experience of transcending the archetypal opposites: conscious and unconscious, union and separateness, male and female. And especially for women, who know we can carry life in us, sex contains the mystery of the life-giving force, the archetype of the Great Mother.

## Nature, Natural Rhythms, and Sexuality

Women's sexuality has been so defined by others—adolescent and parental cultures, men through the centuries, male theologians, writers, and psychological theorists who have not known women's own experience—that we must start afresh with our own experience and even look back at nature itself to see what the fullness of our sexuality might be.

When we are close to nature—vacationing, gardening, walking outdoors, or even looking outside in a free moment—we tend to relax, find our own pace, and feel a sense of being in accord with the world, just as we can find our own pace in our bodies, the grace of our own movements, our sexuality, when we are comfortable in ourselves, close to our own nature. We can tune in to the waxing and waning of our own energy and emotions so that we can be in a mood true to ourselves, not pretending to feel as we *should* feel but being as we are, and not pretending to fit with our partner as we might wish, but being true to the changing patterns of our coming together and drawing apart. When we are attuned to nature, where everything appears a little arrhythmic, a little random, where there are no technologically formed straight lines, we are able to assimilate small differences and transcend them to find a greater underlying sense of rhythm and unity within ourselves and with our partner.

In our culture, however, we seem to have lost our heritage of being in touch with nature. In early times, women were deeply respectful of nature and proud of their womanly bodies. Close to the forces of the earth, early women and their oracles could dip into a reservoir of unconscious knowledge. In those ancient goddess cultures, women looked to dreams and ritual for knowledge and healing. Today we, too, can turn to our dreams, our unconscious, for guidance. And through trusting our experiences of sensuality and sexuality we can restore our sense of earthiness, some of the instinctual wisdom we once had. Not surprisingly, sometimes animals come to women in their dreams to help us know again our basic, sexual instincts under our layers of civilization, cultural attitudes, and standards.

Nature, and our nature, isn't unremitting harmony, nor is it chaos and destructiveness: It is the movement of all living things, the ebb and flow of tides, the constancy and changes in sun, stars, and wind. If we go to the depths of our nature, we find ourselves following an underground river that is often quiet, but sometimes turbulent, and always changing. Isis, the Egyptian moon goddess, is a symbol of the archetypal feminine that we can use as a guide in our look into the depths of our instinctive nature and sexuality. Isis shakes a musical rattle, a sistrum, a hollow ball containing the four elements of earth, air, fire, and water. Isis and her sistrum were believed responsible for turbulence, the movement of nature.

Just as in nature we find the natural flooding of the Nile and the wild, ravaging forest fire, we find unexpected discord in relationships or in sexuality. We are not machines that can produce perfect orgasms every time. And just as the sludge of the Nile is cleaned out by floodwaters every so often, and the thick underbrush of the forest is cleared out by forest fires, so, too, relationships and sex need uncertainty and upheaval now and then. When a relationship becomes stagnant, when sex becomes boring, we should remember Isis. When we find ourselves feeling distant from our partner, distant from our instincts, irritable, discontent underneath, and when frustration dams up the flow of feeling, Isis reminds us of the rules of Nature. Then Isis must shake her rattle!

When we're feeling stagnant, we need to shake loose the sludge of our dark thoughts—that we don't really care or that our partner doesn't care. When we feel unresponsive sexually, we need to scrape out the riverbanks to the deeper layers of our fears, our discontents, where we're cut off from our real feelings and our closeness, sensuality, and sexuality.

Women's monthly cycle, with its natural rhythm of emotions, helps us stay in touch with unconscious feelings we might not otherwise know. When we let go that flood—that outburst of crying, the fire of anger—then we know our darkest thoughts and our real wishes, too. Afterward, surprisingly, we often feel a surge of power and sexual energy. Then we are our old selves again, and restored to our partner—after the partner recovers from the deluge and the fire of the dragon.

The moon goddess Isis and the moon itself remind us that in nature and in ourselves there are cycles and rhythms. Good relations, good sex is not always in the ascendancy. We cannot impose our will on nature: how we want our body to react, how we want another person to be. The process of life follows the wisdom of Isis, of things as they are and as they become. It is the wisdom of following our deeper instincts and the deeper course of nature.

## Sexual Issues in Women's Dreams

Current women's dreams show concern about a great variety of sexual issues. A substantial portion of the dreams have their origins in childhood experiences, and try to resolve anxiety and conflicts stemming from traumatic and confusing incidents. A few dreams in this chapter refer back to early issues, such as a molestation, or parental attitudes toward sex, especially repressive attitudes, but the main focus will be on sexual issues in adult life, the central question being: What keeps women from the fullness of their sexuality?

When working with your dreams, it is important to be alert to current themes that overlay old ones. Even dreams specifically about early sexuality—which usually indicate that your libido or energy is still ensnared in old history and needs to be worked through—are usually pointing out your reawakened hopes of filling in a gap in your current adult life. For instance, some dreams allude to women's early or later teen years, the time of quiet budding—or exploding with agitation and excitement—into emotional passion, sexuality, and womanhood. These dreams often recapture what was important or amiss in girls' lives at that time: Some were dormant sexually, and dormant as individuals, as yet, sleepwalking dutifully through the steps set before them by parents or school. Some burst with energy, emotion, and passion, and searched for a place to put it: great interest in clothes, passion for sports as a young tomboy, a crush on a boy, another girl, a horse, or a rock star, dedication to a life of poetry, medicine, religious service or public service, demonstrating for a cause. In their teen years some girls fall deeply in love for the first time. Women often go back, in their dreams, to such early times, to see not only who they were then, but who they can be in their current lives—when they have another opportunity to recapture their original promise.

Women who have followed the traditional route of home-school-marriage-children-outside work-grandchildren may look back to the one time when they were free and independent and life was full of promise. Perhaps they had summer jobs and money of their own and there seemed to be a world of choices before them. These women in middle or later life may want to find again certain passions and strengths once important to them that were lost through the years—the vigor and tonus of their bodies as lithe teenagers, the intensity of their first loves, their spiritual awakening, their exploration of the world outside the home with freedom and confidence. These desires may be symbolized in their dreams.

Similarly, women who have pursued less traditional routes in their lives (e.g., home-school-career or marriage-and-divorce) that leave them single in midlife have the opposite problem. They may have freedom and confidence in the world outside their home, but look back to the early days when they thought they could "have it all": security, relationship, children, and work. They may wonder: Where is the companionship they could cherish now. Where did all the hopes for romance go?

It is especially difficult for any woman, no matter what her choice of lifestyle, to "have it all," especially the fulfillment in relationship and sexuality of which she is capable. Yet, despite the realistic barriers, we try to fill those important gaps in our life, and our dreams sometimes show us the way. From the broad array of sexual issues that emerge from women's dreams, a few have been selected to highlight what affects women's sexuality and what the nature of feminine sexuality is. For example, some dreams depict cultural attitudes toward women's breasts, in which dreamers try to reclaim the erotic and nurturing part of their bodies as their own, and other dreams feature those things that inhibit or diminish the full expression of sexuality, such as problems of addiction and conflicts about assertiveness. The last section has dreams that, the dreamers felt, touched the core of their feminine sexuality. One woman, in her dreams, tried to combine two passions that had been separated in her upbringing—sexuality and spirituality. In the final dreams, women reveal their deep need for privacy, tenderness, and spontaneity in love-making.

Women's dreams of sexuality range from the erotic to the mystical and encompass myriad concerns and desires. Among all these, dreams about women's breasts appear fairly frequently; they are part of women's own sexual heritage and they express deeply feminine principles. Since women at large are seen as sex objects, a woman must work through cultural attitudes toward her breasts—and her body in general—because they are omni-present issues in her everyday life, which ultimately can also affect her intimate personal life and her self-image as a sexual being.

## Our Womanly Breasts

Women have been so bombarded with how our breasts look to others that we sometimes forget what they mean to us—that they are erotic and nurturing, whether large or small. Our breasts can be a source of erotic pleasure for women. Some women can have orgasms by breast stimulation alone, and some mothers find breast-feeding a very erotic experience. And, symbolic of our deep feminine nature, we all know that from our breasts can come the mysterious flow of life-giving nourishment for babies.

Because our breasts look erotic and beautiful to others, they have become *objects* for others, judged by certain standards, and sometimes even seen as so important that the rest of a woman becomes merely an appendage to her breasts. Women have had to find ways to survive such objectification, cultural judgment, and stereotyping. In fact, breasts have been such an issue with women (as a definition of femininity, as a source of pride, shame, self-consciousness, or potential danger—of being grabbed by strangers) that women's dreams have made some commentaries on the subject.

A woman in middle life had the following dream:

> **Breasts So Small.** I'm in a romantic place with two men: one is appealing and sexy, but the other is indifferent and seems uncomfortable with me about sex.
>
> Then I'm in a high school locker room, embarrassed in front of the others because my breasts are so small. I want to find my car and go home.

The dreamer thought that the two men represented her differentiation of men into those who find her attractive and those who don't. Her concerns about her own attractiveness dated back to her teenage years. She said, "I hated group showers. Instead of feeling affirmed I was embarrassed. I didn't want to be different. Since I was tall and had small breasts—men at that time thought you had to be petite with a good figure to be romantic— I was crossed off by most men. Through the years, though, I've been feeling better about myself. This is the way I am! It's as if I can listen to my instincts come forth like a seed, breaking through the crust of the earth."

* * *

Another woman, Teresa, had the opposite problem of breasts that were "too large."

> **Going on a Dolly Parton Ride.** I'm going on a Dolly Parton ride at a carnival. Gay men stand around the entrance being critical of the carnival ride—in the sense of making fun of it. I'm frightened to go down the ramps where you see all those sexy Hollywood images flash by. Then I'm off the ride, wearing my white spiked heels. Some gay men are waiting at the exit, too.

This dream shows Teresa in the dilemma of how to handle the problem of her breasts that loomed so large to everyone. How much she welcomed the figures of the gay men in the dream, she said, who could make fun of the Hollywood images and the importance ordinarily placed on sexy breasts. They seemed her allies, lighthearted witnesses of her dilemma. "What a relief it'd be in this world to be neuter at times," Teresa said. "I'd like to get through a gynecological exam without being propositioned, or being afraid that I probably would be."

Where do the spiked heels fit into her story? The white spiked heels were the ones Teresa wore the first time she stepped out to date. "Everyone was wearing those heels back then, but I got criticized for looking 'too grown up.'" Teresa was somewhat reserved by nature, not sexually provocative; nonetheless she felt that even ordinary things she did were *seen* as too sexually aggressive because of the way she happened to look. Men either would respond too much to her as if she were seductive, or else would "write her off" as too threatening and not respond to her at all as sexual (a more neutral variation of that being the lighthearted, gay men in the dream). She felt caught between these two extreme responses to her.

It turned out that Dolly Parton herself helped Teresa out of this dilemma. Just before the dream, Teresa had heard Dolly Parton interviewed by Barbara Walters on television. Teresa said, "Dolly Parton was outrageous—popping out of her low-cut dress, with her blond wig poofing out. She was sexy and she accepted it. She was a *real person* whom Barbara Walters could relate to." This somehow broke the spell of being caught in the stereotype herself—being seen as too sexy, or having to deny being sexy at all for fear of others' overreactions. Like Dolly Parton she could wear a *persona*—a conscious way of presenting herself—depending on the circumstances. Some time she might even take a Dolly Parton carnival ride, not frightened by the Hollywood images, but accompanied by her own lightheartedness that would let her enjoy the thrill, the fun, of her own sexuality.

A dream helped another woman sort out a problem similar to that of the last dreamer, and affirm the meaning her breasts held for her as opposed to their importance to others. She remembered this dream from the time when she was working with a male therapist.

> *Give Me Back My Bra!* I had my clothes on, but I became aware that, underneath, my bra and panties were missing! Then I suddenly realized what had happened: My male analyst had taken them without my knowing it. I got very angry and took his arm and twisted it behind his back and demanded that he tell me where they were. "You must tell me! Where's my bra? How did you steal it from me?" I looked up and saw manzanita branches—a decoration—inside the office, holding different bras. I want mine!
>
> The scene changed to my sister recounting in great sorrow that she didn't have the skills to be a good mother; she didn't grow up with them. She had to learn how. . . .

In its wisdom the unconscious protested that this woman's breasts had somehow become a man's possession and a decoration for his office. This is redeemed in the second part of the dream where the sister pointed out their important symbolic meaning for her as a woman: mothering. The dreamer felt a stab of remorse, like her sister, that she couldn't naturally have been a better mother, she had to learn it.

If you look at this dream objectively, it could represent a dreamer's own fear (or wish) projected onto a male therapist—that he prizes her sexuality and undervalues her mothering. This woman, however, was very conscious sexually, and quite aware of how important mothering and grandmothering were to her. So the problem was likely to have been her male therapist's.

The dreamer was probably experiencing the same problem with her therapist that occurs elsewhere in life for women who happen to be unusually beautiful with sensual, sexual figures—and that is, not to be seen as a person (and a patient) but as an attractive and desirable woman. To be very good-looking might seem to be a great asset in life, and it certainly can be, but it is also a problem. "One of the problems," as an older woman—an exquisite beauty all her life—explained, "is that a beautiful woman can be stereotyped, even by therapists, and seen as someone who has everything and is a delight to talk with—or too powerful." Therapists can unconsciously overlook a beautiful woman's vulnerabilities, her doubts, her sorrows, and treat her mainly as a lovely object. But the innermost feminine being in this woman angrily protested being reduced like this and demanded: "Give me back my bra. It's mine!"

## Factors Inhibiting—or Enhancing—Women's Sexuality

Many women's problems with sexuality relate to the quality of their overall relationship with their partner, and, specifically, emotional intimacy, the subject of the last chapter. So this section will focus on things that help or hinder sexual intimacy. Some women find sex too impersonal, and want it more personal. Some need to get past inhibitions and be more lusty; others yearn for a more spiritual dimension in love-making. Dreams reveal various things that interfere with women's full sexuality, and suggest ways to find more fulfillment.

SEXUALITY AND ADDICTIVE BEHAVIOR. It's tempting to dwell on sexual problems in early history, but old difficulties often have parallels in our own contemporary adult life. For instance, a woman who becomes a wife and mother is apt to encounter some of the same problems and dilemmas her mother did as an adult. Instead of blaming her mother for not solving them, she might better resolve her past as much as she can, and confront her current dilemmas as an adult—with a little help from her unconscious.

> **Mother Haggard at the Door. I'm in bed with my husband. He's feeling sexual, has a hard-on. This is our opportunity!**
>
> **But I sense that my mother's outside the door nearby, sewing on her sewing machine. So I say, "Wait. I have to tell her not to come in."**
>
> **I go out to tell her. But she looks so haggard and dishevelled, that I don't feel like going back in the room and being sexual.**

The dreamer, Sue, said, "That's the way it feels sometimes. I'm ready for sex, but then I don't feel like it any more. It's as if something interferes." Could it be her intrusive mother?

Poetic little details—like the sewing machine—often hold a clue to the specific meaning of a dream. "In my high school years, my mother was always at the sewing machine exhausting herself. She sacrificed everything—her looks, her health, her sex—and worked all the time." It turned out that Sue's mother had kept busy as a defense against feeling depressed from losses in her family during those years.

A mother's work addiction can so narrow her life that she tends to envy and intrude on her daughter's more active life. Sue said, "My mother didn't have any life of her own and she didn't have a very good self-image, so when I came home from school, even when I was obviously feeling bad myself, she'd constantly question me about sex. She wouldn't let me alone." Then, an insight came to Sue. "When I feel somewhat overloaded and stressed, I don't feel like sex or affection with my husband—not so much because I'm tired but I don't feel I *deserve* it. I don't feel anything. At times like that I feel haggard. I don't have enough to give, so I pull away from him. It doesn't occur to me that maybe

he can give to me. I always think *I* have to 'prime the pump' with
everyone." As she first understood the dream, Sue saw that the
feelings she had as a teenager were still bothering her. Either she
unconsciously identified with her mother's depression or else slid
unconsciously into her teenager role of fending off sexual interest
as intrusiveness. One task for Sue, then, was to differentiate her
feelings of being tired, overworked, or somewhat depressed,
from feeling "haggard" like her mother—worthless, sacrificing,
and sad.

Sue also blamed herself for recoiling from her husband and
attributed this to her old fears of her mother's invasiveness.
However, another thread of meaning was unravelled from a
particular detail in the dream—that her mother was dishevelled.
Sue said, "That's how she'd look when she'd been drinking:
unkempt, her hair undone. That's when she'd be *sexual*—leave
her dress unbuttoned and tell loose jokes—which sure didn't
make sex look very good to me."

Sue didn't see how her mother's earlier looseness affected her
current life until she considered the question of how she might
feel "dishevelled" or how her husband in any way might seem
"dishevelled" around sex. She realized that when her husband
approached her high on marijuana, she always felt "a wave of bad
feeling come over me. He'd feel cheery when he was high, but I'd
feel like *Don't touch me.*" Evidently Sue was feeling automatically
afraid and repulsed—as she had felt about her mother's looseness.

When Sue worked through how angry she'd been with her
mother, her irrational feelings came under more control. She
could see that her husband was quite different from her mother
and she didn't have to draw away from him as if to protect herself.
Then the problem that remained in the ensuing months was the
real one—of drug use. Her husband didn't smoke much marijuana at the time of the dream, but it still interfered with sex for
her. He thought it made them both feel closer, but she sensed that
he "wasn't there."

This is a common problem. People buoyed by the effects of
drugs can have the strong impression that all's well, and can feel
convinced that the rest of the world shares their feelings. But it is
an illusion. They really aren't responding to other people, and

others resent it. Of course, that is why users want everyone present to be high, too, so it's a shared illusion!

What Sue wanted was something more than illusion. She and her husband loved each other and had lived together for many years. Eventually, she conveyed to him how much she wanted real intimacy with him and persuaded him not to smoke before sex. Later, of his own accord, he decided to quit altogether.

In the course of challenging your partner's habits, attitudes, or behavior, in return you are bound to find your own shadow targeted. Sue's husband, in turn, pointed out that she "wasn't there" either when she was tired from taking care of everything and everybody. She had a tendency to overwork as her mother did. Couldn't they find protected time for sex? Weren't there ways she—or they—could reduce her workload?

Just as living things require special care, so, too, relationships need time for soft talk together and sex, time which this couple worked for and found during the next years. Sometimes a woman has to struggle against those things which diminish intimacy, after settling the conflicts within herself.

EXPLORING FEMININE SEXUALITY. While men generally have been devoting themselves to the realm of work, women, even those who work, have been devoting themselves largely to relationship. They have been outgrowing most men in this area, in personal and interpersonal awareness, including discovering what they want sexually. Although some men are keeping up, the gap seems to be widening, leaving a lot of women dissatisfied.

Margaret had been married many years without much emotional or sexual satisfaction—he was a remote man and an indifferent lover—when she had the following dream:

> *The Female Cylinder.* Two people are standing on top of different giant jars. It's an acrobatic feat to jump into a jar, tumbling through the air and dropping down several stories to land standing on your feet. My husband won't jump, but then I take the dive.
>
> But it's not me diving—it's a lithesome woman in gold, in a leotard of soft lamé. It's a beautiful cylinder

for her to jump into, and her dive is exquisitely executed. She lands on her feet and stands at the bottom waiting for the next person.

Then I, myself, am waiting. I'm caught in metallic ribbon wrapped around and around me, but it's soft like tin foil and only a nuisance. I dive to a ledge, then drop further down, then to another ledge to reach the bottom.

It seemed to Margaret that the woman in gold was her inner archetypal figure of Eros, the one who knows how to express physical love. The gold figure was agile and led the way for her, gave her hope that she, too, could leap into the giant vessel of feminine sexuality. The gold figure showed her something true about women's sexuality—that it is complicated to go to its depths. She herself had to take it ledge by ledge—step by step, as is true in learning more about sex.

Margaret's husband wouldn't leap in the dream and this was true of him in real life as well. He was very intellectual and equated sex with esthetics. Margaret was very intellectual, too, but more emotional, and had a strong sense of touch. In their relationship, she had had to move in his direction—always— because he was a man of habit, and as a result she finally felt trapped with him. Without either of them wanting it to happen, given his limitations and her inability to lead him into her kind of feminine knowledge, the relationship had gradually dried up. In fact, eventually she felt so confined emotionally and sexually that she left him for another man—warm and juicy, who was not afraid to take great leaps with a woman.

However, the dream suggested that it would not just be a matter of changing partners. She had to learn things step by step herself, and disentangle time and again from the metallic ribbon. She thought the ribbon meant her entanglement in the men's world and their definition of things, and her entanglement in her own intellect, which tended to lead—rather than follow—her emotion and instinct, her touch of gold. The dream suggests that she could shed this for the lamé.

* * *

Margaret's next dream a month later showed further inner work on attitudes toward sex, in this case, feeling entitled to earthy sexuality. She thought this entitlement had come from her analyst and from her own inner gold figure who affirmed her sexuality in all its warmth and playfulness, in contrast to the limiting attitudes of her husband, family, and religious upbringing.

> *A Snake Mantle of Soft Brown.* There are two shedding snakes looped around a hook on the wall and hung like tires. Reds, pinks, whites, black spots, brown . . . I stand close by. Another woman, a blonde, throws one to me. It's a brown one, and it becomes a mantle over me, the skin of it like a ruffle. Its various shades of soft brown are like the natural wool of llamas, or feathers. Then that ends. I let the snake mantle drop, and I look up higher on the wall to see the array of snakes. I look at the red snake and think, "That's not so bad!"

Here Margaret is taking up her womanly mantle—that she's entitled to sexuality—and wearing it lightly and easily, this earthy and mysterious wisdom of the snake, an animal close to its instincts, and with the ability to shed its skin and renew itself again and again. This is her own ability to know and renew her sexuality. She said it felt like the snake was tossed to her rather abruptly, as if it were assumed she could catch it, and she *was* determined to do so. Furthermore, it seemed to her that her golden lamé woman in the earlier dream had become an earthy blond, who, like her analyst, assumed that she had a right to her full sexuality. First, she could have soft brown earthiness, warm sexuality, then, perhaps, as the dream foretold, the red—strong emotion and passion.

The feeling of being *determined* in the dream reminded Margaret of a time when she was eleven or twelve and was, at first, afraid to pet an iguana. She had gotten the impression in her restrictive home environment that such things as snakes and sex were slimy unknown things to be ignored or avoided. Margaret had been repulsed at first by the iguana, but had been determined to get used to it. She finally did pet it, and found that it had soft skin and was warm! That's the spirit Margaret needed again at this time in her life—the boldness and curiosity of the eleven- or twelve-year-old. She needed to play, until sex came with more ease—touching and being touched, exploring with curiosity her partner's "snake." The first dream of the gold lamé skin and the second one with the soft-colored mantle of snakes and its association with the surprisingly soft, warm iguana—all confirm the importance to her, and to many women, of touching and caressing in sexuality.

SEXUALITY AND AGGRESSIVENESS.   Sex and aggressiveness (in the sense of sexual assertion, dominance, lust) are more likely to be interwoven for men, just as sex and Eros (affection, emotional intimacy, yielding to feelings and instincts) are more likely to be interwoven for women. We need to learn from each other: women, about such things as feelings of aggressive lust in sex—our own and men's; and men, about yielding to closeness and affection in sex—their own feelings of love and a woman's love for them. Then we can weave both delicate and strong, ever-changing patterns with each other.

Women need enough assertion to let men know what they like—and don't like—in sex; and they need enough power to negotiate safe sex, so that they are not vulnerable to AIDS, venereal disease, and unwanted pregnancy.

Aggressiveness that borders on physical or verbal abuse, by a man or a woman, can make sexual encounters frightening, demeaning, or dangerous. In fact, people who have been abused or mistreated in their past can be hypersensitive to any sign of aggression or coercion—even lighthearted teasing or combativeness that would seem natural or playful to a partner. The next dream shows us how a woman recoiled in alarm from too much sexual aggressiveness in a man, and in the process learned about her own.

*The Bull Spies Me.* I see a big bull below the terrace of my house. It spies me and starts coming at me, inevitably. I wedge myself against the wall on the other side of the table, but it reaches me anyway. It presses against me, nudges me with its head, and licks me. I steady my hand against it firmly, but with a slight rub or caress, and hold it off successfully.

This dream came after a date with a sexually assertive man whom she had placated and resented the evening before, and it shows her mixed feelings toward him. She had to admit that the bull was also her own sexuality, which he had aroused and which she had held in check. This dream poetically shows aggressiveness in sex: the arousing inevitable feelings of a woman's own sexual drive as it responds to the bull in a man and rises and moves to reach consummation. Yet this dreamer had instinctively chosen to stem the tide. In the dream she also had enough counteraggression to hold sex firmly at bay when she wanted, while yet she chose—with a gesture, a slight rub and caress—to do so in a way that showed her desires, her sexual attraction, and her responsiveness to his manliness.

TOO LITTLE OR TOO MUCH SEX. Too little or too much sex are common problems in our sexual matchings and mismatchings. A woman and a man who were well suited to each other, very compatible sexually as well as best of friends, had been happily married a few years. However, at the time of the next two dreams, the couple had become unaccountably irritable with each other, with flare-ups of temper on both sides. These dreams revealed the reason: There had been too little sex for a period of time. In addition, the dreams pointed out two very different effects this can have on a marriage. One dream came right after the other:

*The Seducer with a Rock.* I'm in a new house with many levels. In the bedroom there's a man who's quite appealing to me physically. I feel very sexy and want to make love. My breasts are bare, and I look at him standing there, as if he's almost going to rape me.

Then I see that he's holding up a rock in his hand. He's too dangerous, crouched with the rock so threateningly. I don't want him that way! He could hurt or kill me.

I decide I really don't want this, so I manage to close the door and get outside. He doesn't follow; he isn't aggressive. Then I feel strange.

*Incest with My Brother.* I'm in a spacious house, and there's a lot happening in the basement. I'm with my brother there, and we're lovers. In the middle of making love, I stop and say, "This is incest!" But then, since we've been lovers for years I tell him, "Let's continue anyway." He says, "No, because we're brother and sister!" I say, "But we've done it before." Then I realize we can't.

These dreams crystallized the couple's vague dissatisfactions into a form the dreamer could see. As she thought how sexually arousing the seducer was in the first dream she realized that lately she had missed the early excitement in her marriage—the attraction and the passion. They had had good sex on vacation recently, then had felt even worse returning to their everyday drudgery. Perhaps it was then that their tempers had started flaring up at each other. It was as if the "drudge" in each of them, busy with work, had driven out their playful sexual sides. The seducer, then, was the figure left out in this couple's life, each angry at the other for not being more sexually assertive, each throwing rocks at the other. The first dream showed what can happen when sexual eagerness is not fulfilled: It becomes angry aggression.

The second dream, incest with the brother, showed how a couple can unwittingly let the sparks of excitement between them flicker out. Why was the incest taboo coming up between them in the "basement," the unconscious? Why would they be feeling like brother and sister?

It turned out that the wife and husband were currently together twenty-four hours a day, since they had begun working in the same office. They were compatible partners in their work and best friends besides. They were with each other so much in these other roles, without a good balance of sexuality, that they had become like brother and sister, constellating the incest taboo.

There was no jolt of "the other," no aerating of their relationship, no going apart and coming back together again, no freshness, no longing to see each other again. So sparks of sex became sparks of irritability over not having sexual intimacy. Another reason that their tempers flared up was to keep some distance between them as "brother and sister"! They had the worst of both worlds: Working too much together, they didn't have enough apartness, yet as a couple they didn't have enough real closeness either—the love-making that affirmed their special bond. This dream alerted them to their problem and suggested what they needed.

Too much togetherness—not enough separation, assertion, or sexuality—is a more common problem among lesbian couples, where women are often best friends, more easily close and compatible, often spending so much time together that the lover aspect gets dimmed in another incest taboo, that of sisters or mother/daughter. Often, especially at first, a couple may find all their fulfillment in each other so that other friends fade away and there's no fresh air in the relationship.

A lesbian had been with her partner for a few years when she had this dream:

> ***Showing My Big Stallion.*** An anthropologist friend tells me matter-of-factly that I haven't even tried to show my horse, as others have. Mine is a big stallion, like those big horses in the beer ads. I think, "Yes, that's true. I haven't made the effort."

The problem this couple had was that they were both passive and they each needed to mobilize their sexual assertiveness, their big horses. The dreamer, especially, was by nature more conscious of her inner life or esthetics, than her body and sensations. For women like her, physical awareness, sexuality, and sports did not come naturally; none was conscious or developed. (On the other hand, physical people may find they have to learn esthetics or looking inward, which is an effort for them.) This dream reminded her of the fact that she did, indeed, in her unconscious, have a physical side, a big stallion, her undeveloped sexual energy.

An image came to the woman of what it would be like to mobilize her energy to meet her partner sexually: "It would be like raising a heavy bucket from a deep well—a great effort." It does take a great deal of effort on the part of the conscious ego, the will, to bring something up from the *unconscious*. But the dream promised that it would not always be so for her and her partner, that there would be tremendously vigorous horses, once she let them out of the barn door.

## Feminine Sexuality: Spirituality, Privacy, and the Soft Colors of the Garden

SEXUALITY AND SPIRITUALITY.  When that most powerful of feelings—love—is evoked in a woman, her deepest instinct, the maternal impulse, may be evoked as tenderness toward her loved one, protectiveness, possessiveness, a desire to be together "always." Love also shakes her to the roots of her sexual and spiritual being. For usually sex is, for a woman, an expression of giving and receiving love, and in that act of trust and commitment, the sexual and the sacred are often intertwined—though religion and culture have split them apart, as if one were dirty and one were pure. Yet a woman who knows her heart, who knows the depths of her being, knows that the tender, the sexual, and the spiritual are all aspects of love.

In this dream, a woman reclaims both her sexuality and her spirituality. Maureen was single, and struggling to honor the restrictive tenets of her religion but also experiencing the strong pull of love and her passionate nature. She came to therapy because of severe anxiety attacks at night, which she thought were somehow "both spiritual and sexual." She turned out to be right; she needed to find a way to combine these two very important parts of her life.

> *The Druid Priestess.* I'm in another realm. I walk along the ocean beside a stone wall with my name on it,

which means it's the wall to my own ancient estate. Inside the castle walls, I find a chapel and go in. A girl of seventeen comes over to me from the other side of the altar and we kneel together at the altar rail. The girl looks like a mystic from the 1200s. She's wearing the gold crown of the Blessed Virgin, and inset in the crown are eyes that move! The eyes are pure blue, real, alive. They're watching me: I feel weird! Then the girl slips off the crown of gold to wear a simple one of wood.

Then it's as if I'm kneeling beside a man. I get up and decide to reenact the coronation before the right side of the altar. Suddenly he becomes the king and I'm blessing him with my hands. I've become a Druid priestess. There's thunder and lightning, explosive power. I'm in touch with some kind of power, perhaps the occult; I'm angry and frightened. Then I realize, in the dream, that I must have had an ancestor who was a Druid.

I run out of the castle to get to my car. A Great Dane bounds toward me—as if he's Death—and knocks me over. I lie on the sidewalk near dogshit but I'm okay. I run after him. I won't hurt him; it's a battle of wills, bluffing.

As I jump into the front seat of the car I think, "Now I understand the secret of myself."

In response to the dream, Maureen said: "I had a religious conversion at seventeen, the time of my first sexual and spiritual awakening, but I must have thought of all that sexual energy— that 'explosive power'—as only spiritual then. The Blessed Virgin—whom I was drawn to—had a pure love that still embraces me. But the other side of that, I see now, is the judgmental, the puritanical—the watchful eyes that make me uneasy."

The dream helped Maureen correct this splitting off of sexuality from religion. The dream took her back to Druid times when religion embraced women's earthy nature, when sensuality and sexuality were part of the mystery of love and life-giving forces, when she imagined, "priestesses were not afraid to be sensual." This vivid dream gave her confidence in her own deep inner beliefs, rooted in the feminine, and also gave her confidence in sensuality, rooted in spiritual authority. Then her own feminine spiritual authority—the priestess in the dream—could properly acknowledge masculine authority, crown the king. The dream also registered her alarm—or awe—at taking such power. Perhaps she was afraid that it was forbidden by the church, but more likely she was afraid because she must handle dark forces, too. In any case, then the dream suggests entitlement and confidence through the realization that she must have had Druid ancestors.

The Great Dane seemed to her to represent both Death and being undaunted by Death. The dog also represented masculine sexuality—a big threat that could knock her off her feet and land her in the dirt. She remembered that in her early teens when she was beginning to feel sexual, but denying it, she repeatedly sprained her ankles. This dream, then, was helping her regain her relation to the ground beneath her feet—good Druid earth.

Women are now reclaiming a spiritual heritage that has been covered over by centuries of male religious authority, which has tended to split off sexuality from spirituality in Western culture. We search in history and fantasy for old truths in the bits and pieces retrieved from early feminine knowledge: early statues of full-bodied goddesses, stories of fairies—the last priestesses—in *The Mists of Avalon*,[1] the girl with healing herbs in *The Clan of the Cave Bear*,[2] the rituals of witches, and the work of modern healers and psychics. We imagine a time when sexuality had an accepted place as part of our wholeness: sexuality as natural, free-flowing pleasure and lustiness; sexuality as an emotional commitment, a spiritual experience, a mystery of coming together that was a consecration of love; sexuality as a sacred act in receiving the mystery of the planting of the seed. All of these.

A few months later Maureen had another dream in which she was thrown into an opposite realm:

*Bitten by a Vampire.* **Someone is bitten by a vampire. If the person bites me, I'll turn into a vampire!**

This dream suggests one of the meanings that the vampire has for a woman's psyche. The vampire can represent a woman's fear of the love-bite, fear of sex, in particular being seduced into sexuality, caught in it, obsessed with it. Sex can be so fulfilling—as lovers know—that it can become addictive and eclipse almost everything else. The fear that accompanies intense eroticism is that you'll be so captivated by sexuality that you'll become bound to someone, you'll succumb to outside masculine force, and perhaps lose your will and be too passive, too accommodating, or let yourself be victimized. Beneath that fear, far below in the archetypal realms of the psyche, is the fear of devouring death, symbolized by the earlier dream figure of the Great Dane, reminiscent of the Greek dog Cerberus or the dog-headed Egyptian god Anubis who guided people to the underworld and guarded the entrance to that place of no return. For in the still point of sex you may touch the finite and the infinite, embrace life and death, experience fullness and the void.

A year later Maureen had another dream that continued the reconciliation between her spiritual and sexual sides.

*I'm Given a Golden Ring.* **I'm being transported through the air—like the feeling of my anxiety attacks—but it's not frightening anymore because there's another power there. I'm taken to a school where there's a spiritual teacher. I'm supposed to pray. Spirits lead me to find the right place, and there's something mystical about my praying.**

**Then the scene changes. I'm in the bathroom with my sister—my actual sister—who says, in the dream, that she's "Maggie," my long-lost sister and friend from a former life. She tells me that she was a former prostitute who nearly died by drowning once, so now she helps others by the waterside. She offers**

**me a golden ring—and I accept it. I pray to Jesus, "If this is true, take me home." Then, in the dream, I remember that I was a Druid in a former life. A male voice says, "The Druid and the priestess shall come together," and I'm transported home.**

As is true for many dreamers and their dreams, what is important is not so much understanding the dream afterward as the experience itself. The dream did the actual work of reconciling sexuality and spirituality, and helped to heal Maureen's terrible anxiety attacks. She said that what happened in the dream was unusual. "I've never been able to talk with my sister about sex—we're so different—and at first I hesitated to take the golden ring. But the ring was radiant, a sacred tie, like a long-lost thread between me and religion."

This dream shows the interplay between dreamwork and what happens in the outer world. For the unconscious can solve problems that the conscious mind or actions cannot solve, even in something as seemingly concrete as sex. We all know that scientists pursuing an idea find that a new thought comes to them after they sleep on it. The conscious mind, even aided by the computer, is limited, and our thoughts often go down a railroad track in linear fashion. The unconscious can be more creative because it is fluid. It is more like a pool of water where every drop is part of the whole pool, stirred up, settling anew. Out of this can come a crystallization of the whole. Words can't describe this process, (although in linear thought words do very well as signposts along the railroad track). Symbols, though, like the golden ring, can do so.

This dream was the result not just of inner work the dreamer had done in therapy but also outer work that accompanied it. For the unconscious registers what happens outside just as our conscious mind is informed by the unconscious. After the first dreams, Maureen had summoned her courage to talk with her sister about sex—apparently the first time people in her family had ever done so! Her sister had always been the "wild one" and she, the "family prude." Despite this, they could talk a little, and sense some unspoken commonality and understanding between them as women. It was this bond—each knowing half of the truth—that formed the golden ring, her own wholeness. Maureen had been in the archetypal realm of priestess and vampire and needed personal sisterly help to bring her down to earth and lay her terrors to rest.

THE FEMININE AND PRIVACY. Privacy is especially important to many women, our sexuality being a more hidden part of ourselves, an inner treasure, a vulnerable core. Men often don't understand this aspect of women's nature. The following dream brought this issue to light. It was precipitated by a male sex counselor's suggestion to a married couple that they do a homework assignment of masturbating in front of each other. For some couples, this kind of exercise may be exactly what is required—to be open about the mechanics of sex—but not for this woman. Her dream protests it.

> *Privacy and the Healing Herbs.* I go through a small town. I find a building on a residential street and go into it to find a bathroom. There are a few people in line ahead of me. When it's almost my turn, a plainclothes policeman comes up and starts taking the bathroom door off. I shout, "Wait! I won't have any privacy." He says he has to take it off, but it can be partially closed.
>
> I have a flashback that the night before, police had swarmed around this area and had taken a crazy woman out from a building across the street. They had beamed listening equipment at her window to overhear her conversation. The more she knew she was being observed, the more paranoid she had become. They got her and took her off to prison.
>
> The scene changes. I'm walking on a dirt road along the ocean. I've just crossed a bridge when I hear a voice. It's a fisherman. I study his face and see that he's Japanese. He's a bit bold and accompanies me to the level below, the level of the river, where there's a more quiet Japanese man, laying out herbs. The herbs are of fresh seaweed, the pink-orange color of shrimp

> or salmon eggs. If the two men can put the herbs on
> my hand, they will be healing for me. Although the
> men look a bit coarse, they seem safe to me, so I close
> my eyes and one or the other of them lays some herbs
> on my palm and I let it be. I could learn their lore.

This dream shows how much the woman felt an inner revolt
against the prescription of the sex counselor that the couple use
a method of sexual openness. In the dream the woman feels jolted
by the idea of the door ajar, and watches a crazy woman become
more and more frightened at being observed.

This dream challenges the male bias toward openness about
sex as a curative, and suggests that perhaps this woman needs
another kind of healing from her unconscious side, the kind she
could accept with great trust in the dream, with closed eyes and
open palm. The dreamer didn't know what the seaweed herbs
meant, but this salmon-colored gift from the sea suggests something that has life and grows in the watery depths of the feminine
unconscious, something that her inner Japanese fishermen—
coarse and bold, safe and quiet—could offer her. They could
show her the lore from the sea, how she might give herself up to
trusting the natural and the mysterious in sexuality. This she had
to discover through time. Meanwhile, the dream showed her
deep inner recoil about being too mechanical or open about sex,
and pointed out to her clearly the deep importance of privacy in
sexuality.

THE ESSENCE OF FEMININE SEXUALITY. The last dream in this
chapter is from a woman who wished her husband could be more
attuned to her sexual needs as a woman. This dream expressed to
her the essence of her own sexuality in its natural array of wild,
soft, heartfelt, and—she was to discover—awesome qualities.

> *The Garden of Flowers.* It's a beautiful garden, a wild
> English garden with tons of blues, oranges, and
> yellows—all thrown together. The colors are soft.
> This is beauty, and it's *mine*! I had planted the seeds
> two or three years ago in the garden, and hadn't paid
> much attention to it. Now I'm taking people to see

> it—my husband and friends. I think, "This is my
> garden, even though it's overgrown, and it's mine." I
> wonder why I think it's so beautiful. I realize it's the
> shape of the flowers: like women's sexuality. That's
> why I'm so enamored of it.

Her associations were that the flowers had petals and folds
and softness. What made the flowers beautiful was that they were
blended. She had just thrown forth the seeds—all together—and
they had cropped up wherever they happened to land.

Was this true of sex for her? She said that the essence of sex
for her was a mood of fantasy and romance that sprang from the
heart. The flowers looked like a calico country print—an array of
soft colors—which seemed to her very feminine, "like sex when
it's a blend of the light touch, the gentler feelings, the more
tender words of love." The petals reminded her of Judy Chicago's
exhibition of women's artwork celebrating women's history.

Flowers also meant to her freshness and the ephemeral
quality of sex. "Flowers are fresh, right there, and then they go.
They're just for themselves." To her, sex meant immediacy,
spontaneity, and easy regeneration, rather than work and effort:

> Flowers close and open. That's the opposite of cutting
> the lawn every Saturday morning or having sex every
> Sunday morning. My sex fantasies are wild, eager, in
> touch, not sexual ruts. I do different things for him
> in sex; I wish he'd do them back. He just doesn't click in.
> There are some things I really like, things our baby
> likes—soft touches all over, that soft connection. Some of
> his touch is hard or even painful.

What the dream did was underscore her feminine sexuality.
She knew what she wanted, what she could offer to their sexual
life together, but had been stuck in following his lead, which
meant being passive and in a rut. She had often subtly hinted at
what she might want from him through the years, but had not
found her husband particularly responsive, so she had lapsed back

into her cultural role of the passive, compliant female, and he had stayed in his role of defining their sexuality. The dream had compensated for their conscious positions. It would take much more work to start to move them out of their sexual lethargy, because it had many sources.

One month later she dreamed of an elaborate array of food, and it made her wonder why she hadn't given sex the same attention she always gave food! It also called to her attention how sex was *different* from food—more than just pleasure, in fact, a deep bond between them, awesome, hushed, taboo—so important that she should remember to reserve a special place for it.

Yet, the question remained of why this couple had neglected sex. Some deeper reasons finally emerged. Sex was so ready, instinctual, and intense for her, she said, that she was "afraid of the sharp hunger of it." It was likely that this was more than being afraid of her strong sexual drive or her fear of not being fulfilled sexually. She must have been afraid of something lying beneath sexual lust—devouring and primitive possessiveness—which she must know and transform in order to have a truly loving sexual relationship. Her husband was undoubtedly afraid of this intensity. Apparently he was also reluctant about sex for reasons of his own. She said, "Sex seems remote and archetypal to him, something out of control. He's overwhelmed by awesome feelings as if they're from the realm of outer space." Awed herself at sex, she had not let loose her sexuality in the marriage, so she had unconsciously colluded in keeping it unsatisfactory. Both of them were afraid of her wild side, and the depth of the emotional and spiritual bond between them. These dreams contributed to helping them both on their way toward the banquet—and the bouquet—of love-making in their marriage.

# 7

# The Wise Heart

My mind can't tell my heart how old I am.
—EVELYN HICKEY[1]

As a woman matures into middle and old age, she hopes and expects to develop greater inner and outer harmony. She becomes selective in what she protests and more effective in her actions. Her wisdom in the ways of the world has prepared her for the art of accepting what life brings. In the middle phase in her life, she treasures the late fruits of her creativity, her "generativity"—passing on knowledge to others to ensure its continuation—and the work of completing her spiritual path. An older woman knows her years are limited, as her energy and resources may also be, so she appraises what she truly values in life and these things settle into her heart.

The symbol of a rose window, which came to one older woman in her dreams, epitomizes this harmony of feeling that can be achieved in the second half of life. If you imagine the rose window of Notre Dame in Paris, you can see a great circle of beauty containing a multiplicity of vibrant colors arranged in a unity. Likewise, a woman in later life encompasses a broad diversity of values and a fine discrimination of feelings, sorts them into their rightful places, so they radiate from her centeredness in herself. The rose window, then, is a particularly evocative archetypal symbol of the integrative and harmonizing center, the Self, that belongs to the Wise Woman of Heart.

As a woman grows older, the outer structure of her life generally settles into patterns of contentment (or at least routine), allowing her further inner growth. When she may be jarred by inevitable losses, such as divorce, separation from children, illness, incapacitation, deaths, or other limitations (circumscribed finances, mobility, or social intercourse), she needs a stalwart inner life to sustain her all the more, since society often will not. Some of the dreams in this chapter attest to how women find what they need, and these wise women's stories can be helpful to women of different ages, especially younger women who may be caught up in their roles at home and work with little time or energy left over for tending their inner life.

We instinctively gravitate to a woman who has a full heart. In the interpersonal sphere, she reflects back to others the mature qualities of love: wholeness, authenticity, commitment, and acceptance of the light and dark of her own and others' shadow side. The wise woman knows the range of love: a young mother's tenderness for her infant, a mature woman's fierce defense of her own integrity and protection of those within her boundary of care, the passion of lovers, humanitarianism, and spirituality. Her loving is more conscious, broad, and deep. She may not find the earlier fire of passion, fusion, and fascination with her opposite as much as she finds steady embers of love in truly knowing another and coming together from a position of separateness.

As a woman grows older, she also reaps the inner harvest of her life experience with others. She has distilled within herself the essence of her masculine side from all her years of being with men she has loved, tangled with, and known; and she has also resonated deeply with her own womanliness from a lifetime of kinship, struggle, and fellow feeling with women. In quiet and silence, she may feel attuned to herself, her mate, and her soul. She may touch, at times, love that is beyond the ordinary, transpersonal love in moments of grace, revelation, or mystical experience.

We may all experience Eros welling up within us as healing energy, the Healing Heart, a sense of well-being, harmony, and oneness within and with the universe. We may feel an acceptance that is beyond words and philosophy, beyond our usual human capacity to face the indifference and design in Nature, our place in it, our part in it. This sense of acceptance from Eros helps us come to terms with what our life has been, what has been missing, and what might be.

As we cultivate inner wisdom in the realm of archetypal Eros, and tap knowledge and energy from love beyond the interpersonal—from the transpersonal dimension—our dreams may present us with the archetypal forms of a Wise-hearted Old Woman (or man), Sage, or divinity or with images of older, spiritual people we know or know about, such as Mother Teresa, Kwan Yin, Mary, or Christ. As we saw in the dreams about the Self, one hazard at this stage is to identify too much, and too unconsciously, with a sage or religious leader either by thinking you are one or by being with one. This feels like basking in the sun of the Great Mother, the Great Father, or the Self, but is actually inflation, being burned up in the fiery intensity of the False Self, denying the shadow and insulating yourself from the world, instead of integrating spirituality into everyday life.

The wise woman knows the harsh facts of life. Her inner confidence comes from her descent to her own dark depths. Unlike the hero who slays the dragon to rescue his feminine side, a woman must know the dragon in all its beastliness, be healed by contact with it, absorb its energy, and bring it back, along with the treasure. Although men and patriarchal mythology depict a passive woman to be rescued by a hero or led by a sage, these images pertain to men's own feminine. A woman undertakes her own journey, especially in older age. She may be aided by a helpful animus with good feeling or thinking, a sister figure, or wise man or woman, but she alone must take the initiative.[2]

The wise woman is grounded in the real world. Her convictions are powerful—born of her many years of experience as well as her intuition[3]—and she is not all-accepting. Others know this and are afraid of her critically appraising eye. In fact, this fear, as well as envy and awe, may account for some of the systematic depotentiation and diabolization through history of the old woman—and the Wise Old Woman—in fairy tales and in society.

We can assume that long ago women elders were highly regarded. Recently, *women* scholars have established their own interpretations of symbols, myths, and archeology, and, together with methods such as carbon dating, have established the existence of prehistoric societies which honored feminine values, had priestesses, and worshipped goddesses, including the Crone. These were not matriarchies, a mirror image of patriarchies, but egalitarian and peaceful societies.[4] All phases in a woman's life were honored, especially that of the older woman. Postmenopausal women—those who survived—instead of being disregarded as if their aging were a source of embarrassment or weakness, undoubtedly had enhanced status. People believed that the sacred blood of women's earlier menstruation was retained within them and turned into the "wise blood" of sage and seer. This is a poetic truth: women's great accumulation of experience does yield insights into life, and turning inward does give intuitive knowledge that "goes beyond" what is generally known. These are the kinds of poetic truths that appear in women's dreams today.

Some of the dreams that appear in this chapter are from older women, but most are from early middle-aged women cultivating the Wise Old Woman within themselves and later middle-aged women anticipating older age. Women's dreams here fall under three sections. The first, Missing Elements in the Development of Wholeness and Wholeheartedness, shows important steps a woman takes throughout life in the slow evolution of her inner wisdom. The next section, Accepting the Gift from the Wise Old Woman, demonstrates how wisdom is sometimes offered to a woman, who must decide whether to accept its responsibilities. The last section, Archetypal Changes, reveals images of transcendent power that spontaneously appear in dreams at times of great need. These may help heal wounds, give a woman a "change of heart," or bring about a shift in perspective on the universal dimensions of human experience.

## Missing Elements in the Development of Wholeness and Wholeheartedness

You can view psychological development as a spiral staircase winding upward around a center. You meet the same problems again and again, but at a higher level each time—and as they pertain to your later phases in life. As you progress you can also descend further to the depths of the spiral, at times, to bring back what you find of value. For instance, you may think you have put your "mother problem" and the Great Mother to rest by your thirties at the "third floor," but you may meet them again in your seventies, at the "seventh floor," where they have very different meanings to integrate into your present life.

Dreams sometimes show a woman those elements she lacks in her life, so that she can acknowledge those gaps, mourn their loss, or finally fulfill them to some extent in her movement toward wholeness. Dreams can help her in various ways. A dream may form fine discriminations of feeling that allow her to change her outlook on herself, others, or her circumstances. Or she may realize something about herself that has been holding her back all her life and is essential to accept or change as she passes into an older phase in life. In gathering her strength to meet a midlife challenge, she may find herself able to establish more firmly her full instinctual or intellectual powers, perhaps by acting as a bridge between generations. As she grows older, she may need to reclaim her spirituality if it was lost through feelings of alienation from a particular religious background, the rigidity of parental influences, or the lack of validation from others in early spiritual development. The dreams that follow are everyday examples of the small steps women take along their spiral staircase toward their full strength, their sense of community and humanity, and their spirituality.

## Recovering the Early Self in Later Life

Sometimes you must go back to childhood and retrieve the early sense of Self. The early Self is often depicted in dreams as giving birth or finding the young girl within—wounded or buoyant—and bringing her forward into your life. This renewal of the early Self occurs throughout life into old age, and in this evolution, you often return to your early history, finding the weak links or traumatic episodes in your development, and heal them as best you can. In retrieving the early Self, you will inevitably find yourself coming to terms with its opposite—the Crone, gatekeeper to life's hidden mysteries and death. The task of an older woman is to be "pregnant with herself." She must be creative, give birth to herself alone, suffer and endure, with the courage to face her own deterioration, death, and the unknown.[5]

In the following case, a woman returned to the early Self. An older woman, Evelyn, felt as if the center had gone out of her life when her husband died. She had been grieving for him a long time and could not emerge from her depression, when she began to sense that beneath this loss must be some great early loss in her life. The following dream held the clue.

> *The Black Jewels.* I'm on a train. A young girl is sitting behind me, holding a jewel box. It's *mine*—the dark carved box in which my mother kept her jewels, and I wonder how the girl got possession of it. She's evasive, but doesn't deny that it's stolen.
>
> I'm ill at ease in accusing the girl's mother, who sits beside her, but the mother is brazen. She challenges me to identify what might be inside the box in front of a witness. The witness is a handsome young man, all in white.
>
> I sort over in my mind what jewels are in my mother's jewel box at home. I remember one necklace with black stones and teardrops, beautiful and lustrous. I think of how to describe it. It is an old pendant which she wore for years—with a crudely carved fish. Then I realize that the fish is on another necklace at home in another box. I haven't worn either necklace for years, but they have sentimental value, and I get panicky that I can't remember them.

These were actual jewels that Evelyn had inherited from her mother. Her great task was to clarify just what inheritance—of the feminine Self—she had gotten from her mother so that she could discriminate between herself and her mother, her mother's sorrow and her own. When she pondered the black necklace—

black stones and teardrops—it reminded her of the almost-forgotten fact that when Evelyn was an infant her mother, a very young woman, had lost her own mother and her own sister within one year. For as long as Evelyn could remember back in time, her mother had always had an undercurrent of depression.

As a widow herself now, Evelyn also knew her mother's great loss, and realized that through the years growing up she had felt closest to her mother at times of death. The black jewel was Evelyn's dark feeling connection to her mother, and her heavy-hearted knowledge, through her, of death.

Evelyn sensed that the young man in white represented "a hurdle" for her in knowing her own deepest worth, the early Self. In her associations, Evelyn recalled that during her youth she had thought of herself as short, fat, and unlovable. "I was insignificant compared to my handsome older brother, who was my mother's favorite." But now, looking back at her history afresh, Evelyn was struck by the fact that he had been born in the good years when her mother was still buoyant, whereas she happened to have been born at the time of her mother's troubles. "I *know* my mother cared for me down deep, but she could only *show* it to my brother." Evelyn had a further insight. Her mother—and she, too—had felt free to love the brother and other men, but not females, in the unconscious belief that men wouldn't be in danger of dying as females (in the family) apparently were! Unusual early losses can result in superstitious and irrational beliefs like these which reside in the unconscious and mislead us about what to expect in the world. Then we must find them—sometimes through our dreams—work through the unconscious thoughts and feelings, and also correct them with the facts and perspective of outer reality.

Evelyn was panicked in the dream when she confused the different kinds of jewels. These had to be sorted out. The black teardrop jewels, she knew, represented her darker early experiences of herself with her depressed mother, and her own first encounter with death. They were different from the fish, which represent life stirring deep in the waters of her unconscious, symbols of her early individual Self who could endure. So Evelyn had to go back and find her own young girl within: the sad forlorn girl who had entered life under the heavy shadow of her mother's black teardrops, her mother's great sorrow, and her own early loss. It took years of grief work and other inner work for her to heal this early abandonment, and to find, finally, the archetypal fish—her own fresh wisdom about life and endurance coming forth from the waters.

## Inner Autonomy and Strength in Early Middle Age

Throughout life women compare themselves with their mothers to determine how they are similar and different. Time and again they go back to their original model of femininity, their mother, to find their own strength and confidence in themselves. Through their dreams, and subsequent inner and outer work, they have a chance to restore what was missing in their earlier development.

Bonnie had been appointed executor for her parents' estate when they passed away. She was in early middle age and didn't feel ready for such authority. Her powerful mother had always run everything and, in addition, had had a bad temper. Her mother seemed so fierce to Bonnie that she had always felt small in comparison. Partly in reaction to her mother, Bonnie was sweet-tempered and easy-going, like a teddy bear or bear cub to her grizzly-bear of a mother. Bonnie wondered how she could step into her mother's shoes. She was girding herself to take authority among all the relatives when she had the following dream which helped her gather her feminine strength to persist and face the future.

> *Face to Face with the Bear.* I see several large bears walking through the valley. They're headed up the hill toward my parents' house. I'm not quite sure of the bears' intentions, but I'm certain that they intend to come up the hill and right into the house. I rush to alert everyone in the house and get them to positions of safety.
>
> Then I see the bears starting to come into the house, one after another. Slow and deliberate—like

**them—I walk right up to the first bear. It's huge. I meet it face to face.**

This was a powerful act: to walk right up to a bear. Bonnie knew immediately that this was an important dream, as is true for any dream like this where you come face to face with an animal, confront an important aspect of nature in its pure form, and dare to claim it as your own.

Bonnie had seen black bears in the wild, and said that bears seemed mighty big to her. "They're solid, surefooted, certain of their path. They're powerful, but not impulsive—don't make sudden moves without thinking. They're sure of themselves, grounded, centered."

These were the qualities Bonnie needed: slow deliberation and confidence, an introverted kind of inner strength, different from the powerful temper or bossiness of her mother (or of her own unconscious) and different from her usual easy-going manner. She couldn't hide as the daughter any more, but had to come into her own inner strength as a middle-aged woman, prepared to take her position in the family.

This dream also gave Bonnie an initiation experience: to summon her inner determination to meet the bear's potential violence. In the current situation, the adversity she had to meet was the anger and opposition she expected from her brothers and sisters when she would try to take authority. Bonnie also had adversaries in her psyche. Foremost among them was the inner figure of her mother, whose overwhelming power had always intimidated Bonnie. However, the enemy in her furthermost unconscious was her own powerful temper like her mother's. The dream helped her meet these unruly forces with another kind of strength: her natural bear, who knows its own quiet power. It was as if Bonnie had found her totem animal in the wilderness and henceforth could call upon its power in her life if she dared to do so.

What is the inner strength of the bear? Bonnie had always felt an affinity for Native American animal symbolism, and reported some meanings for the bear which she excerpted from a Native American reference book:[6]

Symbolizes strength and introspection. Not hasty—
makes wise decisions from looking within. Knows her
path, and comes into her maturity and power. The bear
is chief of the animal council and takes leadership. And,
because the bear knows her own heart, she can look into
the hearts of others and help them learn.

From prehistoric times bears have been sacred. Ceremonial
arrangements of cave bear skulls have been found, radiocarbon-
dated back to about 50,000 B.C., drawings before 10,000 B.C.,
and bear sculptures thousands of years before the patriarchal
era—and continuing into the present.[7] Bears have gripped
human imagination as very powerful, mystical animals and as an
archetypal symbol of the one who gives birth, the Great
Mother—fearsome, warm, and independent. Bears have fascinated us with certain qualities that give them an uncanny
resemblance to human beings: their furry coat, occasional two-
legged stance, their prolonged teaching of the young, and the fact
that they can get angry and do great violence.

The female bear presents a strong image of independence.
Except to mate, she lives alone and rears her cubs without
help—a single mother. Our images of a bear with her cubs at
various phases of life express basic instinctual maternal qualities:
the furry mother with her clinging bear cubs, the fiercely
protective mother bear, the firm mother who teaches her young
and even slaps them, the mother bear who abruptly leaves the
young bears when they are truly ready to be on their own. It is no
coincidence that young adolescent girls in ancient Greece were
called "young bears" to honor their independent status. The
mature bear, then, is a symbol of independence and maternal
strength. It is an apt symbol for a woman when she must take
charge of things alone.

It represents introverted wisdom and maturity. Through
history the bear's slow pace, its poor eyesight, its solitary
existence as well as its preparation for winter, and its long
hibernation—all have suggested to humans inner instinctual
power and calm introspection. Native Americans refer to "the

time of the bear" when you consolidate your growth and take responsibility for other generations. They associate the bear with different times of maturity: twilight, autumn—the time of harvest and preparation for winter—and the middle years of human life.

The female bear emerges in spring—every other year with her young. So the bear, with her mysterious "coming and going" like the moon, and with her obvious maternal qualities, has been considered a lunar animal since early times. In astrology, the Great Bear, or Artemis, is the most important constellation of the northern hemisphere, with its tail pointing in the direction of each season as it emerges.

The archetypal symbol of the bear suggests that we, too, at certain times respond to the movement of nature and retire to our own cave, to our inner world, and emerge after long gestation with our spring birth, our creativity, and knowing. It's no wonder that a shaman wears the bear coat with great respect, that the young girl in *The Clan of the Cave Bear*[8] had the cave bear as her totem of awesome strength in order to survive alone, and that in modern times this easy-going dreamer, Bonnie, came face to face with a bear to find her kind of strength and take her place as head of the family.

### Logos and Eros: Wielding Power, Justice, and Generosity in Middle Life

Often, a woman living in Western culture, with its alienation from the feminine, must somehow develop her own feeling-connectedness to others and to life processes. The laws and values are not ready-made for her. Lip service is given to the importance of the feminine values of life and Eros, but winning and rational thought, Logos, seem to be more honored in general. How different it would be for a woman to grow up in a world truly honoring feminine values of life and love! So it takes a long time for a woman to find her strength and confidence, which may not come until she is older.

For some women, intuitive wisdom may be harder to come by than for others. A woman who overvalues her thinking and judgment must develop her feeling and relatedness or she will get further and further from her woman-base, especially in matters of the heart. As she becomes more senior and more successful, her strong thinking may prevail at work and at home, and be less subject to correction. She may typically marshal quick arguments or plans of action at crucial emotional times when she might better pause to see how she feels and find out what really matters to herself and others. Conversely, of course, a woman who overvalues emotion must develop mature thinking so she can defend herself, remain true to herself, and not be dissuaded from her own creative, well-conceived, intuitive judgments by others' patriarchal arguments. A blend of feeling and thinking is required for a good balance of generosity and self-protection, mercy and justice.

Women associate patriarchal kinds of thinking with the masculine principle, so in our dreams various aspects of Logos—clarity of thinking, abstractions, objectivity, logic, judgments—are often represented by the archetypal Great Father or male figures. In dreams these male figures can be a scholar or teacher, a Man with a Lantern, a Wise Man, a Chinese sage, or else a challenging and argumentative man, a Senex—a cynical old man, or a Saturn—a cautious, controlling, heavy-hearted old man. Female figures of thinking and wisdom also appear in women's dreams, notably a grandmother, a teacher, a therapist, and versions of the Wise Old Woman such as the owl, a cat, an oracle, goddess, or saint. In our dreams we find echoes of mythological goddesses: Sophia, the goddess of quiet, passionless wisdom; Kali, merciless in her pursuit of truth; Iris, the goddess of creative imagination; Athena with her clear thinking and directness; Hecate, who probes the secret crannies of knowledge about harsh truths, decay, and death.

The following is an example of a woman struggling between thinking and feeling, success and sharing, justice and generosity. Jennifer was a hard-working, down-to-earth, cautious person who had struggled to become quite successful by early middle age. At the time of the dream, she had just secured a good position at work, and had received a modest inheritance from a relative. She was surprised and pleased that the entire inheritance had come to her alone. This windfall, in addition to her new salary, gave her more than enough financial security for the first time in her life. She wondered if she should keep it all or share it with others in the family? Jennifer knew that the others were still struggling, as she had been recently, yet she also felt she was entitled to it. The others didn't necessarily expect anything. Jennifer had a reputation for being very careful of money—in fact, selfish, which bothered her a little.

Success in the outside world often brings up new issues in the inner world. Jennifer's dreams showed some missing pieces in her character that needed to fall into place. The following dream, in particular, helped Jennifer sort out her feelings and find a course of action.

*Snakes up My Sleeve and Grandmother's Fox Fur.* I'm driving up a steep mountain road. The road's not banked well, so an older man and I must lean way out to keep our balance around the curves. It feels precarious. We finally reach the top. Once at the top, we see someone begin to hack a better path down, a road that's better graded. We see a big rock being moved out of the way with ease.

[The scene shifts.] There's a garter snake, then there are snakes all over the tree branches only a few inches from my face. I take this in stride, more or less. I see a snake that seems to be swallowing itself. Then I feel a snake starting to come out of my sleeve! It's intertwined with another going in the opposite direction. I still don't panic—just feel uncomfortable. I know that I should wait for them to emerge. It's anything but easy!

[The scene shifts.] Grandmother wants me to have her fur coat, saying, "I might as well pass it on to you now." Not her all-fur coat, but one that's reddish fox fur on the inside with green wool sleeves. She has me try it on, and it fits okay except for the left sleeve held tightly to the side. I take it off to figure out what's the matter. It's too narrow across the chest, but it'll be okay if it's put together right.

In this dream Jennifer went from unconscious identification with the Old Man in the struggle toward success to an even more unconscious entanglement with the snakes—her basic instincts—to a more conscious and redeeming gift from the Grandmother figure.

In reaching her pinnacle of success, apparently she had almost lost her balance. The winding road up the mountain looked like a spiral (a symbol of the natural development of centeredness in the Self) but on the way she leaned over backward, almost losing her true center of gravity with the earth by aligning herself with the Old Man. Jennifer wondered if the dream depicted the strain for her of all the plodding and saturnine thinking that had gone into her work, culminating in her position. The Old Man, however, seemed a false guide in the dream. He reminded Jennifer of her father, who "bent over backwards" to be fair in a very rational way, or else was too "mushy" in his feelings of Eros, too sentimental, soft-hearted, and doting.

However, upon reaching the top of the mountain in the dream, Jennifer paused to regain her perspective. She found the road down from the top of the spiral, the way of centeredness, which somehow removed saturnine impediments (like the big rock) with apparent ease.

Then the dream showed what was in store for her: snakes up in the trees in front of her eyes. These were garter snakes, so they seemed relatively harmless to her, but a sign, nevertheless, that the unconscious could suddenly appear and meddle in her affairs. The snakes seemed to Jennifer an archetypal symbol of temptation, especially temptation about material things. She wondered if this was a warning to her that her new job and her inheritance could place her in the position of dispensing good or evil, or being resented. Perhaps she should be more aware of her own snakes—her clever, secretive materialism—and be alert to others' snakes, so she wouldn't be too gullible or too suspicious, but rather have the wisdom of the snake, her intuition, for conscious use.

The snake swallowing itself is the archetypal *uroboros*—symbolizing the Great Mother and the self-sufficiency of nature, the continuity of life and infinite time. This symbol suggested unconscious identification with the Great Mother. That is, Jennifer's mothering instinct might be unconscious and therefore extreme—either too sacrificing of herself and bountiful to others, or too withholding, selfish, and self-protective—rather than more conscious, balanced, and in tune with nature and common sense. The implication was that she should nurture with selectivity and within the context of the whole situation around her. The next dramatic scene shows how she does this.

In a crucial test of courage and endurance, the dreamer let intertwined snakes go up and down inside her sleeve. These are the two winding snakes of the caduceus—symbol of the power of medicine to do harm or heal—which has come down to us from the Greek goddess Hygeia and the later god Aesclepius. Despite her discomfort in the dream, the dreamer waited for them to unravel naturally and emerge, that is, let her mixed feelings straighten out to see what she did, indeed, have "up her sleeve." Jennifer suddenly recalled Hermes/Mercury, the flexible god who knew how to escape entanglement, but who also stole what rightly belonged to Mother Nature; and that mythic image led to further insights which brought about some change of heart.

Jennifer noticed that after the snakes straightened out she received the gift of more conscious matriarchal authority, as if she shifted from cold-blooded, clever, snaky thoughts to receive Grandmother's foxy fur—more warm-blooded foxiness. The warm fur on the inside of the coat meant to her caring for her innermost feelings, that is, taking care of herself; and the fur on the front seemed like showing her own warm feeling or humanity on the outside. This coat was a gift, yet it was faulty. It required modification—freeing up her unconscious left side for action and expanding the chest, that is, releasing her unconscious generosity that had been artificially held back.

Apparently the dream's message seeped into Jennifer's consciousness, for she did stop to sort out her feelings and gain an overall perspective. She became acutely aware of how much she wanted power—power in her new position, and power to give money (or not) to her relatives. Being conscious of this freed up her own "green sleeves," her ability to do this in a new way. She arranged with a lawyer for modest trusts her relatives could count on, while she kept a good share for herself and emergencies.

The crucial thing in this process was that Jennifer followed her deepest feminine centeredness. She endured the discomfort of waiting and seeing instead of acting so that she could unravel her unconscious feelings, confront the conflict between her power motive and her instinctive motherly generosity, and integrate them for more flexibility and balance. Instead of bending over backwards with the old man or stealing like Mercury, she related consciously to the bountiful Great Mother and her shadowy materialism so that her cunning could work for—rather than against—herself and others.

## Finding One's Spiritual Side

The last dream in this section gives a striking symbol of the gradual development of wholeness and wholeheartedness. The dream helped fill in a missing element in a woman's life: the connection to her spiritual side.

Movement toward the spiritual dimension in life can take the form of deeper religious commitment, a spiritual or meditative practice, a philosophical quest, a wider sense of humanity or feeling of communion with others. From this outer and inner growth may emerge a numinous symbol in a dream or a spiritual experience. This may evolve into a very personal kind of spirituality, or rediscovery of spiritual roots and some kind of reconciliation with religion in a renewed form.

However, some people have been so disappointed with their families' religion that they eschew organized religion and anything spiritual. When society has become too secular, or a religion betrays its trust and its message and symbols are no longer pregnant with meaning for contemporary times, people will not experience the human warmth and sense of community which is the life-force of religion, nor moments of awe, mystery, and oneness—the essence of spirituality.

A woman who had been in analysis many years, and usually adopted a cynical air about spiritual matters, said one day that she hadn't ever had any "spiritual experience," and wondered if something might be missing in her life. She was a preacher's daughter, and felt bitter that her father's words hadn't been matched by enough caring about his own family. In reaction, she found herself especially alert to hypocrisy. She also chafed at the way religion had always been presented to her as an absolute—unrelated to the changing and subtle reality of her own experience. She remembered the repeated question, "Are you saved?" She hadn't *felt* saved. To be religious, then, meant to her the pressure to pretend something, which left her with feelings of personal failure and rebellion. These feelings became more troubling in her early teens when friends, one by one, went to the altar and called themselves "saved." She felt skeptical, wondering if they had felt anything special or were just hypocritical—what she thought she would be if she went forward and declared herself "saved."

Later in life, when she established her own home, she quite matter-of-factly devoted herself to caring for her family and relatives, and did volunteer work. As she approached later middle age, she could imagine—intellectually—that others might have a spiritual experience or an encounter with the transcendent, but she herself couldn't. "Love" had become a tarnished word for her. She thought that her grownup daughters were loving, generous people, but not that she was, too. One day when talking about how she couldn't ever have any kind of "numinous" experience, she suddenly remembered a dream many years earlier which she had dismissed at the time.

> *Communion and the Apple Tree.* My niece comes to take me to church for baptism and communion. She leads me to an old church, but we go into the back churchyard, where we find an apple tree, next to my old Sunday school building. The tree has grown in such a way that the tree and the Sunday school building have become intertwined and form one roof. The apple tree has been there all the time! It has been growing there all the time while I've been gone.

This dream suggested some alienation from her religious side, but also her continuity with it. In the dream, her niece—her inner spirited girl—took her to church. But it was not in rituals of baptism or communion in the old church where she found something special, but in the backyard. Perhaps her expectations of the old church had always been too high and she had been caught between inflation and deflation. "To be saved" had always loomed too large for her, so that she was afraid of going up in flames, or else being left among the ashes. She didn't realize other possibilities: that you can turn yourself toward the spiritual, that you might truly touch it, momentarily, but that an ordinary person cannot expect to maintain a state of blessedness. Even if one has touched the numinous dimension in life, one is likely to have an ebb and flow of doubt and faith. Though a spiritual experience can affect you profoundly, you may still have difficulty integrating it into your life—as did the dreamer's father in his home life.

The dream surprised her. It showed that, in continuity with her Sunday school faith as a child, her spirituality had somehow been growing within her as naturally and slowly as a tree. The dream symbols told her about her own kind of spirituality. The apple tree is a sign of simple, natural abundance, fruitfulness, and love. It doesn't represent sudden, special revelation, mystery, and communion, but the dreamer's preference for direct, unpretentious, steady, ordinary, natural love. This aptly described her everyday faith, manifested mainly in her sense of community, her service to others, and her great care for her family.

The fascinating thing about this dream is that it redeems an old religious symbol: the apple and the apple tree. The apple, if you think of it simply and naturally, is a tasty, beautiful, red or golden sphere and is obviously positive. From earliest times in religion, myth, and folklore, it became a powerful symbol of love, nurturance, healing, magical powers, sexuality, immortality, and the gift of life. In ancient legends, the apple tree was sacred, and to cut it down meant death. Apple groves, also, were sacred; the Isle of Avalon and the Elysian Fields were apple islands. According to legend, when King Arthur was wounded he went to the secret island of apples to be healed. A remnant of Celtic divination with apples still exists in the custom of dipping for apples on Halloween. The apple was sacred to Venus; and there were worldwide folk stories about red apples of love and magical golden apples.[9]

However, the apple has come down to us in Christian symbology as "bad": either poisonous, or symbolic of earthly temptations of pleasure, sexuality, materialism, or knowledge. This highlights the fact that there is, indeed, a dark side to the apple: To partake of the juicy apple of sexuality can lead to an unwanted pregnancy. Also, for immediate gain, humankind can forfeit responsibility for stewardship of our good earth and all its creatures. We poison our environment, and, in turn, are poisoned by it—for generations to come.

The negativity of the apple was exaggerated in patriarchal times in reaction to its esteem in the goddess religion. People misinterpreted early depictions of the Tree of Life and the Goddess offering life and immortality to someone on the way to paradise. They projected onto the pictures their own concerns about temptation, sexuality, the feminine, forbidden knowledge, the fall from innocence, and the finality of death.[10] In the current era, the apple  in its negative aspect—symbolizes our difficulty integrating dark truths: acknowledging human failings and reconciling with death.

In this simple dream the symbol of the apple tree restores some early archetypal knowledge about the life-force and the love-force that the dreamer had missed in religion. The young niece, a fresh inner guide, led the dreamer—not back into the church with its words and ritual that had felt empty to her—but out to nature with its alive and life-giving apple tree for her midlife, and for her older age, its promise of immortality. The dream also suggests that in her unconscious this dreamer has kept an inner continuity with some positive aspect of her early religious experience. The image of the arch or "roof" formed between the Sunday School building and the apple tree represents her own young faith growing naturally through the years.

## Accepting the Gift from the Wise Old Woman

The Wise Old Woman sometimes appears in dreams and a woman may experience the healing power of her presence. She embodies the mature and positive feminine Self and offers a deep symbolic sense of wholeness to a woman. The momentous choice a woman must make is whether to accept "the way." This contrasts with the issues and tasks more familiar to the male psyche: separating from the mother and the Great Mother to become more conscious, challenging the father in heroic pursuits to establish his own strength, finding his feminine side, and conquering the fear of death and aligning himself with the Great Father ideals. A major issue that emerges from women's dreams is whether to accept the Wise Old Woman. Can a woman dare to claim the great gift—and responsibility—of the Self from the Great Mother? Can she accept her rightful place in Nature, in the chain of life and death from grandmother to mother to daughter? Can she throw herself into life: to be herself—good and bad, to love and be loved, to be creative, to work, to raise children, to face loss and death? For to know personal failings, limits, losses, and inexorable death—and yet to embrace life wholeheartedly anyway—takes all of a woman's courage, endurance, strength, and humility. If a woman can trust her, the Wise Old Woman can help her.

Some women have always felt connected to the life-force; and as they mature they also clearly show, in their dreams and in their lives, the power and guidance of the Wise Old Woman deep within them. However, other women must get past some formidable obstacles before finding their vital center.

A problem for many women is coming to terms with the negative mother within, experienced as pervasive pessimism, fear, self-doubt, anger, and depression. These feelings lay siege to a woman who has been so criticized by her personal mother, limited by her culture, or frustrated in her life that she doesn't expect positive experiences or inner satisfaction. If a woman has felt unloved, it is difficult to receive the gift of the Self from the unconscious. Perhaps she hardly dares hope any more because of her fear of being disappointed again. Sometimes a woman's conscious mind is so tightly mobilized against adversity that she rejects anything unfamiliar, even if it holds promise. By trying to vanquish the inner negative mother, however, by blindly opposing or dismissing her, you usually end up more entangled than ever. This conflict is heightened if a woman aligns herself with the prevailing patriarchal negativity toward nature, older women, and feminine wisdom. Rather, a woman must cultivate enough "positive mother" experiences to approach and listen with respect and hope to the Wise Old Woman, who knows how to contain both positive and negative aspects of nature.

The unconscious itself may help you in internal struggles with the negative mother. Just as symbols of the early feminine Self appear throughout life—but especially when you are younger—symbols of the Wise Old Woman appear throughout life—but especially as you become older. If negativity has predominated in your life, you may receive compensatory dreams of the positive side of the mother in the form of the Wise Old Woman. The inner positive mother will help you face your inner negative mother, and know her dark side, to neutralize its effects.

## A Modern Version of Cinderella

A woman in early middle age whose psyche was dominated by an inner negative mother shows us the process of struggling with the question of whether to accept the Wise Woman. Lorraine began therapy because of her fears that she might become "an old hag" or "a bag lady." In our society today, these can be realistic fears, especially for a woman, but they were irrational fears for her because Lorraine was secure financially and socially. Yet these images expressed her inner state. Lorraine had been neglected as a girl, and had always felt like a waif, a modern-day Cinderella. Her mother had not wanted her and had become alcoholic after Lorraine's father left home. The earliest dream Lorraine could remember in her life was one that tried to give her a compensatory experience to her history of neglect:

*The Bountiful Old Woman.* I was with an old woman—gray, dowdy, frumpy. She opened her closet and showed me her beautiful fabrics and beads. They were all different shades and colors. They were beautiful! I asked her why she didn't use them herself. She said, "Because I'm going to give them to you." I asked her, "Are you sure that you want *me* to have them?" She said, "Yes, I want you to have them." But I wasn't sure that I'd take them. I wasn't sure I'd know how to use them.

The unconscious was trying to correct Lorraine's general attitude—that she wasn't entitled to love and security. In the dream she was surprised, for her early neglect had led to such deep feelings of self-doubt and worthlessness that she could hardly believe this good fortune. Lorraine automatically expected the old woman to keep it all for herself! This might have been Lorraine's usual experience with her own mother, who, deserted by a husband and perhaps also lacking in mothering herself, might not have had much generosity left over for her daughter. The dream has a somewhat uncertain outcome. While Lorraine was convinced that the old woman indeed wanted her to have the beautiful things, she wasn't ready to accept them and didn't quite know how to take the next step to use them.

The old woman reminded Lorraine of her mother's housekeeper—the only positive person in Lorraine's early life. To feel entitled to the flow of life and love, it is important to find at least one person who passed on the positive mother to you. Lorraine's psyche had searched in her childhood and found someone who had indeed bestowed love upon her. In the dream, the old woman gave her beautiful fabrics and beads in different shades and colors. This should be understood symbolically. To let a girl—especially someone who feels like a waif—adorn herself with an array of beautiful clothes is to entitle her to the rich textures of life, to endorse her womanhood and let her shine and feel attractive to someone who can love her.

There is a magical quality to this dream, and something

extraordinary about the old woman, and a deeper archetypal pattern to the story of this woman, a waif afraid of the old hag. It echoes the story of Cinderella: the daughter in the ashes who is neglected by the stepmother, but is offered beautiful clothes by the fairy godmother, i.e., redeemed by the positive mother. The popularity of the story attests to how many women have felt like Cinderella, estranged from the good mother, without a father at home, suffering in silent servitude to the envious mother and sisters, but with romantic hopes to be chosen by the prince. How difficult it is for a woman to be caught between these two extremes: in everyday life feeling like an oppressed drudge in the ashes, yet, in her hopes, yearning to be an enchanted princess.

The most popular version, among the thousand variants of the Cinderella story, highlights the maiden being chosen by the prince. This indeed presents the task of early life: to marry and come into the fullness of your love and power. However, in real life, you can wish for this in vain. The problem is not just the lack of enough good princes who appreciate women, although that is indeed a real problem; nor is it just the romantic ideal with its attendant inner problem of being suspended between the two extremes of ashes or princess, and thus unable to see a range of real-life choices. The problem is that first you must find enough positive feminine within you to overcome the negative feminine—for this stage of womanhood as well as for later stages.

A Russian variation on the Cinderella story speaks more directly about Lorraine's current fear of being a bag lady and her archetypal concerns about midlife. The Russian fairy tale "The Beautiful Wassilissa," as told by Marie-Louise von Franz,[11] highlights the same crucial part of the story that this dream does: the necessary evocation of the good mother to restore the Self, to sustain the heroine in her struggles. And this story shows more of the whole picture than the Cinderella with its romantic ideal of the dutiful, helpless maiden waiting for the prince. Wassilissa is more of a heroine for today's woman. She first goes through many trials to overcome the negative mother, handles her vengefulness, and slowly learns how to integrate positive and negative aspects of the Self. To summarize pertinent aspects of the tale:

As Wassilissa's good mother was dying she gave her daughter a blessing and a doll to keep with her always for its wise advice. This reminder of her mother's love, and symbol of the feminine Self, gave Wassilissa the comfort, resilience, and wisdom to survive. Wassilissa's father remarried and then abandoned the family, so Wassilissa was left alone with the stepmother and stepsisters. One night, they let all the candles in the house burn out so Wassilissa would have to fetch some light [fire] from the great witch, Baba-Yaga. Wassilissa was afraid to go because anyone who approached the great witch was "eaten up like a chicken." The doll told her to go ahead, but to make sure she took the doll to help her. So Wassilissa went out to learn about the world. She became terrified when she approached Baba-Yaga's house. It was surrounded by a fence of human bones and a hedge with skulls whose eyes glowed. Baba-Yaga appeared with a mortar and pestle and broom [signs of the Earth Mother and her great powers] and ordered Wassilissa to do various tasks before she could take back the fire. If she didn't complete them, Baba-Yaga would eat her up. But the doll helped her complete the seemingly impossible tasks, one by one.

Then Baba-Yaga challenged the girl to ask her questions, and in her answers the great witch revealed her special powers over night and day, her true identity as Mother Nature. Wassilissa wisely refrained from probing too deeply into the mystery of death, that is, she did not let herself be devoured by curiosity, or eaten up by Baba-Yaga. Finally Baba-Yaga asked the girl a question, "How did you manage to do all the work I gave you?" When the girl answered, "The blessing of my mother helped me," Baba-Yaga let her go and gave her the light: a skull with flaming eyes. When she got home, the glowing eyes stared at the stepmother and stepsisters wherever they went and burned them to ashes.

Wassilissa buried the skull in the ground and left the

house for town. She stayed with a helpful old woman who gave her thread to make linen, and through her fine work she met and married the king. Her father returned to be near her in the palace, and so did the helpful old woman with whom she had stayed. And she kept the doll with her to the end of her life.

This story begins with the death of the good mother who leaves the daughter an amulet of great power and wisdom, and shortly afterward, the departure of the good father. This resonates deep and true as a picture of what the human condition has been for a long, long time: The good mother and the good father have both been lost. No wonder this fairy tale has flourished since the beginning of the patriarchal era, when the positive side of the goddess was eclipsed, and along with it, positive feminine qualities and positive paternal qualities. When this happens, what is left is the negative feminine, depicted here as the stepmother and stepsisters who deliberately put out the flame and persecuted Wassilissa, in jealous destructiveness toward any remnants of the life-giving force that they couldn't understand. What is also left is a false kind of positive feminine. This was depicted in the figure of Wassilissa (or Cinderella), whose reaction to the mother's early death was to become too passive, too dutiful, and to remain too innocent. In order to come into her true feminine power, Wassilissa must confront the archetypal feminine, which appears first only in its terrifyingly negative form, the death-dealing side of nature, the powerful witch. It is her doll amulet, an early Self figure representing her deep connection to the archetypal positive mother, who sustains her through her many tasks, so she can wrest something of great importance—the fire—from the witch.

When Wassilissa returned with the flame, the stepmother and her daughters were destroyed by the staring eyes of the skull—their own guilt and their inability to withstand negative archetypal force turned against them. It is crucial that Wassilissa buried the skull and left the house. That is, she could forgo this powerful tool of vengefulness and leave the past behind her. How difficult it is not to dwell on all the wrongs that have been done to you!

Then Wassilissa was open to the positive old woman who gave her the thread to make linen. The story at this point bears a remarkable similarity to Lorraine's dream: The positive old woman opened the closet and offered the dreamer beautiful fabric. This rings true psychologically. Women who have been waifs in early life and generally deprived of the positive feminine, cannot receive it freely, especially in middle and late life, but must make some effort and slowly learn how to let it take shape so they can integrate it into their lives.

It is noteworthy that only after all these efforts did Wassilissa marry the king; and only then was the father, the positive older man, restored, along with the positive older woman. This also rings true: Positive parenting, wise protectiveness, can prevail from both the masculine and feminine sides after restoration of the positive feminine. And the ending of the story makes it clear that a woman's great ally, always, is the positive feminine Self.

How does this bear upon Lorraine's fear of becoming an old hag or a bag lady? Just as Wassilissa wisely refrained from looking too closely at archetypal death, and just as she had to learn many tasks to reach the security of the palace, so, too, Lorraine must take many steps first. She must have the helpful old woman show her how to weave the fabric into a good life for herself. Then she can hope for security in her old age and the ability to face death. For the waif in us is more afraid of dying alone than of dying, and needs some comforters in the palace.

## Wary of the Cat and the Wise Old Woman

An eager and ambitious young woman, Joan, who was very politically aware, had an archetypal dream precipitated by an archetypal event in United States history: the 1986 explosion of the *Challenger* space shuttle in which the schoolteacher Christa McAuliffe died, leaving behind her young children. People across the nation were startled into questioning the risk of someone being blasted into space. The fact that a woman and mother was killed made us question whether authorities were so concerned about national heroism that they had become careless of personal risks. Perhaps we should not trust authority so much, for heroes can be "used."

The incident had especially shaken Joan because she, too, had taken a heroic path in life. She had always been thrilled by her father's world of competition and success. Joan had been fortunate in having had a good family background and education; she was also talented and self-confident. She sought challenges that few would dare, worked like a dynamo, and seemed to thrive on it. She loved the "highs" of success at work, but she hadn't noticed the toll it took, nor had she bothered to seek the remuneration that was her due.

Although Joan had developed her extraverted side to be successful at work, she had neglected her social life to some extent. Introverted by nature, she had come to analysis to cultivate her inner world. She also felt discontented and mildly depressed about her personal life. In fact, what had precipitated her starting analysis was a sad love affair. She hadn't been aware enough of her own personal needs so that she had come under the spell of her unconscious "other side," taking form in real life as a very dependent lover whom she somehow couldn't leave—even though she suspected deception and affairs.

Joan had two dreams, one a few days after the other. The first has a numinous cat, symbolic of feminine wisdom; the next, a Wise Old Woman.

> *A Wondrous Cat.* I had fallen asleep in my apartment. It was raining, and I was aware of the steady sound of rain and it felt comforting. Suddenly I woke with a start—still in the dream—and sat straight up in bed. I'd heard a sound from the kitchen. I wasn't wearing anything and felt naked as I walked slowly and cautiously into the kitchen. I'd left the door to the deck open a bit. Lo and behold, there was a wondrous cat! It was bigger than life. Dark brown with gray horizontal stripes. A thick coat.
>
> I don't care for cats; I'm somewhat allergic to them, so my first thought was: I don't want this cat

here! I thought about what to do. I couldn't throw it off the deck; it's too high off the ground. But how could I shut the door on it when it's pouring rain outside? Just as I was about to shut the door on it, it suddenly ran in as if it had made up *its* mind.

It seemed very needy. It jumped onto the kitchen table and started eating off a dinner plate. I was intrigued and felt compassionate toward it, and not angry anymore. I wondered, Do cats drink milk or water? I put a bowl of milk on the table.

Then I sat in a chair and heard Vivaldi's *The Rites of Spring* begin playing. I started to look at the cat. It looked up. It had exactly my eyes! I started crying and took the cat onto my lap. It felt warm and licked my hands and face.

Joan had this dream shortly after she began analysis and had just begun to discuss what she personally wanted instead of what others demanded of her. The dream portrays inner work on this issue. Near the beginning of the dream Joan was lying in bed, and was awakened from her sleep, the unconscious, to investigate something wrong. She had gone naked, without her usual defenses, to the kitchen, a place of nurturance. What she found was a cat—her own needs—left outside in the rain.

Whatever is not fulfilled in conscious life becomes an unconscious petitioner at the door. People usually try to maintain rigid controls or illusions to avoid seeing such gaps in their lives. Some people don't want to hear the truth even if others tell them or circumstances force it upon them. They avoid new experiences and new possibilities. Perhaps, at times, that's a wise choice: They can't afford the stress of the truth. If they were to open the door a flood of possibilities and anxiety might lead to more discontent or else drown them.

However, Joan had begun therapy to open herself up to new parts of herself. When you leave the door open like this, the instinctual and archetypal forces often know what to do, as this dream shows. At first in the kitchen she was torn between two extremes: whether to let the cat in, or leave it out in the cold. It seemed as if her dream ego had to make a conscious decision. She tried to decide intellectually—between protecting herself or being kind. But some decisions can't be made that way: *The cat ran in!* The instincts knew what was needed!

The dreamer's first impulse had been to get rid of the cat. Joan had always liked dogs because they were friendly. She probably identified with dogs because she herself was generous, likeable, and willing to please. She considered cats more introverted, more needy, and yet also more independent. She said, "Maybe I need to have my own raw instincts—to be needy with my lover, too."

Joan's initial anger in the dream shifted to compassion when she saw how hungry the cat was, and she became intrigued with how bold it was, taking what it wanted. Ordinarily, you can disparage such needs in others or yourself, unless you see them clearly—and up close—that is, relate to them. This is what happened next. Joan sat and really looked at the cat. It looked up, and she said that it had "exactly my eyes." So she actually encountered "the other." Joan saw herself in the cat. She said, "I know this is a raw part of me." Her sensitivity and aggression felt very real, but perhaps were too raw and unconscious to serve her well yet.

Then in the dream came her tears, the liquefaction of new consciousness, the dissolving of her defenses to find her own soft center—her compassion for the cat and for herself. It was as if the pouring rain at the beginning of the dream had come home to her as her own crying, letting go, getting wet, being vulnerable—which restores you, as it does the earth.

She had followed her impulses, which showed the deeply instinctual mother cat within herself as well as her own desire for a warm lap. The tears might also have been ones of relief that she could be bold and aloof like the cat who doesn't care so much what others think. Probably it was all of these. For they all need to come forth, not in subtle underground ways, so you're at the mercy of your own or others' instincts, but all the instincts right out there like a cat's. Then you can try to negotiate with them or handle them in some way, difficult though that may be.

The "wondrous cat" in Joan's dream is more than an

ordinary cat. The cat has been an archetypal symbol since at least Egyptian times, when it was so sacred that to kill one was to risk being put to death. However, the cat has also been viewed with great ambivalence through history. This dreamer didn't like cats, but liked dogs, which has been true for other people, too. In a study of how much people like different animals,[12] dogs were people's first choice, but cats were further down on the list, after swans, butterflies, elephants, and turtles, barely edging out ladybugs for the twelfth place. You might expect cats to be second or third, since many people love cats, but some people *dislike* them, and that brought their average rating down.

Why do people like—or dislike—cats so strongly? Although there are sometimes personal reasons, unconscious cultural reasons also permeate people's attitudes. During the Middle Ages cats were unmercifully tortured and killed on a large scale, just as today they are occasional targets for sadistic persecution. One reason for this widescale violence may be that the cat has been an archetypal symbol of the feminine throughout history. It was a prime scapegoat for man's wrath against the old goddess religion. During the centuries of witch hunts, cats were often burned, crucified, or drowned alongside women. We see remnants of this cultural negativity in Halloween images of the ugly witch and her familiar—a black cat with its hair standing up on end, looking terrified or terrifying. In modern times, the cat has continued to be a handy target for men's displaced fear and disdain of independent women, and their antipathy toward natural or feminine qualities in themselves.

What qualities gave cats such numinosity that they were sacred to the goddess Isis and were venerated in Egyptian temples?[13] What do they tell us about the essence of the "feminine," which seems so valuable and yet so dangerous? One thing that makes the cat special is that it represents the independence of the unconscious from our control. The unconscious is wild, like the cat. It won't come at our bidding and can't be tamed. At night it pounces on us unawares. The cat sees in the dark with the faintest gleam of light, and its eyes glow with a strange luminosity. Its eyes are different from the velvety, responsive eyes of the dog. The cat's meditative stare suggests unfathomable insight, and it does have uncanny intuitions about impending disasters, such as earthquakes. Because the cat is so much itself, disappears, but always comes home, it seems mysterious to us, like "the other," which seems so close and yet so far.

The cat also represents instincts, neglected parts of our own feminine nature—positive and negative. The cat has body-consciousness, demands its creature comforts of a safe warm place and food to its liking. It hates to be disturbed in its sleep or meditative languor. Female cats in heat screech to attract males. The cat tortures its victims—the only commonly-known animal, besides the human, to do so. Yet it also mothers its young, is sensuous and loves to be petted—when it pleases.

Of all the animals, the cat defines itself, maintains its individuality and essence, impervious to its keeper's wishes. That was one of the main meanings for Joan, who dreamed of a cat with her own eyes: to be true to her deepest instinctive self, to shift attention to herself, to be bold—like the cat in the dream—in asking for what she wanted and protecting herself from the rain.

Following the dream, Joan had a soul-searching talk with her brother, in which they both questioned whether they themselves had chosen their ambitious professions or whether their parents had chosen them. In further self-inquiry over time, Joan decided that she truly liked her work, but wanted better recompense—which she got. And, so that she would be less influenced by others' demands, she sketched out long-term career plans for herself.

In the personal sphere, Joan learned to take better care of herself. She gave up her role as the "good one" who endlessly rescued the relationship. She questioned her lover's obvious infidelity. She woke up from her long sleep of self-deception, which had left her open to another's deception. Joan had needed her own cautious, suspicious cat, and it found the rat. It was not easy to come down from her inflated view of herself. Joan was depressed to discover how much she had neglected herself and had let herself be "used" in her relationship, as in work.

In the time following the dream, Joan learned how to become more boldly self-protective. In shifting careful attention to her own self-worth, she became liberated from her extremes of giving to others freely and then recoiling in depletion and resentment. She became more freely generous toward people who would appreciate it, and more aloof, like the cat going her own way, when mistreated. She gained perspective on her role of being the heroic rescuer at work, oblivious of the personal cost. She learned the lesson of the *Challenger*: Heroines beware and choose well.

Several days after the Wondrous Cat dream, Joan had another emissary from her own introverted wisdom in a more advanced form—a wise old woman.

> **The Wise Old Woman Beckoning.** I'm driving to my lover's house in a convertible with the top down, open to the sun and wind. I stop because I need to go to the bathroom. In a field near the parking lot I see a woman getting up out of the tall grass. She looks at me with a beckoning look. She's dressed in a big full skirt and a black shirt, and she's old and wise. I see her looking in one direction and I follow her gaze: over the open fields toward the forest. Then I see her walking toward the forest. I watch her, feeling confused about what I should do.
>
> I get back in the car. Then, within a mile, I hit the wheel. I passed up an opportunity! I hope it's not too late to find her. I go back, but she's not there. The whole forest is gone. One thing she was to tell me about was death.

Joan woke up mad at herself for having missed an opportunity. "The Old Woman had a weathered face as if she'd experienced the elements. She didn't look American. I was intensely curious: She could have told me something about death, dying, letting go, surrendering to my own path. She *knows*."

Yet the dream ego hesitated to follow the old woman. Just because someone beckoned didn't mean that she had to follow! Since Joan had just begun analysis, perhaps she sensed her analyst

beckoning her to enter the forest, go deeper into the unconscious, when she didn't have confidence yet in her analyst—and
her own inner guide—as positive forces. Joan might have been
worried that the woman, though old and wise, would prove to be
a false guide or too much of a threat. She shouldn't follow just
because opportunity beckoned, or because she thought that her
analyst might want her to do so. With her intuitive and enterprising nature, Joan usually leaped at possibilities and opportunities in the outer world, but needed more caution to enter this
strange inner realm.

Moreover, the wise old woman in a big full skirt and black
shirt suggested to her a witch—a foreboding figure to us today.
However, if the inner witch is made conscious, it can become a
source of independence, strength, and spirituality. Can we trust
our own deepest intuition and imagination, our feminine knowledge about the dark and mysterious aspects of life? Someone like
Joan shouldn't necessarily entrust herself, like an innocent child,
to such a potent figure until she can hold her own. For, in fairy
tales, the innocent young girl must know—or learn—how to
approach the witch: when to ask questions and follow her
curiosity and when to be silent, when to stay and when to escape
and return home.

What did this dream mean specifically about Joan's life at the
time? Its meaning was not as obvious to her then as it became
later, in retrospect, when she saw more clearly how it had
poetically described her situation. Joan started the dream driving
a convertible, open to sun and wind; that is, she was apparently
in an open mood, open to nature and her own nature. She had to
stop and urinate on the way to her lover's house: She couldn't
hold back her negative, suspicious feelings any longer, so she had
to interrupt her trip to let them flow forth. Then she was
beckoned into the forest of dark intuitions about her lover:
suspicion, anger, and revenge. Deeper yet in the forest were
disturbing questions about her own loyalty, her own unwilling-
ness to commit, to live together, to marry. And farthest in the
forest was the truth she concealed from herself about her own
neglected, demanding side that wanted everything and ended up
alone. For these were all the things she did eventually find in her

unconscious when she listened to her dreams, when she asked the questions she had been afraid to ask.

Over the next year Joan moved forward a few steps toward confronting these issues, then retreated, forward and back. Finally, she ended the bad relationship. This was the "death" the wise old woman knew about in the dream, and which Joan survived, eventually much relieved.

Joan ended analysis over a year later when she had embarked upon a more promising relationship, one with more equality and commitment on both sides. By then, she had more of the weathered, wise old woman within her and less of the innocent woman with only vague, dark intuitions. She had to forgo some of her great wishes for "everything," and the denial of certain realities that inevitably accompanies that, for her dreams showed her the price of illusion: being left outside like a wet cat and passing by the opportunity to make difficult but wise choices. As the years passed, she continued step by step, glimpsing the Wise Old Woman, sometimes refusing her, yet becoming more and more open to her as time went by, in the process claiming more of her own strength—and weakness—which is what wisdom is.

## Courage from the Wise Old Woman

In contrast to the preceding dreamer, who was initially wary of the Wise Old Woman, a much older woman felt too eager initially, then paused and made a firm decision from her inmost heart to accept this figure into her life.

> *The Old Russian Refugee.* **There are some tattered Russian refugees in the back of a truck. I'm eager to see them, curious about them. I walk rapidly over to them, and help an old lady down from the back of the truck. She has dark, bright eyes and looks frail and wise. She puts her hand over my arm. We have a feeling of good humor, and we smile at each other.**
>
> **I find that it will take all my strength to support her! Then I realize that my smile is too bright. I**

**suddenly have doubt, from fear and from my false eagerness. As soon as I realize that, however, I have a surge of strength: I feel responsible and know that I want to do it! I'm no longer afraid.**

This dream came to Charlotte, an elderly woman, the day before she had to undergo another operation—one of a series of such ordeals in her life, and it gave her the inner experience of overcoming fear. She had had a difficult childhood. Her mother had been sick, and then had left her. Her adult life had been full of real hardships, which she had borne with denial, humor, and lightness of spirit. Her older age was also likely to be difficult because friends had moved away or died and she faced increasingly severe health problems.

The dream suggested that this time Charlotte was evolving another way. She couldn't dance lightly over difficulties, but would have to come to terms with real weakness and take certain kinds of responsibility for herself. She must take the frail old lady by the hand. In her childhood, this was something as a daughter that she couldn't do for her own sick mother. She had been too young to take on so heavy a burden. However, at the time of the dream, facing a great hardship herself, she couldn't deny the burden, couldn't escape it by her usual means, such as keeping busy and being philosophical and humorous. She must pause and muster her innermost integrity. This happened symbolically in the dream. From the archetypal layer of the unconscious, and from her compassion and fortitude, came guidance. Remembering the feeling in the dream, she said, "A wise old woman doesn't say or do. She *is*. She trusts her intuition, her experience, the knowledge passed down to her. There are no shortcuts. And it is enough. In the dream, the wise old woman and I gave each other courage."

Then she recalled one of the few positive women figures in her life—a nun she had known as a girl. "She was a powerhouse of wisdom and love. I was a show-off and had gotten a 'D' in deportment, but she shaped me up. She had courage in her faith, and she had eyes that could twinkle but also look into the depth of your soul. There's a type of woman who just *is*." And, she added, "You do the work you must do." This is the fortitude of the older woman.

What does this dream tell us about getting to know the Wise Old Woman? The dreamer's first step was to follow her compassionate impulse, which echoed her deeply buried sympathy for her mother and herself in hardship and suffering. The crucial turning point was to recognize "false eagerness." Why did this recognition give her such a surge of strength? In important matters of the heart, a woman must be true to her inner feelings. To pretend to feel something, or practice acting in a certain way, doesn't help you or anyone else. You lose your center and scatter your resources, and it feels false to someone else. As a young girl, Charlotte had to act too brave with her ailing mother, an additional hardship for her. This dream, then, helped her shed the burden of false bravery.

This dreamwork helped Charlotte gather up courage and strength and weave together the real strands of her life: her girl-like bravado, her compassion—and helplessness—regarding her mother's frailty and her own. She found her own show-off and her powerhouse nun. Charlotte faced a great ordeal at the time of the dream and she couldn't put on a false front, nor make light of things, nor shrink from hard realities. Her psyche was preparing her for older age and incapacitation, which would require all her compassion and fortitude. And the Wise Old Woman would give her true grit, perhaps without losing a twinkle in her eye.

A month later Charlotte had a dream where she affirmed her inner, introverted strength, and differentiated her way from her grandmother's more extraverted one.

> *Great-Grandmother's Mirror.* I look at myself in an oval mirror. I look at my dress: a long gray dress with a white collar—big and broad like a nun's collar. My grandmother stands nearby to see if I want it. I can have it if I want. What that means is: I can have my own strength.

Charlotte's actual grandmother had seemed like a negative crone to her: thorny and controlling. In her extraverted way, the grandmother was always disciplining her and telling her what to do. In contrast, this dream presented another kind of positive crone, and gave her the experience she would have liked. It was as if the dream re-did history to give her what had been missing. The psyche often does this to quicken in a woman the potentials that haven't had a chance to come to life in outer experience.

In the dream, the grandmother stood nearby and respected the granddaughter's own self-assessment, affirmed her own introverted view of herself. This experience came not only from the outside, somehow salvaged from the grandmother's structure and discipline, but mainly from Charlotte's own sense of wholeness, seen in the full-length mirror. Charlotte mentioned that the mirror was oval—an interesting detail. Not to be perfectly round, but to be elliptical, suggests an idiosyncratic, individualistic, feminine shape. In the mirror, then, Charlotte saw a reflection of her inner basic feminine Self.

The mirror is generally a symbol of self-reflection, self-knowledge, and truth—separate from surroundings. It represents the wisdom born of contemplation more than the wisdom that comes out of activity. It reflects an introverted sense of yourself, which you know by self-scrutiny more than you do by deeds—who you are, not what you do. In this dream, the grandmother stood by and let the granddaughter choose to identify with the models of feminine strength who fit her: introverted nuns she knew who were strong. They were some of the few women she knew back then who, she said, "ran their own things." The mirror also reminded her of her great-grandmother—another positive model for her.

A woman's psyche unerringly finds a way to remind her of the models she needs from the past. The mirror had special meaning to Charlotte because it had belonged to her great-grandmother, who had owned a trading post on the Western Plains. The mirror, six or seven feet high, had stood in her great-grandmother's parlor, and since it was the only big mirror in the territory, the Plains Indians walked in to see themselves in ceremonial dress. This mirror, then, represented the openness, the extraversion, the positive crone aspect of her great-grandmother. The great-grandmother was interested in others, and, with the true pioneer spirit of the West, she had opened her house to others, however different, and had discarded the pretensions and conventions of society at the time to make her own rules, be her own person—and be a model of feminine strength for her great-granddaughter. So this great-grandmother was there, backing her up, behind the figure of the grandmother. They were both mirrors of herself, and who she could be, as an older woman.

Like the stern mother with authority, the Wise Old Woman can also help someone say "no" when necessary. For example, a middle-aged divorced woman had decided to get involved in a relationship with a man very similiar to her ex-husband, with whom she had a destructive relationship. At this crucial turning point, she had a dream of her analyst suddenly appearing before her with arms raised in a strong gesture, saying, "No. Absolutely No."

One of the Wise Old Woman's roles, especially as the Crone, is to help a woman come to terms with limitations and the unknown, as she helped Charlotte mobilize inwardly for her operation. In her cold aspect of facing the truth, the Wise Woman is an unflinching witness who *knows*, and can be an ally for a woman who must withstand unavoidable hardship and suffering, such as taking care of a husband with Alzheimer's disease, so she doesn't feel so alone. And, in the end of life, the Wise Woman with her fierce heart lends a woman the compassion and courage to make decisions on when to comply with heroic patriarchal measures of prolonging life and when to counter them and let death come naturally with less suffering, indignity, and loss of personhood.

## Archetypal Changes

In contrast to the gradual changes of the previous sections, the slow growth of the apple tree and the process of approaching the

Wise Old Woman within, sometimes important changes occur as a result of encountering the archetypal dimension in life. Archetypal events in the outer world evoke great turmoil and require archetypal resolutions within a person. The inner world of dreams provides an arena for this process, sometimes for repetitive nightmares, and, if a person is fortunate, for transformation. An experience of transcendent feelings and symbols can precipitate a major shift in your relation to the Self. You may feel the lifting of a burden, or a "change of heart" toward those you love. You may find a gift beyond human compassion—transpersonal love or grace. Sometimes this happens at times of great need.

## The Circle of Plenty

Maxine had been undergoing an acute physical problem—excessive and prolonged bleeding for many months, requiring medical care. This physical upheaval was also reflected in her dreams of feminine and masculine figures in trouble. At about the same time these inner figures settled into place, the excessive bleeding stopped. So we know that she was experiencing great psychic movement.

At this time, Maxine received a big grant she had sought for a project. Like most women in her family as well as in her work place, she had never been in a position of such potential authority—an administrator. She was surprised to get the grant, and had to decide what she wanted to do with it. A dream helped her:

> *The Wise Old Black Man and Sharing the Cake.* I'm in a subway under an unknown city, perhaps Chicago or Paris, but the subway actually looks more like the Boston MTA. I get on a train, since you can get off at any station and easily get back on.
>
> I'm still underground, and go over to a sidewalk stand where someone says there's plenty extra of a big round cake. I cut a piece—one-fourth of the cake—and offer it to an older black man. [I see each person in the dream, and yet I'm also each person, so when I offer a piece to the black man, I'm also offering it to

myself, and so forth.] He, in turn, cuts it into pieces for me and four other black men—a total of four [sic] of us.

The black man looks like a composite of three black men who come to mind: an old railroad steward; Paul—an older, close confidant of mine; and an even older and wiser man with graying temples. I'm concerned that the wise old man will have some cake left for himself, but he cuts the last part in half—for himself and me. It's a spongy kind of cake, almost unreal. It's good—the way it worked out.

These figures are all parts of Maxine, activated at a time of her journey into a new life, a new inner position. She is apparently reaching far into the unconscious to make this change. Generally, dream figures who come from another era, another sex, another race, age, culture, or remote parts of the world imply more distant parts of your own psyche. This is just a general framework, though, and personal associations are all-important. What did the three black men mean to this dreamer?

Maxine's associations to the railroad steward and the subway trip harkened back to an earlier time of great change for her. She remembered that when she was a young teenager right after World War II, she had left home and had taken a long train trip across the country to live with relatives. At that time of great outer and inner transition, the old black railroad stewards represented "safe passage" to her in their position of professional protectors and with their personal qualities of kindness toward her. Maxine felt a pang at the memory of those figures from another era whom she had to leave behind, because they no longer fit modern times: the young, innocent woman in a position of privilege, and her counterpart, the steward who protects and serves others. Yet she needn't abandon everything she valued from that era. The dream suggested that she could salvage and bring forward into her life some of her young girl's trust, and some of her own inner steward's professional and personal qualities of protectiveness, devotion, and kindliness.

The next figure in the composite Wise Old Man was

someone more contemporary in her life. Paul, in reality, was a somewhat older close friend. She felt some kinship with him, partly because of their somewhat similar positions in this society—she as a woman and he as a black. He was more experienced in the world, and a model for her of someone who quietly but firmly took authority, and handled things with some give and take. Despite differences in background, their relationship was reciprocal, so Paul represented a different position from the steward: a current, more equal position with an inner figure with reciprocity, "one who is served and serves."

The third figure was a more archetypal Wise Old Man who was beyond her personal knowledge, but who imparted to this dream a transformative message and underscored the fact that this dream could not be understood rationally. The confusion of the dream was that she and the black men were one and the same; they were three and one or four in one. The confusion of dividing the round cake—symbolic of the Self—was that it could actually be endlessly divided and shared. The supposed confusion to the rational mind of "giving is receiving" could not be figured out rationally, only accepted as a mystery. Giver and receiver were the same. This was true wisdom of the heart.

The dream reminded Maxine—who had gone to Sunday school—of the Miracle of the Loaves in the Bible (Matt. 15.32–39), when Jesus broke several loaves of bread before the multitudes and the pieces multiplied and became enough bread for everyone. One rational explanation of the parable that Maxine had heard was that everyone who had brought bread was afraid of bringing it out and having to share it with others, so no one had anything to eat. However, when Jesus broke bread and handed it out, everybody could follow his example and there was plenty for all. The practical message of the parable, then, was that there is enough to go around if everyone trusts and shares. At the same time, Maxine felt very moved by the story as a miracle, for she sensed its transcendent meaning: the Self contains endless bounty. To partake of the Self does not diminish the source. Or, God is bountiful.

In Maxine's dream, there was also enough to go around; and to share and receive was the same. That is, what augments another person augments us all, just as what diminishes another person diminishes us all, because we are all one family. This goes beyond the usual rules of ownership and fairness that the ego knows by its being bound mainly to material realities.

The dream, with her associations to it, left Maxine with a change of heart about the new grant she had received. It cut through her unconscious sense of being "high and mighty" and possessive—or even perhaps greedy—about it. Rather than feeling awed about becoming a grant administrator, she felt a shift to another kind of spirit altogether—appraising the whole situation as simply one person "among the multitudes." These Wise Old Men helped her find an original solution. She could be someone who serves and parcels out, and is also served herself. This fundamental change in attitude—not even something she could put into words—was manifested months later as the surprising, but easy and appropriate, decision to turn the grant over to someone else. Maxine saw that a colleague was especially well situated to be the administrator and would gladly accept the position. Maxine retained one slice of the pie, to be a consultant, freeing herself for what she preferred—to follow her heart in more enterprising pursuits. For the mystery of the Self—the round cake—regenerates ever anew.

## The Inner Man of Heart

Previous dreams in this chapter had important male figures—an old man who leaned over backwards and a Wise Old Man of transcendent humanity. Negative male figures of archetypal inhumanity in dreams are the devil, Hitler, and other extremely cruel or powerful men. A woman who has a difficult background with men in her life may focus on the negative aspects of a male figure in her dreams for a long time. She may feel at the mercy of Merlin's misuse of power, or feel pressured to conform to judgments and rigid rules of an inner figure like Moses, until she can gradually come to know their more positive paternal aspects, too. What other male figures can bring a woman knowledge to round out her feminine wisdom of the heart? While inner female figures of authority and mercy, to which women feel entitled, may be quite straightforward, male dream figures may, especially at first, be heroes like D'Artagnan of the Three Musketeers, the Count of Monte Cristo, or Robin Hood, who try to right wrongs by revenge, plots, or intrigue. Or, a woman may have a figure like Percival, the young knight of pure heart and ideals, searching for the Grail. Other males in dreams may be archetypal figures of transcendent love and wisdom such as Buddha, Gandhi, a priest, an inner masculine voice of authority.

A woman may dream of an ordinary man on the street with special qualities, her father, mate, or someone else she knows who brings her the kind of wisdom she needs. The figures may display human qualities seen as traditionally masculine: fairness, reciprocity, protectiveness, humanitarianism, perspective, teamwork—an ease and objectivity in tolerating the shadow of others and working well together. They may also exhibit special emotions, heartfelt empathy, or maternal qualities usually seen as feminine, if a woman lacks these in her repertoire, for inner figures are not necessarily stereotypic.

Older women sometimes have dreams with youthful figures whose energy complements that of the Wise Old Woman. On the eve of embarking on a new enterprise, one woman in her older age had a dream of an exciting man in his forties who swept her into his arms and carried her into the bedroom. A middle-aged woman had dreams of a man who reminded her of Pan, the earthy, lighthearted goat god who plays the flute and delights in dance, music, sexuality, and nature. In dreams, women can find connections to the masculine within themselves in very traditional forms—perhaps through a passionate lover—which can prove to be transcendent for them. These animus figures often have an aura of the numinous about them, and have a great impact on women that is healing.

One of the tasks of old age is to review your life and come to terms with life and death. This involves accepting what has and hasn't been fulfilled in life, coming to terms with the great gaps and healing old wounds. Sometimes you can fill in missing parts in an outer way—but more often only in an inner way. Just as a woman grows older biologically—through her hormones—and becomes both more feminine and more masculine, this is true psychologically, too. She reverberates with feminine and masculine strength. In her dreams she may retrieve the sensitive, whimsical young girl or the energetic, dauntless, young woman whom she lost long ago simply by growing up female in this culture. These inner figures may gradually get older in the course of her dreams until she reaches her full womanly strength. In a similar way, masculine figures may be constellated in her psyche, as illustrated in the previous dream, so that she may encounter her own masculine side, and the masculine side of boys and men she has known, and bring her masculine side to its fullness in her inner and outer life.

An elderly woman had worked long years in analysis on her father problem. In all her years of growing up, she couldn't recall any time when her father had called her by name. He was a very intellectual man from an austere culture, and he had wanted a boy, not another girl. A main issue for her, then, had been to overcome this early rejection and make some kind of positive bridge to men in her life and to the masculine within her. It is never too late. At the end of her seventies she had a dream that was very moving for her, as if the earth had shifted on its axis.

> **In One's Late Seventies: Passion for a Well-Formed Man.** I was with a man who was pleasing to me in every way. His body was well muscled, well formed, and strong. He seemed calm and intelligent, and very much "there" in the moment. We were nude and our bodies were in close contact. I was participating in our arousal by slowly moving my hand down his body. As my hand came in contact with his testicles, our mutual passion culminated and I woke up with an orgasm. I had a feeling of completion and relaxation that was wonderful.

She said that it was totally unexpected—such a great orgasm. For a woman truly knows things through her passion. She had not had an intimate man in her life for a long time, but her dream had given her the experience for which she was ready. This experience, taken together with recent events in her life, "felt," she said, "like the ultimate correction of my father problem."

In the days before the dream she had had an especially meaningful conversation with a male colleague over lunch. She had revealed her feelings to him about personal troubles and he had responded to her with such feeling that she had been deeply moved. In a body therapy session the same day she had been greatly helped by the sensitive and effective touch of a gifted male body therapist. She said, "At one point, as part of the maneuvers, I held on to his arm and was acutely aware of how strong and solid it was. After the session I experienced a soul-shaking sense of gratitude for his ministrations. I went for a walk in nature to stay close to my feelings. On the walk I recalled how unrelated my father had seemed to me, how I felt unappreciated with no fatherly affection or closeness from this profoundly introverted man all the years of my growing up."

The deepest wounds, the greatest gaps in life, can be where true intimacy was missing, both emotional and physical. But where the wounds are: There lies the healing. How profound it is for a woman to open up herself wholeheartedly—body and soul—to a man who truly "meets" her! And how healing it can be. In thinking over the dream and the men with whom she had felt close during the previous days, the dreamer said, "I've had affairs with men and have experienced a deep transference to a male analyst, but I haven't ever had the *inner* sense of intimacy and gratitude that I've now experienced with these men." She had restored a great personal and archetypal dimension in her life: her bridge to the masculine and men—whom she could love. In the very earth of her womanhood, she had known a well-formed man and he had moved her, heaven and earth.

Sometimes when the outer world has dealt us a blow and we feel hopeless or worthless, as if we have lost our center and our resilience in life, something unexpected happens. From the innermost core of our being comes a transcendent experience of renewal which links us once again to the flow of life and hope. This sense of renewal feels unexpected, impossible, like grace, a gift from God. And it is "from beyond." For, no matter how much we might have wished it, no matter how determined we might have been, we could not have actually brought it about. We can give problems conscious attention in our outer life. And we can prepare the ground through attention to inner life— dream and fantasy work and openness to healing experiences— but the transcendent life-giving force still comes out of the blue. Often, it just comes when we most need it. Then the proper attitude is not to scoff at it in modern disbelief, nor be dazzled by it, but be grateful.

A middle-aged woman, Shirley, received devastating criticism from another woman at work, which seemed to stab the same place where Shirley had been wounded by her mother while growing up. Shirley could hardly maintain the usual cheerful facade required in her job. She had started to become depressed when she had this remarkable "big dream."

> *The Fourth Dimension.* I'm in class with a well-known Tai Chi master. In fact, he's my own teacher's old master. He's a master of masters. It's a three-sided room, with the fourth wall missing. The master suddenly leaps up and out—where the fourth wall "isn't." He falls down and goes *into* the sidewalk and becomes one with it, leaving a black and yellow spot on the sidewalk. Then he comes up again!
>
> Everyone is amazed that he could go into the sidewalk and *come out* again. He comes up and resumes teaching and posturing, lifting his knee and turning, as everyone watches amazed. I look nonchalant, not feeling anything, as if I assume everything's fine and nothing big has happened, although I know it has.
>
> The Tai Chi master comes and sits beside me. I sense his caring, that there's caring between us, and that it took tremendous effort to do what he did. He's feeling very vulnerable, but no one knows it except me.

This dream felt to Shirley like an impulsive leap forward, and she realized how depressed she had been. In her high-pressure urban life, she had lost contact with her own feelings. Perhaps that was why she had chosen Tai Chi, a moving meditation, in order to feel harmony in her body and perhaps keep the creative, spiritual side of her alive.

Shirley had been feeling good until the recent jolt at work when she crashed against hard realities again. In the dream, this is expressed in the poetic image of crashing into the sidewalk. The sidewalk is an apt metaphor for urban life with its segmentation, uniformity, and its hard barrier of cement covering Mother Earth. However, instead of smashing himself against it, the inner figure, the great Tai Chi master, "became one with it." He represented the dreamer's innermost capacity to leap forward impulsively, go through the cement of her defenses to the pain of her emotion, and bounce back relatively unscathed. He also left evidence that a miracle had truly happened.

Evidently Shirley's natural propensity, as described in the dream, was to stiffen herself against feeling anything and act blasé, although she did know intellectually that something miraculous had happened. In the dream she noticed how amazed everyone else was, but felt reluctant to join the crowd. That is, evidence alone—a demonstration of a special feat—wasn't enough to reach her. What it took was personal caring. When the Tai Chi master of masters sat beside her, she could sense his kindness, and then she could acknowledge and respect what he had done.

In working through her associations, it turned out that this dream also gave Shirley renewed hope about her relationship with her partner. She could go beyond the three walls of reality to a wholeness or completion, a fourth dimension, the dimension that can't be seen, but can only be imagined and felt: a special dimension of human connectedness. It would require a "tremendous effort" to take this leap of faith and confront vulnerability, to make a wordless bond with a figure of the Greater Self, a connection to her own deepest emotional, caring center. This is what had been wounded by the critical mother and the critical woman at the office, who made her feel unloved and hopeless. So this is what needed to be healed. And Shirley realized that in her personal life this is what she needed to do with her partner if she wanted to realize the love they could have—to take the risk to do something dramatic, take the impulsive leap forward, dare to be inspired without being inflated.

The dream hauntingly illustrates the archetypal theme of the three dimensions of reality and the leap of faith into the fourth dimension, the realm of imagination and spirit. This is archetypal imagery, which has existed throughout human history in various forms—the fall and the resurrection, death and rebirth. It is difficult to leave the ground of our everyday reality and take a leap of imagination to know about another existence. And it is very human to be afraid to do so. Shirley's initial reaction of denial registers a psychological truth similarly experienced in the Bible. Even Peter, Jesus' most trusted disciple, had a lapse of courage or faith.

If you look this up in the Bible, you will see that during the time of Jesus' trial before the crucifixion, Peter was afraid to admit he was a disciple, or had a lapse of faith. As had been prophesied, when he was questioned he denied Christ three times, saying that he had never known Him. ("And the second time the cock crew. And Peter called to mind the word that Jesus said unto him, Before the cock crow twice, thou shalt deny me thrice. And when he thought thereon, he wept." —Mark 14:72) How profoundly human this is. It is indeed difficult to accept the spiritual dimension in life, and we depend on the personal presence of someone we love to overcome our doubts, withstand others' doubts, and sustain our faith through certain times.

This dreamer had long "put a hold" on her spirituality and her creativity in life, but they emerged spontaneously to affect her life. And this dream helped her depression begin to lift.

## Archetypal Darkness: Hearts That Break—and Endure

A woman's usual way of knowing is to empathize, to move closer, to relate personally to someone or something. This is what happened with the previous dreamer: Someone's caring in the dream softened her so that she could reach her center. However, there are some forces that must be related to on their own terms.

The reality of great negative archetypal forces must be acknowledged. It is futile to try to deny or diminish them.

In everyday life, people in middle-class Western culture are largely insulated from confronting deep moral issues or issues of life-and-death, but sometimes we personally encounter archetypal events that resonate with important issues. For example, if a woman is pressured to make an immediate decision to terminate an unexpected pregnancy, something deep inside her may recoil at making a quick answer with the rational ego alone, trivializing and glossing over its importance. She may need to weigh carefully the human and real-life consequences. This kind of decision must come from the core of a woman's feeling, her whole being, and the dark side of the Self. This requires inward preparation. She may get in touch through her dreams with not just the nurturing side of nature, but the destructive side—the Kali side of nature that can say No and let life go sometimes. A woman may need to search deep within to know her spiritual concerns and relate properly to the awesome archetypal forces of nature—the power to give or destroy life.

Archetypal decisions cannot be made in a rational, heartless way as if there were a simple answer. Other cultures closer to nature provide images of other ways. The Native American hunter pauses and takes a moment for a ritual that acknowledges reverence for the life he must take. Medical volunteers at the Thai camps for Cambodian refugees saw a mother, who was holding two infants, let the healthier one suckle, and the sicklier one die, so that at least one might live. That mother was accepting archetypal, impersonal reality with a deep instinctive mother-knowledge. In this one image can be seen natural relatedness and natural coldness. It is terrible, but understandable. It is poignant; it is detached, but respectful of human feeling: This is the way it must be. There is no fascination, no place for complicated intellectual thought, no place for emotional hysteria. This is different from human evil, where there is unconscious fascination with power and emotional intensity yet blunted sensitivities. Human evil is warped, cruel, dehumanizing, and repetitive, such as in atrocities of war or compulsive abuse.

Of course, even if we do relate as appropriately as we can,

negative archetypal forces—like earthquakes or storms in the physical world—can still devastate us. The same is true for positive archetypal forces. We know this instinctively. Artists have depicted people being struck blind when they encounter the archetypal force of angels. These artists have acknowledged the awesome energy in the mystery of things far beyond our power and understanding.

What happens to women who don't have choices but are the victims of destructiveness, such as abuse, rape, street violence, war, or terrorism? They may be haunted by nightmares—repetitive re-living of the events which cannot be integrated. Over time, the nightmares may evolve to help heal the wounds. However, some dark betrayals of humanity cannot be fully healed, cannot be transformed; they can only be endured.[14] What happens to survivors? They suffer a sudden loss of innocence, a loss of trust in the world and themselves, and react with such feelings as fear, rage, denial, avoidance, helplessness, depression, guilt, self-doubt, or the breakdown of their physical, mental, or spiritual strength. At these times, human warmth, or the quiet presence of someone nearby, can help a woman keep alive her life-force against the forces of darkness. At a deeper level, nightmares register the wounds in the core of a woman's being. It helps to have someone witness nightmares—to listen and share some of the terror, the raw pain. Even small changes in imagery can give a woman some hope and the sense that the Self is her inner ally, trying to help. People who have lived through similar trauma truly *know* what it is like, and can be the most healing.[15]

We cannot find, yet, any signs of transformation in the following nightmares. We can only witness these women's stories, be unsettled by them, and do what we can so other women do not suffer similar tragedies. One solution for these particular women—Salvadoran refugees—lay in social support and action. They are examples for us all of how the human heart might be shattered—and yet persevere. These are the women's stories recorded by the journalist Lonny Shavelson.[16]

After Laura's husband refused to take a job that he feared was associated with the death squads, he was shot to death.

*The Dreams of Laura Montero.* I am so afraid of these dreams I try not to sleep. I travel each night in my dreams to see my children. I am afraid they are suffering, that they are ill. I tell them we will soon be together. The older is very happy to hear this, but the little one cries. And sometimes when I wake I reach him by phone and hear these same words: "Mama, take me with you."

I dream we are all together in our home as we were before. Then *they* arrive, and the children's screams begin. My husband falls on top of me and I fall to the floor with him in my arms. I look at my hand and see his blood on it. And I wake up in horror. Because this dream is exactly what happened.

Laura has been granted political asylum in the United States, and is trying to bring her children to safety.

When she was eight, Gilma Cruz would run to her church to watch Father Rutilio feed the doves. The death squads killed Father Rutilio and a 15-year-old boy who was walking to mass with him. She remembers his face, and the blood. "This is how children grow up so quickly in El Salvador," Gilma says.

*The Dreams of Gilma Cruz.* After I dream I awake with the memory of people crying out for me to help them, screaming in pain. "Come help me!" I am always hearing the marching feet in my dreams. I can see the uniforms but not their faces. And then they get to me—and I wake up.

But my dreams come in the daytime also. When I go to church and there is the smell of candles my mind fills with the feelings of when I was small. And I am standing by the table with Father Rutilio's body, and all the people are crying and asking, "Why? Why?" And the mother is hugging her dead child. All this comes back when I smell the candles of the church.

At age fourteen, Gilma escaped from El Salvador, and three years later in the United States she began a hunger strike for other refugees to be granted political asylum.

When Rosa and Antonio Alvarado's son was "disappeared," they began working for the Families of the Disappeared, and became a thorn in the government's side when they spoke out at human rights conferences—internationally. When the body of Rosa's brother was found, naked and burned, they left the country. "Every day, every day, something reminds me of my son," Rosa says. "I have developed sores on my knees from praying." "There is this permanent nightmare," Antonio says, "of never knowing what happened."

> *The Dreams of Rosa Alvarado.* Last night I was taking care of a neighbor's baby and I fell asleep. The mother came to me in my dream, asking for her child. But in my dream I couldn't tell if they had taken her child or my own. I became confused and woke up and ran with great fear to the other room—and the baby was still there.
>
> I dream there is a big party in front of my house in El Salvador. Everyone is dancing and I feel so happy to be there. Then everyone sees me, and the party stops. I am so frightened by the expressions on their faces that I hide in my house. The need to speak is like a weight on me when suddenly I see the shadow of a soldier in the house. And I wake up with the lasting feeling of the menace of the soldier. And I cannot go to sleep again.
>
> I have so many dreams. But I never dream of my son. I never see his face. I always dream that they are chasing me and I am running. But at the moment when I will either be caught or escape I wake up. There is never any resolution, never an ending.

In these stories we can see that great adversity can also bring forth great spirit. In the first, Laura continues to search for her child; Gilma undertook a hunger strike for others; Rosa lent her efforts to a group for the "disappeared." Mothering and loving spirit are such powerful forces in women's lives that mothers of young children cannot afford to give up, and in fact, rarely commit suicide. Though their hearts may break at terrible losses, they keep the flame of humanity alive, comfort and are comforted, and try to spare others from mankind's inhumanity to children, women, and men.

Let us not insulate ourselves from these women and their suffering, but share their burden. For their nightmares are ours, too. They portray the dark shadow of "heroic" patriarchal society with its terrorism, politics of violence, and commerce in weaponry.

## Grace

Religion, the religious community, spiritual practice, and spiritual images can sustain people in great distress through times such as the death of a loved one. Even though a person may not have been raised in a religious framework, when something in the realm of the spiritual occurs, the psyche may use whatever religious imagery may fit. Often the psyche uses the religious imagery of the dominant culture in the society—even though the person may not have been raised in that faith, because it is the particular language that the culture generally uses to speak about certain archetypal events.

In this particular situation, an older woman had lost her husband. She had had a Christian upbringing, but didn't attend church. She was deeply spiritual, but since her husband's death had become alienated from her faith and could hardly pray now that she needed to. She had always relied on her own spiritual practice and counsel from deep within, which finally did emerge. This series of two dreams heralded a quickening of the inner spirit for her.

*Over the Cliff.* **I'm driving my car. I approach the crest of a cliff and keep driving. Right ahead of us, straight below, I can see a body of water. The car goes ahead**

over the edge, teeters for a moment, then gravity pulls
it down in front and it starts the plunge. It's in slow
motion. My mind is racing. I must call on the Holy
Spirit! I must pray hard. The only possibility for me
to be okay is if I totally concentrate—despite the
dilemma—on the Holy Spirit. The car hits the water
before I awaken. I'm praying anyway.

She recalled that during the previous week she had been
driving as usual along the Pacific coast where she lived when she
discovered herself driving fast around a curve. She had noticed
the sign to slow down to twenty miles per hour, and had thought,
"They *do* go off. It'd be *easy* to go off." She hadn't acknowledged
the potential seriousness of her fleeting thoughts about flirting
with death until this dream. It warned her to drive more carefully
for there was a suicidal undercurrent in her unconscious which, in
an impulsive moment, could take over.

The woman's husband had recently died of cancer. They had
had a good marriage; in fact, it was a fortunate and rare match.
There was a deep bond between them and they were good for
each other. They truly enjoyed each other and expected to live
together into very old age. It was indeed a great loss for her to
bear. And in a great love like this, a woman sometimes projects
the Self onto her husband, and that means that she also grieves
her loss of soul, her connection to life itself and the universe. She
had been keeping a journal, doing grief work in therapy, and had
finally reached what she said felt like a "deep, dull, hard place of
neglect." She had tried, then, to pray but it seemed futile, as if she
couldn't reach what she called "that big tin ear in the sky." She
was angry at God! A great loss like this can bring in its aftermath
a sense of abandonment, anger, cynicism, and, as the dream
suggested, a strong wish or "pull" to follow the loved one, if not
an undertow of archetypal death.

She had been casually missing some appointments with her
therapist, but this dream suddenly alerted them both to the fact
that she must keep every appointment. It might be a matter of life
and death. She needed a helping hand at this crucial time in her
life.

The dream meant to her that she was reaching a kind of careless despair. The dream showed that she herself must try to make direct contact with the Self—the healing spirit—instead of passively yielding to the course of gravity and following her husband. She said, "Praying was the most important part! I have to be fervent in making a connection to life."

Two months later, the night before minor surgery, she had a similar dream, but different in important respects.

> **The Holy Spirit.** I'm in the car going over the cliff, then heading down through the air toward the water. I think, "This is it!" I know that it's vitally important to connect with the Holy Spirit. I'm aware that I've made the connection, just in time, as the car hits the water.
>
> Then I'm out of the car, in the water, close to shore. As I'm swimming, I roll over and look at the beautiful sky. It's very *blue*, and the trees are very *green*. I feel as if a miracle has happened, and I feel wonderful.

When she woke up she felt restored, in touch with the Self again. She came out of the water, she said, as if she were a warrior who had gone through an ordeal and proven that she couldn't be destroyed. "It was as if something was healed." And she added, "I can see now how cynical I'd become; but cynicism would've been the easy way." Through her dream, she had glimpsed the exquisite beauty of life which she had forgotten how to cherish.

The dream describes a driver out of control of her car: the ego no longer in charge. Although the woman had a stalwart ego and had always been very sensible, anyone—no matter how strong—falls into disequilibrium at a time of great loss. No one is immune. Most widows have similar experiences and it is normal. Great events *should* affect us deeply. Her ego had lost its grounding and was momentarily succumbing to the unconscious, falling into depression, considering the idea of a car accident. However, in the dream, the near-experience of losing her life brought forth the opposite: conscious commitment to life again.

How beautiful to taste life! Her ego had realigned itself with the life-force. Like physical pain that wears you down, long sorrow can do so, too. She said, and only someone who has been worn down with suffering truly knows this: "Faith takes *courage*." And she did have the courage, this stalwart woman, and with some help from her inner core of being, she gradually emerged, through the next years, into a sense that life—though never the same again—was quite worthwhile. The Self had been reinstated within her.

# Notes

## Introduction

1. For daughter-father relationships, see Leonard, *The Wounded Woman*, 1985.
2. For contemporary views of the animus, see Mattoon, "Is the Animus Obsolete?" in Nicholson, *The Goddess Re-Awakening*, 1989; Wehr, *Jung and Feminism*, 1989; Young-Eisendrath, *Hags and Heroes*, 1984; Young-Eisendrath and Wiedemann, *Female Authority*, 1987.
3. Although it may appear as if therapy with these women consisted only of work on their dreams, this is because the book focuses on this aspect of therapy. Therapy also included working through early life experiences, internalized oppression, and transference (the relationship with the therapist), as well as issues of fulfillment in interpersonal relationships, work satisfaction, creativity, and the search for meaning and a meaningful place in the community and society at large.
4. Cooper, et al., "The Remarkable Rise of a Widow in Yellow," *Newsweek*, 10 March 1986, p. 34.

## Chapter 1: Understanding Dreams

1. For example, Bolen, *Goddesses in Everywoman*, 1984; Downing, *The Goddess*, 1981; Harding, *Woman's Mysteries*, 1973.
2. For example, see Sjöö and Mor, *The Great Cosmic Mother*, 1987; Gimbutas, *The Language of the Goddess*, 1989; Johnson, *Lady of the Beasts*, 1988; Eisler, *The Chalice and the Blade*, 1987; Nicholson, *The Goddess Re-Awakening*, 1989. Also see contemporary women

poets, for example, Canan's anthology, *She Rises Like the Sun*, 1989.

3. Johnson, *Inner Work*, 1986.
4. The Self is actually the center of the *whole personality*, which includes the conscious ego, but it is easier to talk about it in informal discussion as the center of the unconscious.
5. Jung, *Memories, Dreams, Reflections*, 1963, pp. 158–161.
6. In this book I use one of the other names for the collective unconscious—the "archetypal unconscious"—to designate its contents and emphasize the creative symbolic process which takes place there.
7. I am indebted to Louis Stewart for his insights in his preliminary theoretical formulation, "A Brief Report: Affect and Archetype," *Journal of Analytical Psychology*, 1987; and to Joan Chodorow, "Dance and Movement as Active Imagination," Ph.D. diss., 1988. See also Chodorow, *Dance Therapy and Depth Psychology—The Moving Imagination* (in press).
8. I am grateful to Frances Gilliam Slocumb for bringing the goddess Iris to my attention.

## Chapter 3: Dealing with Aggression

1. Walker, "Psychology and Violence Against Women," *American Psychologist*, 1989.
2. Brownmiller, *Against Our Will*, 1975.
3. Rutter, *Sex in the Forbidden Zone*, 1989.
4. Gilligan, *In a Different Voice*, 1982.

## Chapter 4: The Shadow

1. Graves, *The White Goddess*, 1966, pp. 383–386.
2. Auel, *The Valley of Horses*, 1983.

## Chapter 5: Relationship

1. See next chapter on sex.
2. For a feminist view of the meanings of Greek goddesses and gods for contemporary women and men, see Bolen, *Goddesses in Everywoman*, 1984, and *Gods in Everyman*, 1989.
3. Bottigheimer, "Silenced Women in Grimms' Tales," *Fairy Tales and Society*, 1986, pp. 115–131.
4. See also Leonard, *On the Way to the Wedding*, 1987, pp. 39–60.

5. Gimbutas, "The Temples of Old Europe," *Archaeology, 33,* 1980, pp. 41–50; Gimbutas, *The Language of the Goddess,* 1989, pp. 147–48.

## Chapter 6: Sex

1. Bradley, *The Mists of Avalon*, 1984.
2. Auel, *The Clan of the Cave Bear*, 1981.

## Chapter 7: The Wise Heart

1. Hickey, "Six O'Clock News." Unpublished poem, 1988.
2. I am indebted to the insightfulness and scholarship of Claire Douglas, "Christiana Morgan's Visions Reconsidered," *The San Francisco Institute Library Journal, 8,* 1989, pp. 5–27.
3. Dreyfus and Dreyfus with Athanasio, *Mind Over Machine,* 1986.
4. In fact, in these societies, such as Catal Huyuk, archaeologists have found no signs of warfare (no weapons, no fortifications) and have found no signs of personal violence (no skulls dented by blows), which has changed our usual beliefs about violence in human nature and the inevitability of war. See Walker, *The Crone,* 1985; Eisler, *The Chalice and the Blade,* 1987.
5. LeGuin, "The Space Crone," *The CoEvolution Quarterly,* Summer, 1976, pp. 108–110; see also Downing, *Journey through Menopause,* 1987; Walker, *The Crone,* 1985.
6. Sun Bear and Wabun, *The Medicine Wheel,* 1980, pp. 146–149.
7. Johnson, *Lady of the Beasts,* 1988, pp. 337–345; Gimbutas, *The Goddesses and Gods of Old Europe,* 1982.
8. Auel, *The Clan of the Cave Bear,* 1981.
9. Graves, *The White Goddess,* 1966, pp. 251–258; Walker, *The Woman's Encyclopedia of Myths and Secrets,* 1983, pp. 48–50.
10. Ibid.
11. I am indebted for much of the story and interpretation to Marie-Louise von Franz, *Shadow and Evil in Fairy Tales,* 1974, Part Two, chapter III, pp. 157–162.
12. Kellert and Berry, "Knowledge, Affection and Basic Attitudes Toward Animals in American Society—Phase 3." NTIS #PB81-173106, 1980, p. 34.
13. Dale-Green, *The Archetypal Cat,* 1983.
14. Irvine, "Untransformed Toads and Talking Frogs," *Psychological Perspectives,* 1984, pp. 9–26.
15. See reports by Jungian analysts Harry Wilmer, on dreamwork with

Vietnam veterans with post-traumatic stress, "Combat Night-mares," *Quadrant*, 1986, pp. 120–139, and "The Healing Night-mare," *Spring*, 1986, pp. 47–62; and Randa Diamond, on dreamwork with rape survivors, "Persephone Today," *Clinical Social Work*, 1983, pp. 78–86.

16. Summarized and excerpted from Shavelson, *California Tomorrow*, 1989, pp. 22–29.

# References

Auel, Jean. *The Clan of the Cave Bear*. Toronto: Bantam, 1981.

———. *The Valley of Horses*. Toronto: Bantam, 1983.

Bear, Sun and Wabun. *The Medicine Wheel*. Englewood Cliffs, N.J.: Prentice-Hall, 1980.

Bolen, Jean Shinoda. *Goddesses in Everywoman: A New Psychology of Women*. San Francisco: Harper & Row, 1984.

———. *Gods in Everyman: A New Psychology of Men's Lives and Loves*. San Francisco: Harper & Row, 1989.

Bradley, Marion Zimmer. *The Mists of Avalon*. New York: Ballantine, 1984.

Bottigheimer, Ruth B. "Silenced Women in Grimms' Tales: The 'Fit' Between Fairy Tales and Society in Their Historical Context." In *Fairy Tales and Society*. Edited by Ruth B. Bottigheimer. Philadelphia: University of Pennsylvania Press, 1986, 115–131.

Brownmiller, Susan. *Against Our Will: Men, Women, and Rape*. New York: Simon & Schuster, 1975.

Canan, Janine, ed. *She Rises Like the Sun: Invocations of the Goddess by Contemporary American Women Poets*. Freedom, Ca.: Crossing Press, 1989.

Chodorow, Joan. "Dance/Movement as Active Imagination: Origins, Theory, and Practice." Ph.D. dissertation, Union Theological School, Berkeley, 1988.

———. *Dance Therapy and Depth Psychology—The Moving Imagination*. London/New York: Routledge (in press).

Cirlot, J. E. *A Dictionary of Symbols*. Trans. J. Sage. New York: Philosophical Library, 1972.

Cooper, Nancy, et al. "The Remarkable Rise of a Widow in Yellow," *Newsweek*. 10 March 1986, 34.

Dale-Green, Patricia. *The Archetypal Cat*. Dallas: Spring, 1983.

Diamond, Randa Carmen. "Persephone Today: Use of Dreams, Imagery, and Myth in the Treatment of Raped Women," *Clinical Social Work Journal. 2*, 1983, 78–86.

Douglas, Claire. "Christiana Morgan's Visions Reconsidered". *The San Francisco Jung Institute Library Journal. 8*, 1989, 5–27

———. The Woman in the Mirror. Boston: Sigo.

Downing, Christine. *The Goddess: Mythological Images of the Feminine*. New York: Crossroad, 1981.

———. *Journey through Menopause: A Personal Rite of Passage*. New York: Crossroad, 1987.

Dreyfus, Hubert L. and Stuart E. Dreyfus with Tom Athanasio. *Mind Over Machine: The Power of Human Intuition and Expertise in the Era of the Computer*. New York: The Free Press, 1986.

Eisler, Riane. *The Chalice and the Blade: Our History, Our Future*. San Francisco: Harper & Row, 1987.

Fordham, Frieda. *An Introduction to Jung's Psychology*. New York: Viking Penguin, 1983.

*Funk and Wagnalls Standard Dictionary of Folklore and Legend*. New York: Funk and Wagnalls, 1972.

Gadon, Elinor W. *The Once and Future Goddess*. San Francisco: Harper & Row, 1989.

Gilligan, Carol. *In a Different Voice: Psychological Theory and Women's Development*. Cambridge: Harvard University Press, 1982.

Gimbutas, Marija. *The Goddesses and Gods of Old Europe 6500–3500B.C.: Myths and Cult Images*. Berkeley and Los Angeles: University of California Press, 1982.

———. *The Language of the Goddess*. San Francisco: Harper & Row, 1989.

———. "The Temples of Old Europe," *Archaeology. 33*, 1980, 41–50.

Graves, Robert. *The White Goddess*. New York: Farrar, Straus and Giroux, 1966.

Hall, James A. *Jungian Dream Interpretation*. Toronto: Inner City, 1983.

Harding, Esther M. *Woman's Mysteries*. New York: Bantam Books, 1973.

Henderson, Hazel. *The Politics of the Solar Age*. New York: Anchor/Doubleday, 1981.

*The Herder Symbol Dictionary*. Trans. ʙ. Matthews. Wilmette, Ill.: Chiron, 1986.

Hickey, Evelyn. "Six O'Clock News." Unpublished poem. 1988.

Irvine, Florence. "Untransformed Toads and Talking Frogs," *Psychological Perspectives.* 15, 1984, 9–26.

Jobes, Gertrude. *Dictionary of Mythology, Folklore and Symbols.* Parts 1 & 2 (2 vols.). New York: Scarecrow Press, 1962.

Johnson, Buffie. *Lady of the Beasts.* San Francisco, Harper & Row, 1988.

Johnson, Robert A. *Inner Work.* New York: Harper & Row, 1986.

Jung, Carl G. *Dreams.* Trans. R. F. C. Hull. Bollingen Series XX, Princeton, N.J.: Princeton University Press, 1974.

———. *Memories, Dreams, Reflections.* Recorded and edited by Aniela Jaffé. New York: Vintage Books, 1963.

Kellert, Stephen R. and Joyce K. Berry. "Knowledge, Affection and Basic Attitudes Toward Animals in American Society—Phase 3." NTIS Document #PB81-173106, U.S. Fish and Wildlife Service, Springfield, Va.: National Technical Service, 1980.

LeGuin, Ursula. "The Space Crone," *The CoEvolution Quarterly.* Summer 1976, 108–110.

Leonard, Linda Schierse. *On the Way to the Wedding: Transforming the Love Relationship.* Boston: Shambhala, 1987.

———. *The Wounded Woman: Healing the Father-Daughter Relationship.* Boston: Shambhala, 1985.

Mattoon, Mary Ann. *Jungian Psychology in Perspective.* New York: The Free Press, 1981.

———. *Understanding Dreams.* Dallas: Spring Publications, 1984.

———. "Is the Animus Obsolete?" In *The Goddess Re-Awakening: The Feminine Principle Today.* Edited by Shirley Nicholson. Wheaton, IL.: Theosophical Publishing House, 1989, 142–165.

Nicholson, Shirley, ed. *The Goddess Re-Awakening: The Feminine Principle Today.* Wheaton, IL.: Theosophical Publishing House, 1989.

Pascal, Blaise. *Pensées. IV.* In Louis Lafuma, ed., 1973.

Robinson, Edwin Arlington. *Tristram.* New York: Macmillan, 1927, 206.

Rutter, Peter. *Sex in the Forbidden Zone.* Los Angeles: Tarcher, 1989.

Shavelson, Lonny. "Dreams From a Tortured Land," *California Tomorrow.* 4, 1989, 22–29.

Sjöö, Monica and Barbara Mor. *The Great Cosmic Mother.* San Francisco: Harper & Row, 1987.

Stewart, Louis H. "A Brief Report: Affect and Archetype," *Journal of Analytical Psychology.* 32, 1987, 35–46.

von Franz, Marie-Louise. *Shadow and Evil in Fairy Tales.* Zurich: Spring

Publications, for The Analytical Psychology Club of New York, 1974.

Walker, Barbara G. *The Woman's Encyclopedia of Myths and Secrets*. San Francisco: Harper & Row, 1983.

———. *The Woman's Dictionary of Symbols and Sacred Objects*. San Francisco: Harper & Row, 1988.

———. *The Crone: Woman of Age, Wisdom, and Power*. San Francisco: Harper & Row, 1985.

Walker, Lenore E. A. "Psychology and Violence Against Women," *American Psychologist*. *44*, 1989, 695–702.

Wehr, Demaris S. *Jung and Feminism: Liberating Archetypes*. Boston: Beacon Press, 1989.

Wilmer, Harry A. "Combat Nightmares: Toward a Therapy of Violence," *Spring*. Dallas: Spring Publications, 1986, 120–139.

———. "The Healing Nightmare: A Study of the War Dreams of Vietnam Combat Veterans," *Quadrant*. *19*, 1986, 47–62.

Young-Eisendrath, Polly. *Hags and Heroes: A Feminist Approach to Jungian Psychology with Couples*. Toronto: Inner City Books, 1984.

Young-Eisendrath, Polly and Florence Wiedemann. *Female Authority: Empowering Women Through Psychotherapy*. New York: Guilford Press, 1987.

# Resources

**A Jungian Psychology Resource Guide.** James and Tyra Arraj, Inner Growth Books, 1987, Box 520, Chiloquin, Oregon 97624.

A complete guide to Jungian resources: mail order book services, journals, films. Includes a listing of local Jungian groups and professional societies in the U.S. and abroad as sources for lectures, workshops, and referral to local analysts. Free catalog.

**The Centerpoint Foundation.** 33 Main Street, #302, Nashua, New Hampshire 03060.

The foundation produces courses in Jungian psychology for small, informal groups, and provides a newsletter of Jungian programs in the U.S. and Canada, and a discount book service. Brochure available.

**C. G. Jung Bookstore.** 10349 West Pico Boulevard, Los Angeles, California 90064.

A large selection of books on Jungian topics, general psychology, mythology, fairy tales, symbolism, and religion. Mail order catalog available.

# Recommended Books*

## Symbol Dictionaries

*The Herder Symbol Dictionary*, 1986.
> Handy pocket-size dictionary that often goes to the heart of a symbol's meaning.

J. E. Cirlot, *A Dictionary of Symbols*, 1972.
> Reasonably priced for such an excellent general guide.

Gertrude Jobes, *Dictionary of Mythology, Folklore and Symbols*, 1962.
> Well worth its great expense for its complete coverage of symbols' meanings.

Barbara G. Walker, *The Woman's Encyclopedia of Myths and Secrets*, 1983, and *The Woman's Dictionary of Symbols and Sacred Objects*, 1988.
> Walker's two books complement the above symbol dictionaries by describing what symbols originally meant to women in pre-patriarchal cultures. The *Woman's Encyclopedia* is twice as large as the dictionary and is organized alphabetically. The *Woman's Dictionary* is a very useful and extensive reference book for dream images with its many illustrations and its organization by the type of symbol, such as Round and Oval motifs, Animals, and Supernaturals.

*Funk and Wagnalls Standard Dictionary of Folklore, Mythology, and Legend*, 1972.
> Especially good for animals and fairy-tale figures.

---

*See References for complete source information. All recommended books are in print at this time, and most are available in paperback by mail order from the C. G. Jung Bookstore in Los Angeles (see Resources).

## Jungian Dreamwork

Mary Ann Mattoon, *Understanding Dreams*, 1984.
  An excellent, readable, and comprehensive book for general readers and therapists.

C. G. Jung, *Dreams*, 1974.
  Rich material extracted from Jung's writings. Includes over 100 pictures.

James A. Hall, *Jungian Dream Interpretation*, 1983.
  A simple, practical guide to common motifs and techniques in analyzing dreams, organized around basic subjects.

## The Feminine

Jean Shinoda Bolen, *Goddesses in Everywoman*, 1984.
  A feminist view of the Greek goddesses within us and how they relate to our everyday life.

Janine Canan, ed., *She Rises Like the Sun*, 1989.
  Vivid poems by eloquent women poets who evoke the presence of the feminine spirit.

Christine Downing, *Journey through Menopause*, 1987.
  A beautifully written personal account of a woman's rite of passage that illuminates the deep mythic dimensions of the feminine.

Riane Eisler, *The Chalice and the Blade*, 1987.
  A very readable distillation of scholarship on early goddess cultures and their implications for peace in the world.

Elinor W. Gadon, *The Once and Future Goddess,* 1989.
  An exciting, down-to-earth, bountifully illustrated book. Perceptively feminist in discussing goddess cultures and the reemergence of feminine images and values today.

Buffie Johnson, *Lady of the Beasts*, 1988.
  Beautiful illustrations and in-depth descriptions of certain animals in goddess cultures across the world, seen through an artist's eyes.

Shirley Nicholson, ed., *The Goddess Re-Awakening*, 1989.
  An exciting treasury of articles by an array of authors on the essence of the feminine. Includes articles on the Black Goddess of Africa, Oya; the Navajo Changing Woman; and the Jewish Schechinah.

Barbara G. Walker, *The Crone*, 1985.

> In this readable book, Walker redeems the Crone as a vital figure of strength and wisdom for mature women, with important implications for wider issues in society today.

## Jungian Psychology

Claire Douglas, *The Woman in the Mirror,* 1990.

> A very comprehensive and enlightening history of Jungian thinking about women and the feminine, from Jung's concepts — shaped by his personal psychology and the culture of his time — through contemporary feminist views.

Mary Ann Mattoon, *Jungian Psychology in Perspective*, 1981.

> A scholarly and very accessible discussion of Jung's ideas, which gives clear definitions, comparisons to Freudian thought, and research evidence. Includes how to apply Jungian insights and methods to personal life, psychotherapy, and social issues.

Frieda Fordham, *An Introduction to Jung's Psychology*, 1983.

> A slim volume which outlines Jung's main concepts and includes a brief biography of Jung's life.

C. G. Jung, *Memories, Dreams, Reflections*, 1974.

> Jung's autobiography which shows his personal inner journey.

# Index